THE
EDGEMASTER'S HANDBOOK

THE EDGEMASTER'S HANDBOOK

A Comprehensive Guide to Choosing, Using, and Maintaining Fixed-Blade and Folding Knives

LEN McDOUGALL

Skyhorse Publishing

Skyhorse Publishing books may be purchased in bulk at special discounts for sales promotion, corporate gifts, fund-raising, or educational purposes. Special editions can also be created to specifications. For details, contact the Special Sales Department, Skyhorse Publishing, 307 West 36th Street, 11th Floor, New York, NY 10018 or info@skyhorsepublishing.com.

Skyhorse® and Skyhorse Publishing® are registered trademarks of Skyhorse Publishing, Inc.®, a Delaware corporation.

Visit our website at www.skyhorsepublishing.com.

10 9 8 7 6 5 4 3 2 1

Library of Congress Cataloging-in-Publication Data is available on file.

Cover design by Tom Lau
Cover photo credits: Len McDougall

Print ISBN: 978-1-5107-2769-4
Ebook ISBN: 978-1-5107-2771-7

Printed in China.

TABLE OF CONTENTS

PREFACE

I am grateful for the opportunity to be invited to write a few lines for a good friend, Len McDougall, respected writer of numerous books on the outdoors, a field guide and expert tracker, and a man who lives life on the hard side. He has handled many of life's ups and downs, and with his perseverance and the assistance of an incredible wife, continually beats the odds. His writings carry not only a message, but a great transfer of knowledge that makes one feel that he is right there in the thick of it with Len. His book *The Edgemaster's Handbook* will be a great source of inspiration and knowledge.

–Mike Fuller, founder and president of TOPS Knives

INTRODUCTION

Another knife book? Before you groan, and put this book back on the store's shelf, be assured that this treatise on mankind's original tool (several species use inanimate objects as hammers, but only we manufacture cutting tools) is intended to be unique on a number of points. If I thought that it would be just another book about knives, too many of which have regarded them as jewelry, knick-knacks, and status symbols, I wouldn't waste my waning lifetime composing it.

As this portable butcher's kit from Outdoors Edge illustrates, cutting tools have evolved to take many forms.

Sure, it delves into some of the same facets surrounding knives as can be found in other knife books, because to leave out crucial information concerning alloys, edge designs, and the like would leave the book incomplete. As an author, I must presume that at least some readers have opened this book to answer questions, and that a few may be less than expert.

Where this book is intended to differ from other treatments is that it doesn't consider knives to be just manicured shards of steel, but as valued friends. Not as accoutrements of ostensible badassery, or icons of some usually imagined warrior status, but as the necessary, genuinely loved tools of life that good knives represented to our forefathers. There have been a lot of years in my own life when my knife (I often only had one to my name, because one was all I could afford) represented one of my most precious and relied-upon possessions.

Mostly, my knife has performed mundane chores, like opening a bag of livestock feed or trimming branches. But on occasion it was called upon for uses of a more severe nature, like dispatching wounded animals, and in a couple of instances, for more serious uses—you'll understand if I'm reluctant to divulge some of the particulars of those incidents. Suffice it to say that the techniques and tactics described herein are not cocktail party hypotheses—I place extreme value on my credibility.

Only a few generations ago, and for hundreds of generations before, a woodsman's knife was precious and unique, as prized as anything he or she owned.

I have taken the liberty of using factual anecdotes to illustrate points I want to make whenever possible. I hope that these snippets of stories will prove entertaining to read, as well as helping to clarify pertinent details concerning edged tools and their uses. It has been my often unfortunate observation that learning to do a thing correctly is most effectively done by paying a penalty for doing it wrong. That's how I learned too many of the skills I've acquired while using cutting tools, and I don't recommend it. Learning to handle edged implements through attrition leaves scars, so if you can learn the things I've learned by vicarious means, without the blood loss, you'll be better for it than I am.

One of the goals that this book most fervently strives to attain is to reduce the number of people who learn the lessons in its pages the way its author has—the hard way.

Finally, a quote about this book which makes me especially proud comes from *Brian Tighe*, a Top Ten knife designer of more than three decades, who Columbia River Knife and Tool (CRKT) describes as a "Canadian Renaissance Man." In his words: "Inspiration and insight; there is more to a book than just reading."

Why we like knives:
"There will always be a place for knives in society. Whether it be cutting open boxes, whittling a stick, or carrying a knife in your purse or pocket for a task that requires a sharp edge, knives are necessary tools."

— Lindsey Phelps, Licensed Brands Manager, Columbia River Knife and Tool

CRKT calls Brian Tighe, a Canadian knife designer with thirty-one-years experience, their "Renaissance Man," because his designs are definitely outside of the box.

There may be no other icon of human history that has inspired such feelings of magic, romance, and groin-deep self-confidence in its possessor as a good knife. Romanticized accounts of William Wallace's gigantic Scottish broadsword, James Bowie's meteor-forged Iron Mistress, Miyamoto Musashi's extra-long katana, and the vicious sickle-sword of King David's armies have been written about and portrayed in movies many times. Mystical attributes of power and destruction that we instinctively apply to handheld blades have spawned legends like *Excalibur*, Anduril of *Lord of the Rings*, the *Sword of Damocles*, and even He-Man's *Sword of Power*. Almost universally, regardless of race, gender, or religion, a knife, big or small, imbues its wielder with a feeling of pleasure.

Some people try to deny the fascination that knives hold for humans in general, imagining that to exhibit interest in the very implements that forcibly brought civilization to society, and which most courts of law view as violent weapons, would be to somehow brand themselves as proponents of violence. But there are genuine, instinct-deep reasons for the strong attraction that blades have always held for men and women of all ages. It is no exaggeration to state that the rise of humankind has been inextricably linked to the creation of, and to innovations in, knife manufacture.

On September 16, 2017, a twenty-one-year-old student named "Scout" Schultz was shot to death in a brightly lit parking lot at Georgia Tech while holding a closed multi-tool; a disturbing indication of how dangerously warped the official view of knives has become in this world.

Even today, when nearly every calorie eaten has passed through a battalion of hands before reaching our mouths, and an ability to render live animals into tablefare is seldom a life skill, ownership of a knife is still perceived by some as one threshold of adulthood. For millennia, the presentation of a blade from father to son marked the day when a young man was entrusted with the power to hunt and butcher, and to kill in defense of kin, kith, and hearth, if it came to that. Many an adult grandchild still holds his or her grandpa's deer hunting knife in a special place, and fate willing, they will hand it down to their own son or daughter.

This seventy-three-year-old Western Bird & Trout Knife has been processing deer and other game since the Prohibition Era.

The warm feeling that holding a fine blade engenders is more than just imagination born of childhood fables. The rise of Australopithecines from easy prey to Earth's most feared species can be linked directly to their discovery of cutting tools and weapons. Like the ripping canines and scissoring carnassial teeth of a coyote, a cutting/hammering/ripping tool shaped from bone, stone, or

even wood enabled a comparatively weak, slow, and naturally unarmed hominid to hurriedly strip meals from large carcasses left temporarily unguarded by napping predators. By slashing off flesh and bone, then escaping to a safe place—which itself evolved into an armed encampment too dangerous for any but the biggest and most starved predators—early humans took in a diet rich in meat and fat.

Anthropologists say that it was this intake of super-rich animal proteins and fats that gave our species the nutrition required to grow a large and complex brain—and the idle time to relax, free of fear of predators, that allowed our ancestors' developing brains to dream up innovations for making life easier and longer. Long before the discovery of fire, survival knives of stone were used to hammer open bones too thick for carnivores to crack,

Earliest humans, stripping out super-rich marrow from the bones of prey killed by other, better predators, who could not themselves crack the bones like a man-ape with a rock, soon learned that bones opened in this manner were sharp, opening an entire toolbox of possibilities.

Among all the species inhabiting Earth, Homo sapiens is alone in being denied the natural tools and weapons that every other animal receives naturally; we have to manufacture our own teeth and claws.

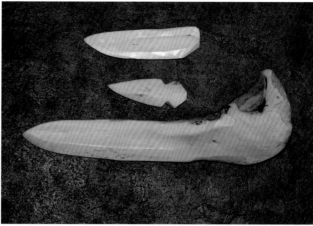

Examples of early cutting tools and weapons made from bone.

and then to scrape out the super-rich marrow within, so it might be posited that discovery of the knife is an original cornerstone of human evolution.

The Stone Age became the Bronze Age when someone learned that naturally occurring deposits of pure copper, already used to make jewelry and cooking vessels, could be melted with tin at relatively low temperatures to form bronze, history's first metallic alloy. The pure forms of either component metal are too soft to be of use in cutting instruments, but their blending resulted in an array of new characteristics, like springiness, strength, and better edge retention, with easier resharpening, than was possible with bone, stone, or either metal by itself.

Like every great innovation, the new bronze alloy was immediately integrated into social life in the form of plowshares, shovels, axes, arrowheads, and weapons, and again human existence was changed forevermore. With creation of a durable, lightweight knife that could be manufactured to any desired length, in any configuration, early humans virtually removed themselves from nature's food chain. A lone wanderer armed with dirk, shortsword, spear, and shield soon became recognized as too dangerous to try by nature's most fearsome carnivores.

Contrary to movies and cheap novels, the secret to long life for a lion or brown bear has always been to get a meal of meat with the least amount of danger to itself, and that means avoiding the possibility of receiving a serious wound. In tribes from Africa to Norway, it has long been a rite of manhood to hunt down the mightiest meat eaters that competed with human societies for food. Within a few centuries humans had become the most feared animals in their world, completely wiping out large predators in many locations. Even today, whole prides of lounging African lions will up and relocate at the approach of Masai tribesmen armed with their traditional long spear and rawhide shields. With predators, it's always about getting a meal with as little harm to oneself as possible, and some outdoorsmen believe that most large carnivores still instinctively fear a large knife brandished toward them.

Many political groups today would have you believe that the instinctive appreciation nearly all of us feels for the tool most responsible for the rise of humankind is some sort of psychological defect.

Armed with metal teeth and claws that were far superior to anything that nature had created from keratin or bone, our ancestors stabbed, plowed, shoveled, and chopped their way to a place of dominance over every other large species on earth. It can certainly be argued that discovery of fire was the real key to the rise of humankind, but it was the invention of the knife that kept those first humans richly fed, warmly clothed, well defended, and gave them the leisure time to dream about concepts like friction and combustion.

In that sense, it could be said that discovery of the knife was the turning point when early humans separated themselves from the natural order. The sense of romance that a fine blade engenders in a person isn't a fetish toward violence, or anything to feel self-conscious about. In fact, it's quite the opposite, because those emotions connote recognizing a connection to your own ancestors. To feel the vibrant life energy that emanates from the hilt of a quality knife held in your fist is merely to acknowledge a genetic memory of how vitally important this original multi-tool has been to the very existence of us all.

You might also notice that many of the knives illustrated by photos throughout this book look anything but new. That's because this book is not a catalog of macho porn. Its purpose is not to sell you a knife, but rather to educate readers about knives in general. A new knife is a stranger, an unknown commodity whose dependability and trustworthiness has not been established. The knives in this book have proven that they are capable of by passing or failing the most comprehensive, toughest, real-world field trials in the business. In light of that, the usual beauty shots have been supplanted by pictures of tools that have been worked hard, maybe even abused, and sometimes broken, as true-life field trials demanded. And for that reason alone, you can rest assured that the information related in this book isn't just believable; you can bet your life on it.

With six decades of life in the North Woods , most of it living on an income below national poverty levels, the author has butchered, built, whittled, netted, trapped, carved, drilled, and done just about anything that can be done in the backcountry with a knife.

Knives Today

Knives in the new millennium are different on all counts. Whereas a good fixed-blade sheath knife was once as much a part of the uniform of the day as a wristwatch or smartphone is for today's on-the-go world citizen, carrying any kind of cutting instrument is now severely restricted.

United States citizens narrowly dodged a bullet in 2009, when the Customs Department attempted to prohibit importation of assisted-opening knives, in an obvious first step to having those types of knives banned altogether under a re-definition of the 1958 Switchblade Act. Fortunately, Congress did not agree that spring-assist folders were switchblades, and neither did President Obama, when he signed legislation to that effect on October 28. However, I have seen for myself that the cop on the street did not get that memo in a lot of cases, and citizens are being arrested for possession of perfectly legal folding knives

Despite President Obama's display of good sense, the rest of the world is a surrealistic, nonsensical collection of extremes where knives are concerned. In Iraq and neighboring states, victims are murdered at will with long-bladed knives that are not only carried concealed, but specifically as weapons of violence. In such places, a stabbing murder has the same gravity as a parking ticket in New York.

Then there are "civilized"—spelled *disarmed* countries, like England—where governmental attempts to legislate nirvana have resulted in more or less tyrannical environments. Following is a recent message about knife laws there from a friend in Great Britain:

"UK laws are prohibitive in the extreme. Less than two-inch non-locking is the only carry option. Grown-ups are out of the picture. I would risk several years in custody for carrying a

regular, decent, folding knife. Pathetic. But sadly, teenagers keep stabbing each other with their mum's kitchen knives, and we all suffer. Terrible legislation."

Despite the hedonistic ideals of politicians who would prefer that blades were made from foam rubber, the knives of today are the finest ever made. First, the alloys are much more homogenous, meaning that they are blended more smoothly. Think of a batch of molten steel as a cake batter; the steels of yesteryear often had "lumps" of impurities in them that resulted in knife, and other, blades that were hard and brittle in one spot, but soft an inch over. The real result of that was a blade with uneven levels of sharpness and edge retention and, most important, toughness. Some blades would just break in two at one of their harder points, as if they were made out of glass. Unfortunately, I know that to be true.

And just as a better batter makes for a better cake, so too have better alloys served as the basic building block for better knives. And just as there are different flavors of cake to suit different tastes, today there exist so many alloys with so many different qualities that one cannot help but find a knife suited almost perfectly to his or her needs. Just two weeks before his tragic death in 2011, the legendary knife maker Walter "Blackie" Collins confided in me that if he had to choose "just one knife to do it all, it would be one of the four-forties." I've had, and do have, numerous blades made from this original stainless-steel formula—and I'm hardly qualified to argue with perhaps the greatest knife maker of our time—but I'd probably go with a blade of S30V, or one of the high-carbon tool steels, like the extraordinary D2.

Better alloys have been accompanied by improvements in metal hardening, once known simply as "tempering." Put simply, this process uses heat to help align the molecular grains of a steel to make it evenly hard and strong throughout. Hardening processes of today would have seemed like magic spells to even the most skilled Japanese swordmaker of old. More than just coaxing the greatest edge retention out of a blade, and making it precisely the same throughout its length, contemporary tempering methods bring out maximum toughness and strength, too.

So although it might seem as if some of the evaluations in these pages are overly kind, they are not. The truth is that even

This sadly discontinued big folder is a Benchmade RUKUS with an almost spectacular blade of S30V stainless steel; it stands as an example of how far the arts and sciences of knifemaking have come in recent years.

cheap knives in the new millennium are merely outstanding by the standards of yesteryear. The 440A steel that was virtually a trademark of those cheap, under-five-dollars, rosewood-handled, Pakistan-made folding knives of the early eighties has benefited from the aforementioned advances until blades made from the same alloy today are almost indistinguishable from the best knives of that era. If you want a knife that you can be proud to own, you really don't have to look hard, and you don't have to spend a lot.

Knives and Children

My favorite nephew was just four years old when I gave him his first knife. It was a small, inexpensive brass-and-rosewood Bearclaw-style lockback folder, the kind that were made in Pakistani garage-factories in those days, and sold at cut-rate retailers and flea markets for just a couple of dollars. It had brass bolsters, and a soft, polished blade of 440A or B stainless, which dulled just from quartering an orange.

The blade I gave to my nephew was razor sharp, although I knew that it was incapable of retaining that keenness for long. My sister's philosophy was that I should start him with a dull knife, to allow him to "safely"—in her mind—discover what a knife was capable of. I failed to see the logic in that philosophy, and the knife that I gifted the boy whom I loved as dearly as if he were my own son was honed keen enough to pop the hair off your forearm with only a light stroke.

I handed the lockback to the lad with a few simple, sternly put warnings about what it could do to him if mishandled or used carelessly, and I made him acknowledge that he'd heard my rather didactic cautions—knowing fully well from the gleam in his eyes that his head was filled with visions of He-Man, the Sword of Grayskull, and other childhood icons of his generation.

Sure enough, he'd been slicing and eating an apple for barely five minutes when he snapped the still-sharp blade closed onto his finger. He uttered a squeal that conveyed the pain of it all, and I swiftly removed the half-folded knife from his lacerated forefinger. I'd been standing by with gauze, safety tape, and antibiotic ointment, because I'd predicted this, and I had him staunched and bandaged in a minute.

He'd just learned his first, and arguably most important lesson in knife handling. It was one that he never forgot. He cut himself many times over the next thirty years, to be sure, but it's a given that his first experience with that cheap little folder helped to mitigate both the frequency and severity of those subsequent injuries. In fact, I take more than a little pride in admitting that, at the onset of an age of "zero tolerance," my nephew, Josh, was the only student in the Boyne City, Michigan, public school system who was permitted to carry a keenly sharpened Gerber EZ-Out folding knife clipped to his pocket while in class. Even his teachers borrowed his knife to open boxes and such.

How old your own child is before he or she is old enough to have a knife can only be determined by you. Would you trust your child to prepare a simple stovetop meal, like tomato soup? Can your son or daughter operate a power lawnmower safely? If your answers to questions like these are *yes*, then your kid is probably old enough for a knife. On the other hand, children do not mature at equal rates; the nephew to whom I gave the knife was ready for his first gun by age ten, while I didn't trust his older brother to handle a firearm safely by the time he'd reached legal drinking age.

Sharp or Dull? Which is Safer?

Note that I elected to give my own nephew–and several other children in my family–a first knife that was sharp enough to skin a deer. Here's my rationale: A knife that's sharp enough to lacerate skin with a touch is less likely to inflict a serious wound, because as soon as it begins to cause pain, a sensible human being will pull the blade away from his skin. No one in his proper mind willingly cuts into his own flesh.

A sharp knife parts what it's cutting with relatively little pressure. A dull knife, however, requires greater force to drive it into a material. Needing to apply more muscle means that you will have decreased control over the blade because you're pushing harder, and that translates into an increased possibility of slipping. If you–or your child–slips while pressing hard against a knife's handle, it's quite likely that the resultant wound will be both deep and severe, because there will be more force behind its blade.

No matter what the age, a neophyte knife handler (and occasionally the expert, too) is going to cut himself, and most lacerations will be to the fingers. It pays to have a quick-and-dirty blood-stopper, like this self-adhesive medical-grade gauze tape from General Bandages.

Conversely, the slightest slip with a very sharp knife is probably going to instantly make a user pay for his mistake in blood. But it most likely will be only a little blood, just enough to remind him not to do that again. For that reason, I prefer to give neophytes in my family a very sharp knife to learn with; a keen knife actually leaves fewer scars and spills less of its user's blood.

Kids' Knives

You've made the decision to gift your child a knife. It's a very special gift and, if it comes from me, that's a very special child. To me, you don't just give away a knife, you find a home for it, and the process is very much like homing a puppy. I recall once, decades ago, when a long-time acquaintance, after seeing me gift a knife to an actual friend, complained most pitifully that I had never given him a knife in all the years that I'd known him.

There was, indeed, a reason for that. But I had a new Ontario-made USAF Survival Knife that I'd honed skinning sharp. Although that particular model owns a special place in my heart, because of our long history together, it wasn't an especially expensive or valuable knife, because I knew how it was going to be treated. Predictably, not a month later, I spied it lying, rusty, on the floor of his garage, sans its sheath, which he had lost. My "friend" didn't comprehend the profound sadness his thoughtlessness had invoked in me. He only knew that the only thing that I was willing to give to him after that was a communicable disease.

That this thirty-something father of three had so casually disrespected a woodsman's most precious tool confirmed something that I'd known about him for a long time: This fellow's upbringing had failed to instill respect for anything or anyone in him. You most certainly would not be smart to lend this person your car, or to give him the keys to your home while you went on vacation. The problem is that people like this guy rarely wear signs that identify them as the bozos that they are.

Conversely, children who are given a knife as soon as they seem capable of safely using and appreciating its value always seem to mature faster, and with a higher regard for the importance of taking care of their possessions. That respect and esteem, ideally, transfers to everything else, from clothes and computers to automobiles, homes, and family members. In short, giving your child a knife, in my experience, contributes to forming him or her into a better adult.

One of the first purpose-made survival knives, and one of the best fixed-blades knives for a beginner, the 1095 steel USAF Survival Knife still costs a mere $45 from Ontario Knife Company (OKC).

Which knife you choose for your progeny is important. Until a child reaches the age of cognitive thought, learning is more of a conditioned response for him and, like any skill a child learns, he'll remain interested if the experience is as pleasant as possible. There's no contradiction here, because learning to use a knife necessitates scars, and one or two of them is a fact of life. But never make the mistake of thinking that a child should "grow into" a knife. A knife that is too heavy for undeveloped muscles to control, too lengthy to be handled dexterously, or too large to be grasped firmly by little fingers is going to prove unwieldy, and that's going to lead to inevitably bloody mistakes that could turn your son or daughter away from carrying the tool that defines them as a human being more than any

SOG's SEAL Pup knife ($64) is especially sized to smaller hands.

other. Get your little skinner a knife that fits smaller hands, like SOG's excellent Seal Pup model.

No kid needs a double-edged knife; these are ultimately dangerous to their users, whatever their age. I believe that youngsters (and small-framed adult beginners, who don't use a knife every day) are best suited to a blade length of no more than five inches; my own choice for my four-year-old granddaughter was a Seal Pup, but there are numerous qualified alternatives. Choices should have a smaller, textured handle diameter, a secure grip, with a rough texture, a good finger guard that prevents hands from sliding forward, and a sheath that holds securely, but releases easily.

Folding knives should have blades that lock open, but should be easy to open and close. I prefer the newer styles, with a safety catch that locks blades closed when engaged. Again, double-edged or stiletto-style blades are undesirable. Handle scales (sides) should be textured to provide a good grip, and a knife should not be too large to be held firmly. Out-the-front and spring-assisted openers are never good choices for beginners.

CHAPTER ONE
KNIFE CHARACTERISTICS

Before you can discuss a thing, be it automobiles or the human body, you must first know a thing or two about the design, features, and nomenclature of the item in question. Fortunately, knives are one of the simpler tools to understand, but I don't believe that it's an exaggeration to say that the majority of readers are going to be surprised at how much there is to know about this most defining tool of humankind. This is especially true today, when advanced materials and manufacturing techniques have transformed them into tools that the mountain men of old could only have dreamed of. In its broadest sense, the configuration of knives has remained essentially unchanged, although some descriptive terms have gone out of style through the centuries. Still, even an amateur knife lover should be conversant in the often unique lingo associated with knifecraft.

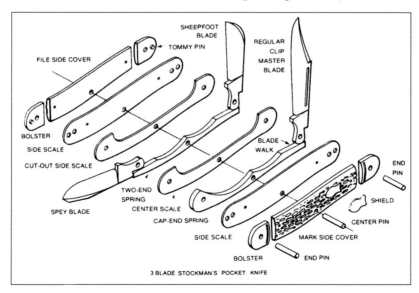

As this drawing illustrates, the language of knives is a vernacular unto itself.
(Courtesy W. R. Case)

Anatomy of a Knife

Any knife is not just a knife. Encompassed by that blanket description of mankind's oldest manufactured tool are numerous refinements that make it more suited to one use than others. There are skinning knives, fillet knives, boning knives, cleavers, machetes, pen knives, and other specializations that make a particular type of knife different from its brethren.

Let's begin with knife anatomy. Because you cannot talk about knives if you don't know what their parts are called, any more than a doctor can get away with not knowing the proper terms for parts of a human body.

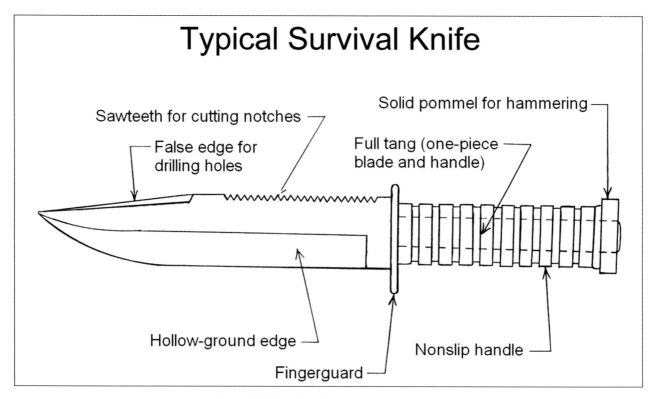

A simplified drawing of a typical survival knife.

Fixed Blades

The original, most basic knife design is a fixed-blade, in which the handle and blade are a single, integral unit. Typically, the knife is carried with its blade encased in a separate sheath, or scabbard, to keep its wearer safe from its cutting edge. The sheath itself has historically been carried on its owner's waist belt to keep it always available and ready to be drawn, but today's scabbards are often fitted with multiple and varied attach points, so that they can be carried in any orientation on virtually any strap or belt.

In fact, it is a real bone of contention with me personally that most modern sheaths tend to be almost an afterthought, the result of experiments with designs that are meant to have a stylish cool factor, but very often, even usually, lack the functionality to make them qualify as useful tools outside of a living room or den. That topic will be covered in rather harsh detail further on in this

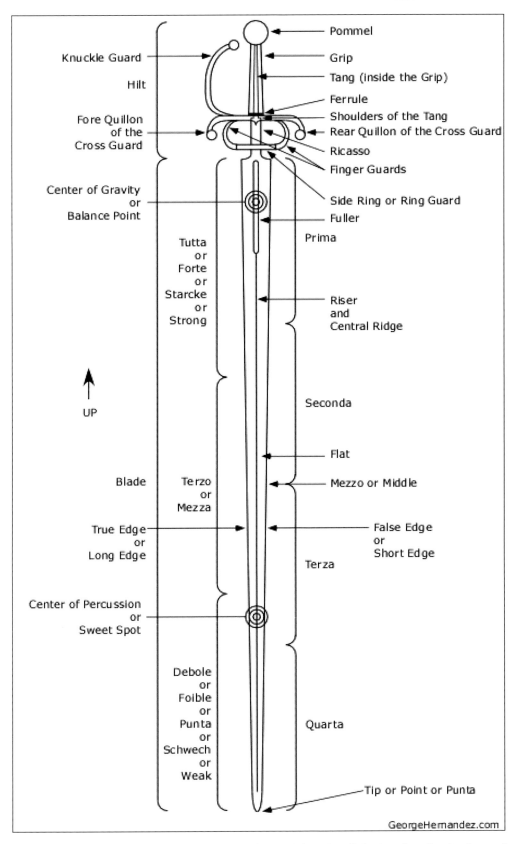

Perhaps it is only fitting that a cutting weapon which has left such a distinct mark on the development of humankind should also possess such a complexity of parts and nomenclature. (Drawing by swordmaster George Hernandez).

The last knife to bear the name of Blackie Collins just before his death in July 2011, the Meyerco CAST was an ignominious farewell whose all-fabric sheath was cut to pieces just during my hurried evaluation for Tactical Knives *magazine.*

book. The knife on my hip has kept me from dying, or at least suffering greatly, too many times for me not to regard every useful feature with the importance that hard experience has proved to me it deserves.

It's not the least superfluous to state that a fixed-blade knife is in every respect responsible for shaping the course of human history. Usually it did that by peaceful, even mundane means. A raw-hide thong, so useful for binding everything from clothing and footwear to snowshoes and boat masts, could not be made without using a sharp blade to strip it from a piece of animal skin. The handle for an axe, hammer, or plow blade could not be fashioned and shaped without whittling, and neither meat nor vegetables could be prepared as food without a keen edge.

A working-size sheath knife, built stoutly enough for daily chores like prying, drilling holes, and a multitude of cutting chores that would be impossible for bare hands, was the original multi-tool. Different cultures used knives that reflected their environments and needs, like the Filipino's bal-isong and the Scot's dirk, but during any of the developmental eras of humankind, a knife that was as common as a wristwatch or cellular telephone is today was logically engineered to meet a maximum variety of needs that were common to the environment in which it was used. Steak knives were redundant when every customer at a local inn had a knife right on his hip to cut up the meat that he was served. No farmer ever had to borrow a

The axe handle, mallet, shovel handle, and spoon shown here are all the result of a good knife shaping the environment to meet our needs, the way Homo sapiens has done since before recorded history.

Modern folks in timber country, like their ancestors, break axe handles, and a dwindling number of wood-cutters simply make themselves new ones—they have the wood.

knife to cut the umbilical cord of a newborn calf, and few travelers lacked a long-bladed dirk—the original sidearm—with which to protect possessions and loved ones from highwaymen.

The original sidearm, a Scottish dirk like this one, able to kill with a single blow, defended travelers everywhere they went, inside and out, for hundreds of years, while always ensuring that a diner had the tool to cut his steak.

When they were the most common tools of the day, knives shared common features in every locale, much the same as plows and saddles, because certain features were desirable. Most had handles and blades that were in a straight, or nearly straight, line with one another, and perpendicular with the hand that gripped them, because that is a naturally comfortable orientation for human anatomy. Notable exceptions include scythes that are specialized for reaping grains, and the early Israelite's' sickle-blade sword, both designed to maximize shearing efficiency (from lopping off arms to cutting sheaves of barley) but good for little else.

Stabbing Knives

Knives designed for stabbing (not necessarily as weapons of crime or warfare—sometimes just for "bleeding" livestock that was intended for the dinner table) tended to have blade points on the center line of their handles to maximize thrusting power, with a crossbar-type finger or hand guard mounted securely at the junction between handle and blade. This, of course, protected a user's hand from sliding forward onto the cutting edge. A good many of us can affirm from unpleasant experience that a cross-guard might be very necessary if a handle becomes coated in greasy, slippery blood and fat—not usually from mortal combat with legions of unnamed enemies, but from more mundane chores, like butchering an elk. Today, many knives have abandoned the cross guard in favor of a molded-in bulge that ostensibly serves the same function, and too many have abandoned that protective feature altogether. In truth, deletion of a cross guard demonstrates that today's wielders no longer depend on their knives for the same multitude of functions that our forebears did. In fact, Jim Bowie's brother, Rezin, almost lost a thumb when his hand slipped forward over his knife blade while fending off an enraged bull. All his knives thereafter featured cross guards.

A knife whose functions might include driving its point into any medium—a task which might be required of almost every working knife except lightly built kitchen cutlery (which should *never* be used as a screwdriver or for prying)—also has a center line that extends from its point through the middle of its handle. Having a point on center with its handle means that a thrust can deliver maximum force, and drive a blade's tip in to the greatest depth possible—important for use as a weapon, but also a necessary feature when digging wood out of a log that will become a dugout canoe, or just hollowing out a wooden bowl. Having point and handle on the same axis is vital for using a blade to drill holes, because if they are offset from one another, the point will wobble as the handle is rotated, wasting torsional energy, and making it harder to drill a nice, round hole. This physical characteristic is why designs like the Kukri (a Hindi and Urdu name, circa 1811) of the Nepalese Gurkhas are primarily slashing tools, and are not well regarded as survival/utility knives by wilderness experts. Conversely, it demonstrates why stabbing weapons like the dirk and rapier are rod-straight, as are survival knives.

Typical survival knives, like this Schrade SCHF1 Extreme, are designed with blade points on the knife's center line, to provide maximum transference of force for drilling, punching, digging, and stabbing.

Another defining characteristic of a knife whose primary purpose is to stab is its narrow blade. As the M7 Bayonet used by GIs in Vietnam, the Sykes-Fairbairn Commando Dagger of WWII, the M-17 Knuckleduster Trench Knife of the Great War, and the dirk used by Jim Bowie at Vidalia universally demonstrate, a narrow blade, sharply pointed, penetrates more deeply with less force than a wider one. This was perhaps the worst flaw in the movie *The Hunted*, in which Benicio del Toro uses an abominably wide Tom Brown Tracker knife to stab to death his enemies. The Tracker knife, like KaBar's Warthog and the new (at the time of this writing) Tracker-Digger from TOPS are great for skinning animals, scraping hides, or any job that needs a long cutting edge, but none of these broad blades are fit for use as stabbing tools.

A dictum of the Renaissance era states that if a man were given a long enough lever, he could move the world. But leverage can work against a wielder when it comes to blade length: Swordsmen and fencers share the trait of having strong wrists, because the axiom "It's all in the wrist" was not a cliché when someone who threatened to "run you through" meant to do what he said. The longer a blade, the more amplified its leverage, and the more wrist strength is required to control its point. The shorter the blade, the more powerful its thrust—that's why you never see a foot-long ice pick—and the more lateral (slashing) force it can deliver. It is that attribute which makes the 1.9-inch bladed Launch 4 knife from Kershaw, which often elicits comments like "Aw, that's a cute little knife," into a decidedly lethal weapon.

Some knives, like the universally popular Bowie design (which was probably designed by Rezin Bowie, and might never have been used by James, the family's most famous knife fighter), incorporate a beveled, but usually unsharpened, false edge into the spine leading up to a blade's tip. This feature reduces the amount of thrusting force that must be applied to penetrate a maximum depth into a given medium.

It is not usually a good idea to sharpen a false edge—I once put a shaving edge on the false edge of a friend's Kabar USMC Knife (at his request, and against my own better judgment), only to have him yank it from its sheath and lay a ten-inch gash into his opposite forearm. His wife, of course, blamed me for his stupidity and the twenty-some stitches that it took for a doctor to close him up.

Slashing Knives

A slashing knife differs from a stabbing tool in several respects. First, it typically has a long blade, to give it a longer cutting edge, as well as more mass. Some knives, like the aforementioned kukri, and the bolo designs, artificially lengthen a cutting edge by giving its blade irregular curves. Making a blade wider toward its tip greatly enhances chopping force by adding mass (weight) at the outer-most and fastest-moving part of its arc, but detracts from penetrating power.

Even without a blade that bellies out toward the point, a machete-type knife is typically too wide-bladed to make it much good as a stabbing weapon. Added width and thickness are needed to give a machete mass (mass + velocity = power, the same as it does with a bullet), and nothing can beat good old weight when it comes to chopping power. For illustration of that point, I present to you the axe, whose long handle and intentionally heavy chopping head can strike (and has done so many, many times) with enough force to kill a half-ton bull before it falls to the ground.

As added illustration, permit me to offer a personal anecdote: I hail from the North Woods, where a swamp-tromper's most prized possession was supposed to be a hatchet. I went against convention by insisting at a young age (almost fifty years ago) that a hatchet was just too narrow, both in blade length and in usefulness, to suit my needs. I tried the classic GI-style machete, like the ones that had served with distinction from the jungles of Burma in World War II to the Mekong Delta in Vietnam. But those razor-sharp lengths of good 1095 high-carbon steel, so effective against lianas and bamboo, were simply no match for beech, maple, or even jack pine. Inevitably, even predictably, the blades would break off cleanly about six inches ahead of their handles. Ironically, the cheaper civilian models with blades of unhardened 1060 that nicked, dented, refused to hold an edge, and vibrated painfully in the hand are tougher than the GI models—at least their blades have never broken.

I remained frustrated, and usually just resigned myself to lashing a heavy roofer's hatchet onto my backpack whenever an outing was more than a couple of days. That changed in 1989, while working at an innocuous little metal fabricating company where we plasma-cut, milled, and welded armor plate components for the M1 Abrams Main Battle Tank. I never did find out exactly what that steel was (the guy from General Dynamics acted like he was James Bond, and the identity of that steel was a national secret), but I could tell from the way it behaved in an end mill that it was extremely tough. So I filched a large piece of quarter-inch-thick scrap one day, and ground it into the shape of a short, wide Bowie knife. It was just what I needed in the woods. The blade held an edge sharp enough to skin a deer, with maybe a touch-up during the job. The alloy proved as tough as I've seen to this day, and a weight of two and a half pounds in a ten-inch blade made it formidable against the hardest wood in the tightest quarters. I had my swamp machete; that thing served me well for more than two decades of very hard use.

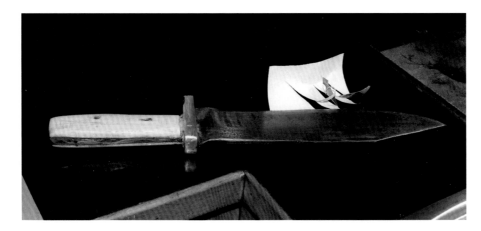

This handmade Bowie, with its twelve-inch blade of M1 Abrahms tank armor, has been clearing paths through the North Woods for almost thirty years.

On the other side of the coin, when John Moore, unabashed genius and founder of Mission Knives, sent me the concept drawing for his MKT-1 titanium-blade knife, with an overall length of fifteen inches, and an intended goal of challenging longer steel-bladed knives in the field, honesty dictated that I throw water on the fires of his passion. Having already evaluated the Katrina search-and-rescue knife from Mission for my survival column in *Tactical Knives* magazine, I'd had some experience with Beta-titanium in a knife blade. John had been absolutely correct when he'd told me that the blade was unbreakable under the harshest field conditions—the *only* knife I haven't been able to break. But the titanium required frequent resharpening (John, who knew his own knife creation, distrusted the sycophantic knife magazine writer who'd claimed to have skinned twenty-four deer before his sample needed sharpening—not all writers are honest, readers), and it was too light by at least half to be serviceable as a machete, unless he made it the size of that huge mythical broadsword that William Wallace was supposed to have wielded. The MKT-1 is a really tough, really strong, and really lousy machete; it just isn't heavy enough.

Today, there exists an abundance of good to great slashing knives. That turn of events started with the square-ended SP-8 Survival Machete from Ontario Knife in 1998, 1.75 pounds of 0.250-thick, epoxy powder-coated, SAE 1095 high-carbon steel with a saber-ground edge and an ability to literally cut 8D nails in two. Enthusiasm for the SP-8 said that this was an idea whose time had come, and soon there were a number of big workhorse blades on the market. One such knife was the Power Eagle 12 from TOPS Knives, a monster with a foot-long 1095 blade—I actually broke this knife chopping a deer's leg bone in two, but it took a year of similar abuses, and TOPS replaced the knife, no questions asked. Or the sadly discontinued Outcast from Kershaw, with its spectacularly tough D2 blade. Or the Woodsman's Pal from Pro Tool Industries, a light, thin, soft, poorly designed tool that I quickly learned to leave at home when I went into the woods, but which seems to have gained a following. If you need, or just like, a big, rugged brush-clearing tool, this seems to be an ideal time to get one. Never before has it been as possible to get such a good working knife for such a modest outlay of cash. Prices, too, are excellent; you can purchase a worthwhile chopping blade for under $50. Or you can pay $200 or more, if you want to.

Folding Knives

The second major category of knives is folding knives, in which the blade pivots into and out of a recess in the handle on a bolster pin. Also called a rivet or hinge pin, this is one of the numerous pins that hold a folding knife together, but it's the most critical in the sense that it also serves as the hinge point for a blade or blades (depending on the type of knife). A bolster pin needs to be strong, of a large diameter, and tight, but without inhibiting a blade's free rotation from open to nestled into the handle recesses. It should also be held in place with threads, so that it can be repaired more easily; a hinge bolster that is made from a rivet is generally the mark of a cheap knife.

Other pins perform various functions, most of them to just hold the knife together. Again, better folding knife designs use a threaded screw or a bolt held in place with a nut. A new (at the time of this writing) and innovative folder called the Home Front, from Columbia River Knife and Tool, features what that manufacturer calls Field Strip Technology, which allows the unit to be completely disassembled in the field without tools for cleaning, then reassembled.

The earliest folding knives were in existence when Jesus preached atop Mount Sinai, created for reasons of portability and safety. Actual origins are lost in time, because many cultures had folding knives. Our ancestors valued their knives more than any other possession, and they well knew the importance of having a cutting tool on one's person at all times. A folding knife whose blade swiveled to recess safely into its own handle was the solution to always having a knife tucked into a pocket, even while sleeping.

Folding Knife Patterns
Like fixed-blade knives, a folding knife is not like every other folding knife. There exists a multitude of different designs. Here are some of the most popular.

Slip-joint
This is the original jackknife design, carried by generations of fur trappers, fishermen, electricians, and men and ladies from all walks of life. From cleaning fingernails and a horse's hooves to cutting

Only a couple of generations ago, this was the knife you found in everyone's pocket or purse, a slip-joint folder whose blades did not lock—and a lot of old-timers have scars on their fingers to prove it.

clothesline and opening a box, the pre-computer civilization when slip-joint knives dominated was replete with citizens who knew how often a sharp edge was needed in daily life.

The simplest explanation of a slip-joint knife is one that is held open or closed by the tension of a torsion bar spring against a cam. A small amount of tension holds the blade in its closed position, so that it doesn't open while being carried in a pocket. Tension increases as the blade is rotated toward its open position—usually by the force of a thumbnail inserted into a notch in the blade—until coming to its fully open position against a wall-like stop that prevents a blade from rotating further.

The same torsion-bar spring tension holds the blade in its open, fully extended position until a downward force against the blade's spine overcomes spring tension, and the blade snaps closed into its safety recess between the handle slabs. Held closed by the same torsion bar, a knife can be safely carried in a pocket, securely closed until its blade is lifted and rotated open again by a thumbnail pressed into a notch in the side of the blade.

The inherent danger with a slip-joint folder is that its blade isn't actually locked, just held fully open or closed by spring pressure. It can, and often has, closed on its user's finger when its point is used as a drill. For this reason, extreme care should be exercised. But remember, this type of knife has served everyone from cowboys to trappers with distinction for centuries, and it is still a fine choice for anyone who will respect its operation. Slip-joints have been mostly replaced by safer lock-blades, but W. R. Case (of Case XX fame) still manufactures a showpiece-quality Muskrat Trapper that, except for its Clip and Spey blades of stainless steel, is a bittersweet piece of nostalgia for this arthritic old trapper.

A gorgeous blend of classic design with modern materials, this Case XX Muskrat Trapper brings a tear to the eye of many an old-timer woodsman.

One-hand Opening Folders

Until the late 1970s, it took two hands to open the typical folding knife carried by every farmer, trapper, fisherman, and schoolboy in North America. The thumb studs, blade holes, and other opening-assist features that are found on virtually every folding knife sold today were not present. Instead, every blade had a thumbnail notch that enabled a wielder to lever a blade open against its cam spring, while holding the knife body in the opposite hand. Clearly, based on the longevity of this type of knife, it worked well enough to become a fixture in every tackle box, possibles kit, and workman's pocket in the world for many generations.

The Importance of a One-hand Knife

The late Jim Warren was a three-time finisher of the thousand-mile Iditarod dogsled race (just finishing that grueling challenge is a win in itself), and he was one of the best friends I've ever had. He was training his team in the vast and wild Betsy River Wilderness Area of Lake Superior State Forest in January of 2009, where eighteen feet of snowfall had compacted down to four feet of hardpack, and you'd generally have a better chance of meeting another person on the moon.

Jim knew that being there alone was taking a chance, but like so many competitive personalities, he was driven to incautious behavior for the benefit of getting a little practice. He got away with the gamble until a combination of rough terrain and a pair of new, untrained dogs caused one of the tangles that every dogsled racer dreads. Several dogs had twisted their harnesses around one another, and one of his newer dogs had the steel-cable reinforced gangline around her neck.

Alone, miles from the nearest road, and with no reason to expect anyone else to come along, Jim was in a real predicament. Sled dogs are powerful, and only adrenaline gave him the strength to restrain the panicked team, who had now started to fight among themselves. Worst of all, he wasn't able to reach the multi-tool he kept zipped into his jacket pocket—ironically, for just such an emergency.

Luckily, and against all odds, another musher who was out training his own team happened along just then and helped Jim to extricate his dogs before any serious damage occurred. For Jim's part, however, the lesson stuck, and a pocket-clipped spring assist folding knife became a permanent part of his daily attire.

Some people, both good and bad guys, needed a knife that could be deployed quickly with one hand. Automatics, known in colloquial vernacular as "switchblades," because they opened from the pressure of a compressed spring with the push of a "switch" button or lever, were illegal under the Federal Switchblade Act of 1958, and were more difficult to obtain than a gun. You could go to prison for possessing a switchblade, but until 1968 you could order a .45-caliber Colt M1911 combat pistol through the mail.

But ingenuity abounds nowhere as much as it does in criminal efforts to circumvent restrictive laws and to procure proscribed items, be it a zip-gun or liquid refreshments from a backyard whiskey distillery. One popular easy open knife with thugs when I was in school was a florist's knife, with its long, slender (and fragile) blade, and faux mother-of-pearl handles. Owners of these inexpensive knives would sprinkle sand into a knife's cam/spring action, then open and close it endlessly, until the cam was worn down to the point that a blade simply fell open. Often called a "gravity knife," it was simply flicked open with a snap of the wrist, and held in that position—dangerously to its owner—by gripping its handle with three fingers and pinching a blade at its choil between forefinger and thumb. Gravity knives were a measure of coolness among guys with greased-back ducktail haircuts, but they were poor weapons, rarely inflicting more than a minor wound—sometimes to their wielder—and often just snapping in two from the stress.

More common from the 1970s and on, when companies began to experiment with bigger and heavier blades, was a "flick" knife. Most of these knives also needed to be worked until cam and spring were polished and rode smoothly against one another (which often introduced a bit of sidewise wobble to an opened blade). At that point, a blade, if it were massive enough, could be flicked open with a forceful snap of the wrist.

Long before folding knives were fitted with thumb studs and other tools that enable one-hand opening, knives like this one could be made to open with a strong flick of its user's wrist.

Some guys liked to cheat by holding a blade between thumb and forefinger, with a thumbnail anchored in its opening notch, then flicking the knife open. Added inertia from the mass of their knife's body, instead of its blade, helped to ensure that it opened, but you ended up with an opened knife in an unusable position, and very often it was just flung half open across a room. That, and the fact that a successfully opened knife ends up in a tentative grasp, and in a decidedly clumsy position, makes opening a folder in this manner a bad idea in real life, especially if the knife needs to be used.

But some knives, like the handsome, all-stainless-steel 440A-blade Silver Falcon from Compass Industries, although intended to be opened with a thumbnail notch, could be snapped open with a hard flick of the wrist. This lockback was sharp enough to shave a beard, and the lightning speed with which it could be deployed probably saved my life on at least one occasion. I've had several pre-thumb stud knives that opened in this manner, and I presume that the reason you didn't hear more about it was because those of us who had used such knives to protect ourselves simply wanted it to be our little secret that the hysteria that proscribed switchblades was in fact a moot point.

Then in 1981, Spyderco introduced a radical, but ludicrously simple design that clipped a closed knife to a hip pocket, and whose blade opened by placing the ball of a thumb onto a simple round hole through the blade. By pushing against the hole with the ball of a thumb, the blade rotated open and locked.

The concept was an instant hit with a public that was craving folding knives that didn't

Probably the most recognized of the original one-hand openers, Spyderco made the thumb hole in the blade a trademark.

require both hands to deploy. Before long, everyone was incorporating a one-hand opening feature onto the blades of their folders. Sometimes it took the form of a traction hole through the blade, *a la* Spyderco, but more often the opener was simply a thumb stud that extended from one or both sides of the blade. There were even a few aftermarket bracket gizmos that mounted to the spine of old-style jackknife blades with a setscrew to give them thumb studs, thereby transforming a knife into a one-hand opener. These aftermarket devices quickly became obsolete as thumb studs became standard features on all folding knives.

Initially, the studs were mostly on the right side of the blade, to accommodate right-handed people, but, as the late, and great, Charles T. (Chuck) Buck once observed to me after a trade show in 1998, "I never would have believed that there were that many left-handed people out there." Apparently no other knife maker could believe that either, because it was about that time when right-hand-only studs all but disappeared. I have a few in my collection, but they're pretty much gone in the new millennium, replaced by a more sensible stud that simply extends from both sides of a blade, making it ambidextrous.

Lock-back Knives

Lock-back knives are not a feature of the modern age, only a more common one. Since the first designers began folding blades inside the handle, it has been a concern that the blade not fold up onto its user's fingers like the old guillotine-type paper-cutter. Typically, a locking-blade folder locks as soon as its blade is rotated to its fully open position, although some are equipped with slide-lock safety catches. Some lock-backs operate from a lever positioned in a recess in the back center, or at the butt end, of a knife's handle. Depressing this lever releases the lock on an opened knife, unlocking the blade and allowing it to swivel back to its closed position, with its cutting edge safely inside its handle. If the lock-release lever and notch are located at the rear end of the handle, instead of the handle's center, the design is probably a Bearclaw-style, made popular as the original Buck Knives style hunting lockback.

Liner Locks

Another means of preventing a cutting edge from closing onto its user's fingers is a liner lock. This design uses a slightly warped spring mounted inside the blade recess between a knife's handles to block a blade from closing. In its fully closed position, the spring lays flat alongside the blade, between it and the frame. But when the blade is rotated to its fully open, deployed position, usually by means of a thumb stud mounted just ahead of the choil, the flat end of the spring pushes toward the center of the blade channel. There it physically blocks the choil, preventing the blade from rotating. To fold the blade back into its closed position, use the ball of your thumb to press the blocking spring usually to the left, until it lies flat against the frame of the knife, out of the way of the blade, and fold the blade back into its resting, closed position.

A liner lock is brutally strong. I have never managed to wear one out after years of service, and the worst that happens is that the lock spring's face wears sufficiently to allow a small amount of up-down play in the locked-open blade. I should point out that this problem is not necessarily a given, and most of my own quality-made liner locks have not worn out before their blades were sharpened down to nubs.

Frame Lock Knives

A frame-locking knife operates much the same as a liner lock, except that in this case, a portion of the side of the handle is warped to act as a spring that moves inward to block a blade you rotate it to its fully opened position. Like a liner-lock spring, depressing the flexible side of the frame enable it to move outward sufficiently to permit the blade to rotate closed. To unlock the open blade so that it can be closed to its safe position, press the lock portion of the frame outward, out of the way of the choil, permitting it to be folded.

Many people prefer a frame lock, and in theory it would appear to be stronger than even a liner lock. This isn't my favorite design because I don't care for its looks; more important, years ago I witnessed a couple of failures due to a broken locking mechanism—the frame simply broke in two at its lock. In fact, that has

A frame lock folder uses part of its frame as a spring to block a blade from closing at its tang.

not been a problem on a frame-lock model for decades—that I know of—but the old prejudice persists.

Push-Button Lock

This type of locking/unlocking mechanism employs a button, usually mounted on the side of a folder, near the front (bolster) end of the knife. Presuming a clean, grit-free operating mechanism, just holding a closed knife blade down and depressing the button causes its blade to just fall free of its recess. Note that no push-button action is actually intended to be opened thus, and all of them have thumb studs or holes that permit them to be opened with a push of the thumb.

Likewise, a push of the locking button will probably also cause an open-and-locked blade to fall back toward its closed position, just from the force of gravity. This is worth mentioning, because a few owners—including this author—have lost a few drops of blood when a surgically-sharp edge rebounded off a finger. But, based on my own Gerber 06 Combat Folder, this is an extremely versatile action that permits a blade to be both opened and closed with a press of the button and a flick of the wrist.

The best push-button lock to date, insofar as actual hard work (it split all of this kindling— without hammering on its blade), the Gerber 06 Combat Folder has performed hard labor for more than six years, with nary a hiccup in performance. (Nothing's perfect, though, and it needs re-sharpening a bit too often).

Flipper Knives

An ingenious, gloriously simple folding knife opener is the "Flipper." This is essentially just a spur on the upper tang of a folding knife's blade. In its closed position, a flipper spur sticks outward from the side of a knife's handle, naturally under the index finger. A backward flip of the index finger rotates the blade out of its recess. A forceful flip is enough to fully snap a blade into its open-and-locked position. In real life, draw-to-deploy time of a flipper knife is as fast—some say faster (and a few can prove it)—than an actual switchblade.

The inventor of the flipper is an unknown, but it's such a simple, logical design that it's safe to assume that any people who could build a waterwheel or windmill might have conceived of it. Earliest known models of flipper knives date back to the 1800s, but the Father of the Flipper as we know it today is the late Harold Joseph "Kit" Carson. Master Sergeant (retired) Carson made history, and helped to put a fledgling Columbia River Knife and Tool Company on the global map in 1999 with his M16 folding knife. The knife was an instant worldwide success that was shipped to the US military "by the pallet." So, even if he wasn't the inventor, today the opening spur on any manufacturer's folding knife will probably be referred to generically as a "Carson Flipper."

Balisong Knives:

No one really knows the origin of what twentieth-century Americans have nicknamed the "Butterfly Knife," after the way its two handles open outward to either side of its blade, similar to butterfly wings. Its proper name, "Balisong," is from the Filipino Tagalog dialect, and translates roughly to "broken antler."

The flipper one-hand opener has proved to be a little bit faster than an automatic in most cases.

This common name probably derives from the practice of using antler and bone—the hardest workable materials on a south sea island—as handles. In its closed position, the longitudinally grooved handles completely cover the blade from either side, concealing it so that it might look simply like a short length of bone or antler. In its closed position, a balisong was safe to carry concealed, it didn't look like a cutting or stabbing weapon, and it was in fact a deceptively effective striking weapon.

Fitted with metal handles, it is also the strongest locking-blade folding knife in existence, impossible to close so long as it remains gripped in its wielder's hand. Or when it's locked open, or closed, with the beautifully simple locking lever located at the butt end of its handles.

Spelled with a hyphen, as Bali-Song, the name of this knife is a registered trademark of Benchmade Corporation, whose CEO, Les de Asis, essentially reinvented the design in the late 1970s. Today the original Model 68 Bali-Song is made using state-of-the-art alloys and technology, and stands as the trademark knife of that company, although Benchmade's line long ago expanded to include other styles.

Introduced in the early 1970s by a little company whose name reflected its mission, Benchmade's Bali-Song resurrected a classic design and introduced it to the world.

I love butterfly knives in general, and Benchmade's Bali-Songs in particular. They are quick, nimble, strong, and just plain fun to play with; flipping them open, then closed, in different ways and orientations is a terrific way to keep the fingers loose and agile. Beware, however, because this knife will bleed —and *has* bled—disrespectful handlers, especially Benchmade's razor-keen models. Learn to grip the outsides of the handles using only thumb and forefingers, and to let only the unsharpened spine recoil off your hand. In common jargon, the "bite handle" is the one facing the blade's cutting edge, and the "safe handle" is the handle facing the unsharpened spine.

I personally think a little blood loss is a learning aid, but if you want to learn how to flip a butterfly knife around like the guys in action movies, without bleeding, Benchmade offers blade-less practice models that won't get a cop called on you if you while away time with it in a doctor's office or at the DMV. In my opinion, looking cool by being able to flip your butterfly knife around in wondrous displays of digital gymnastics takes a distant second to being able get the thing open and closed quickly and surely.

Assisted Opening Knives

A knife that will open (and preferably close) with just one hand can and has been a literal life-saver on many an occasion. By the time lockback designs had begun to incorporate thumb-pushed holes and studs, making them easy to open with one hand, some of us had already learned to flip their blades open using the centrifugal inertia produced by a forceful flick of the wrist. But knowing the prejudice courts had already displayed over one-hand opening knives, this little trick was mostly kept on the down-low by people who could do it.

Spring-assisted opening knives are *not* switch blades. The distinctions between them may seem a bit blurred, but rest assured that they have been absolutely established and set forth by no less than President Barack Obama. It began in 2009, when US Customs, claiming to be acting in the public interest under the auspices of Homeland Security, sought to amend the Federal Switchblade Act of 1958 to re-classify imported folding knives that used the force of a spring to help them open as "switchblades." Alarmed, because the wording of the proposal from Customs was vague enough that, if passed, it might be construed to apply to all one-hand opening knives, the American Knife and Tool Institute (ATKI) issued a legal challenge, stating that, if passed, the proposed amendment would turn, at minimum, 35.6 million law-abiding American knife owners into felons instantly.

Recognizing the far-reaching, calamitous implications of the proposed Customs legislation, Barack Obama, to his everlasting credit, took immediate and irrevocable action to guarantee that no further future attempts at eroding folding knife rights would come about. His own rather clever amendment to the Switchblade Act determined that a knife would be classed as a switchblade if it used a spring action to close the knife, like out-the-front automatics.

This should have forever protected our knives against legal confiscation. Probably. We've seen this before with the gun issue: when anti-gun forces promised that they only wanted to get cheap pot-iron import pistols off the streets, back in 1977, and then included the classic Smith & Wesson Model 29 in that category. Then they promised to never go after long guns, which was clearly a lie, as the war on "sniper rifles" (otherwise known as deer rifles) clearly illustrates. Nirvana-seekers believe that they can forcibly legislate Eden, and until they themselves disappear, they will attempt to outlaw anything that might even remotely be utilized as a weapon. When guns and knives are gone from America, they'll go after screwdrivers and shovels. Ironically, the alleged peace-lovers have historically shown themselves to be quite willing to use lethal force against people who do not go along with their rather colored view of the world.

Spring-assisted folders are sometimes mistaken (even by police) as switchblades, but President Barack Obama interceded, ruling that they, in fact, are not.

Assisted-opening knives can take several shapes, with several different actuating mechanisms. The simplest uses a thumb stud, much like any plain old one-hand opener. Others use a flipper, a hook that is part of the blade that sticks out when a blade is closed, and allows a user to "flip" a blade open. One very cool actuator from Schrade uses a lever located at the top front of the closed blade. In every case, federal law requires that an actuator lever physically move the blade a quarter-inch before its spring takes over and pushes its blade to the open position. That is the main difference between a switchblade and an opening assist: a switchblade opens a knife with a mere push of a button; a spring-assist knife opens only after a slight push of its blade.

Automatic

Automatic knives or switchblades are the classic criminal and special forces folder. James Dean had one in *Rebel Without a Cause,* and in *Dirty Harry* Inspector Callahan stabbed one into the thigh of a serial killer who was garrotting him to death. Out-the-side switchblades, sometimes known as "flick knives," for the way their blades flick into action faster than an eye can follow, were the original one-hand knives. They were probably developed more for fishermen, who often needed to cut lines and nets while holding on for life with their other hand in rough seas, than for any other purpose.

The first switchblades appeared in Europe around 1840, although there seems to be considerable disagreement about the when, where, and who of their invention. The simplest design is the aforementioned flick knife, in which the blade pivots out from the side, like a conventional folding knife.

More complex, and therefore less common, are out-the-front designs. There have been experiments with out-the-front designs that deployed with enough force to actually stab into a victim's innards, but most have just enough spring force to deploy the blade to its locked position with a forward push of the actuator. Most of them withdraw it again when the actuator is thumbed back. The

The classic switchblade folder, whose blade deploys under spring pressure with the push of a button (Kershaw Launch 6 shown).

knives that withdraw their own blades were specifically outlawed by President Barack Obama's amendment to the Switchblade Act.

An out-the-front variant that is not legally an automatic, although it looks like one, is the assisted-opening Schrade Viper. By disengaging the Viper's safety catch, then pressing its release so that it moves its blade the prescribed quarter-inch forward, the spring-assist takes over and thrusts the blade out the front of its handle with sufficient force to engage the blade lock at the end of its forward travel. To reset the blade, it must be unlocked by depressing a release catch, then manually withdrawn into its handle using the same lever that activated it—unlike a proscribed out-the-front switchblade, which retracts its blade under spring pressure.

As mentioned in the descriptions of some other types of modern folding knives—especially, as a prime example, Gerber's 06 Combat Folder, which opens and closes with a practiced flick

Not a switchblade, a spring assist out-the-front knife is often mistaken as one.

of the wrist—any real differences in being able to deploy many styles of modern folding knives are more semantics than practicality. Even before the advent of "one-hand" openers, people who needed to do it learned to snap open many lockback knives with a flick of the wrist.

One potentially important problem that our field trials have uncovered with automatics is that besides their spring-operated push-button opening mechanism, most are equipped with no other means of deploying the blade. The wear, tear, sweat, and dirt from everyday carry can gum up the mechanism to the point that a blade fails to deploy when its release button is pushed. A knife that fails to open when you need it can have serious consequences, especially when it is equipped with no alternate means of forcing its blade to open. SOG has already taken this problem under advisement, and may be the first knife maker to offer an assist device.

Tactical Folders

The term "tactical folder" is credited to designer Bob Terzuola, who used it as a gimmick for marketing his liner-lock knives as street weapons in 1990. The truth was that Terzuola had invented nothing more tangible than a perspective, for weaponized folding blades had been drawing the blood of enemies for more than a dozen centuries prior. But it was a concept that appealed to American urbanites who felt increasingly denied the right to defend themselves in a world that they perceived as growing ever more dangerous.

At the time this book is being penned, the tactical folder movement has ballooned to almost religious status, spawning all types of folding knives, even ink pens, whose purpose—or side-purpose—is to draw the blood of others.

Again, do not get caught up in monikers. When Buck introduced its Strider line of fixed-blade and liner-lock folding knives in 2002, the knife-buying public was not impressed. The pocket-clip folders were a bit thick to be carried comfortably in a hip pocket, but the heavy ATS-34 stainless blades were as fine a cutting tool as you could want. It's just that consumers weren't impressed with the designs.

Then Buck added $100 to the $80 price tags of the Strider folder and fixed blade, more than doubling the MSRP of both, and began listing the knives as tactical weapons. Overnight, buyers couldn't get enough of them. There's a great deal of power in semantics.

The point being made here is that a name is just a word, a collection of letters. The original sniper rifle in Vietnam was a Model 70 Winchester bolt-action drawn from the Army's sport hunting armory. The deadly accuracy that made the rifle so effective against tigers and deer transformed it into a fearsome weapon of war. The only difference between a screwdriver and a murder weapon is the intent with which it is being used.

An ideal example of a tactical folder, TOPS's Mil-Spie 3.5 is fast, strong, and appears to be looking for a fight.

Folding Knife Maintenance

I didn't actually work there, but I liked to hang out at the Army/Navy surplus store that my wife managed in Petoskey, Michigan. It was a fun place to loiter, and, as a writer, I often got ideas from questions and concerns I overheard from customers.

I paid special attention when the group of men—"Roughneck" oil and gas well drillers who were working in the nearby Pigeon River State Forest— came in and started looking at the knives on display. One of them took an interest in a 440-stainless Silver Falcon, the same knife that I was wearing on my belt at that time. But then a buddy of his came over and said to him in a heavy southern drawl, "Yeah, but a foldin' knife ain't no good for skinnin' deer. The insides get all gummed up with blood and guts."

His assertion was news to me, because the 440C Silver Falcon on my own hip at that moment had skinned and at least partially quartered dozens of white-tailed deer, salmon, and an assortment of small game. Its predecessor, also a Silver Falcon, had done the same to more than one hundred deer (several publishers have cautioned me to keep the source of my experience quiet, so as not to offend sports hunters, but to deny the dirt-poor way I grew up, and the way my family fed itself, would be less than honest).

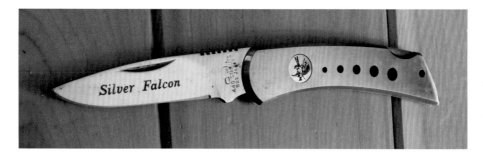

If there were any doubts about a folder's ability to serve as a deer-hunting knife, this Silver Falcon from Compass Industries dispelled them in the early 1970s.

Any machine—that is, any device consisting of an assembly of two or more moving parts—is subject to malfunction. Automatic and spring-assist knives are notoriously apt to fail unless their mechanisms are kept clean, lubricated, and "exercised" regularly to ensure that sand and grime hasn't clogged jointed parts enough to impede their function. A spring-assisted knife that refuses to snap open isn't a big deal, because you can force its blade open with its thumb stud, but automatic openers rarely have such backups.

However, it has happened in real life that a switchblade that has been carried concealed, exposed to just sweat and body oils, for a period of time without "exercise" has refused to deploy its blade when the button is pressed. With no auxiliary opening devices on most automatics, that means a blade will probably have to be pulled open with a pair of pliers—not a great option if you're in the process of being strangled, like Dirty Harry was. (Incidentally, SOG Knives has made a note that there could be a potentially dangerous problem with blades that won't open on automatic folders, and readers may see a remedy in the near future.)

The basics of folding knife maintenance begin with simply washing your knife with soap and heated water after every use that's more prolonged than cutting a string; even just cutting the packing tape on a box can get sticky adhesive on your blade. And definitely wash your knife if you've used it to slice cheese and sausage, to cut pizza, or on any type of food, before and after the fact.

As for using a folding knife to clean and butcher meat, that's pretty much a moot point, because it should go without saying that you'll wash your knife after exposing it to hair, blood, fat, and entrails. All of that removes easily with nothing harsher than soap and water, and anything a meat animal might get in or on a knife will also wash off (knives used to remove oily, strongly scented tarsal or other musk glands merit an extra-thorough washing). Urine, feces, stomach contents . . . none of these are harmful to a knife (except for glandular musks) or the meat, either, providing it is washed off with *cold* water). The old-fashioned Muskrat Trapper 2-blade knife stands in contradiction to the recent, and mistaken, belief that fish and animal residue from cleaning cannot be washed off. And if you don't wash the fish guts and animal entrails from your folding hunter, well, there probably isn't much point in trying to educate you, anyway.

Lubrications have always been a sticking point, because there is good reason that the adage "well-oiled machine" is a metaphor for smooth operation. Despite the truth in that axiom, lubrication of any kind should be applied frugally, because oils attract grit and dirt that actually do more harm than good. Any type of folder that is used as an everyday work knife by a carpenter, drywaller, etc., is usually best kept clean, but un-lubricated. As soldiers in the arid desert were quick to discover, the best lubrication for an oft-used and relied-upon weapon is little or none at all; just keep the moving parts clean, grit- and obstruction-free. Historically, oil has been used less as a lubrication than as a rust inhibitor.

If moisture or a tight fit requires that some sort of lubrication be used, a go-to has long been vegetable-based cooking oil. Be aware that cooking oil, while providing adequate lubrication and good rust resistance in a non-toxic coating, develops a denser viscosity (it gets thick) in a cold environment, which causes operation to become slower. A more or less amusing life lesson about that occurred with an SKS rifle whose trigger I'd sprayed with Pam® cooking oil for storage over the summer. When I tried to zero the carbine's sights just prior to deer season, the thickened oil caused its trigger sear to stick, and the gun went uncontrollably automatic, ceasing to fire only when its magazine was empty—even though I'd immediately taken my finger from its trigger. A particularly frightening happenstance.

A relatively new, and I think outstanding, food-safe lubricating product which was designed by a retired Navy SEAL for lubricating hard-used field weapons is Frog Lube (www.froglube.com),

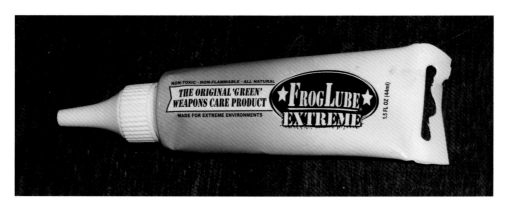

The latest and, based on extensive field trials performed by the author to the Navy SEALs, most effective knife and gun lubricant is a food-grade product called FrogLube (www.froglube.com)

a vegetable-based multi-viscosity oil that has minimal attraction to dust and grime, refuses to thicken even in sub-freezing temperatures, leaves a protective film over bare or coated metal surfaces, and provides almost friction-less contact between bearing surfaces. Wintergreen-flavored FrogLube CLP lubricant has actually been approved for human consumption by the Food and Drug Administration, so it is safe for use on knives that will be used for cutting food—just be sure to wipe off excess FrogLube before cutting any food that you don't want to taste like wintergreen. This is the only lubricant that I use whenever possible.

For cleaning the mechanism of a dirty, gritty folder in the field, when soap and warm water are unavailable, FrogLube has a good answer and, again, it's an all-natural, environmentally friendly solvent that was meant to clean firearms in the field. The company's Super-Strength Carbon and Metal Cleaner is ideal for restoring smooth operation to gummed-up folding knives, and it's safe to apply to blades used to cut food.

Breaking In a New Folder

When he was thirteen years old, my nephew inherited a Gerber EZ-Out from me. He carried that knife daily for the next six years, until its blade was diminished from re-sharpening to the point that it no longer fit into its handle properly. Not surprisingly, the knife that he bought to replace it was also an EZ-Out.

When I next saw him, he showed me his new knife, and expressed disappointment that it felt tight and gritty compared to the knife that he'd just retired. His question to me was, did I think that quality of Gerber's products had diminished?

I chuckled and informed him that the knife I'd given him was one that I'd broken in to meet my personal standards, and that I'd tweaked as much smoothness and performance from it that I could. Some folding knives come straight from the factory with a watchmaker's precision—Benchmade is renowned for the silky smooth operation of its folders, right out of the box. But expect to pay for such a glassy action, because it requires extra steps at the factory—like de-burring and polishing individual components in a vibrating tumbler, and burnishing them to a high gloss, often by hand. It just isn't reasonable to expect a high level of hand-worked craftsmanship in a less expensive knife.

Nonetheless, a fairly astonishing level of slickness can be coaxed out of a well-made folder. The Gerber EZ-Out mentioned is a fine knife, but it is a working person's knife, intended to open bags of livestock feed, strip electrical wire, and whittle parts to fit. It isn't a "gentleman's folder," meant to be carried inside the vest pocket of a suit coat, where drawing it to trim the end off an expensive after-dinner cigar will elicit murmurs of admiration from other diners. A knife meant for that latter purpose will be expensive, it will glitter like the piece of jewelry that it is, and it will exhibit the silky operation of a Swiss watch. Most of us fall between those extremes: we want a rugged, strong, everyday knife that'll do whatever job we demand of it, but without feeling and acting like it was hammered from scrap metal by troglodytes.

To begin, give your new folder a thorough washing with ordinary dish soap and water (being mindful that most of today's new knives are sold with surgically-sharp edges). A kitchen-sink type sprayer is ideal for pressure washing inside to rinse away metal filings and grit, and a good sudsing loosens particles inside the mechanism, so that they'll wash away. An old toothbrush helps to remove stubborn grit from hard to reach places; I keep two of them in my sharpening kit.

Beyond frequent washing, the real secret to why my own folders perform so smoothly and easily is simply because I exercise the hell out of them as soon as I take them out of their packaging. I truly need the knife I carry and rely on to perform flawlessly in my daily life—which might include anything from making a neckline for the swing dogs on our dogsled to swiftly parting a wet hemp rope that someone tied into an inextricably tight granny knot. For example, the rounded cam surface on the inside tang of most folding knives typically comes from the factory with metal dust and oil on it, and often a few tool chatter-marks that cause it to be at least a little jerky when its blade is rotated open or closed. By continuously rotating its blade back and forth to the locked position, then closed, then open again (I like to do this while I'm watching a movie, or just riding in a car), and washing and oiling its moving parts regularly, a relatively inexpensive folder can be made to feel and perform like a more expensive top-of-the-line knife. So much so that, as in the case of my nephew and his EZ-Out, people will say "Hey, I want to buy one of those."

Tactical mavens often say that a folding knife isn't as suitable for that purpose as a one-piece fixed-blade knife because it isn't as strong, being joined blade-to-handle as it is by a relatively small pin. In contradiction to that belief, the Outward Bound survival school once contracted me to author a book they'd titled *The Outward Bound Wilderness Survival Handbook.* The deal died when Outward Bound insisted that I recommend a slip-joint Swiss Army knife as a main survival knife, and not the full-size fixed-blade that a lifetime of near-lethal experiences had shown me was needed.

Stabbing a human to death isn't as strenuous on the wielder or knife as ripping apart a log, and if actual, repeated history is to be believed, even a shoddily built, mid-sized folder is more than capable of killing a large man rather easily. It just isn't that hard to fatally perforate a human being. On the other hand, rending a stump in search of insects to use as fish bait, or levering up a large rock in an actual survival situation—the definition of which is a scenario that you might not live through—could demand more toughness and strength the finest one-piece knife ever created can deliver.

Blade Anatomy

Perhaps a knife's most identifying characteristic is its blade. How a given knife is identified in its broadest sense is often determined by the shape of its blade. Most knives will perform most knife chores, but specialized blades have been developed to accomplish certain tasks better than all others, with particular shapes that enable it to perform specific functions.

For example, a drywaller's utility knife, often known generically as a "box-cutter," is designed to make shallow cuts with its extremely sharp, usually replaceable blade. It has inherent limitations to how far it can penetrate, so that it can cut through the strapping tape that holds a crate closed, without reaching far enough inside to damage the box's contents. Yet, as we saw with hellish clarity on September 11, 2001, the short blade of a utility knife does not prevent it from being lethal in the hands of a mentally ill murderer.

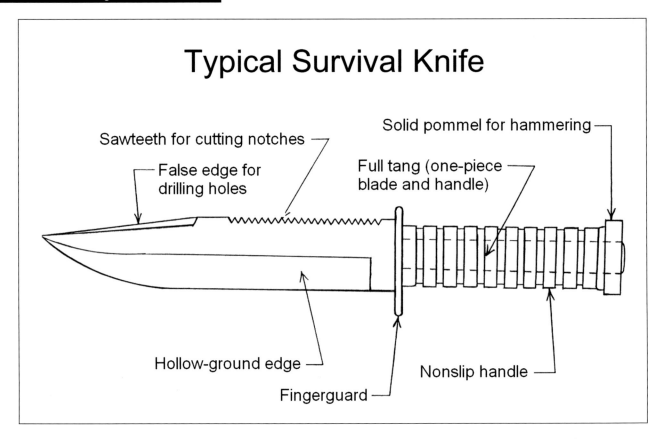

Typical Survival Knife

Sawteeth for cutting notches

Solid pommel for hammering

False edge for drilling holes

Full tang (one-piece blade and handle)

Hollow-ground edge

Nonslip handle

Fingerguard

Basic knife anatomy.

Likewise, a Bowie knife is named for the style of its blade, as is a stiletto, dagger, or fillet knife. A few exceptions include a Stockman's folder, which sports three different types of blade, or a Congress, which has four. Or a paring knife, which has one blade, but might have a number of blade designs, all of which are meant to remove peels and rinds from fruits and vegetables. Except for some of the downright weird Gil Hibben-style fantasy blades, which are neither built nor designed to be functional, cutting tools that are meant to be used possess configurations that reflect whatever tasks they are intended to do. A fillet knife is thin and sharp, to more efficiently slice away a fish's meaty dorsal muscles. A skinner has a broadly rounded tip to effectively peel away hide from flesh. A Tanto is designed to punch through armor . . .

In the following sections you will see some of the same knives listed under different categories. The multitude of reasons for this seeming redundancy will become apparent as you see for yourself that there are multiple categories that pertain to same-style blades, and that overlaps are unavoidable. This is particularly true today, when distinctions that used to be identifying characteristics are becoming blurred and considerably overlapped as new technologies spawn new designs.

CHAPTER TWO

BLADE CONFIGURATIONS AND NOMENCLATURE

Like tires, wrenches, or ink cartridges, a knife is not just a knife. There are different styles for different purposes, made from sometimes very different materials, and that opens a world of possibilities. Generally speaking, a deer hunter's knife is different from a fisherman's knife, which is different from a survival knife, and all of them are different from carpet and flooring knives. If you hope to choose a knife that will suit your needs, you must first know something about the features

Since the invention of a sharpened blade, there have been specialty knives, designed to accomplish special tasks.

that make knives different from one another, and why any given type of knife has the features that it does.

Blade: This is the portion of a knife onto which a handle is mounted. It bears one or two (occasionally three or even four in the case of some old-time spike-type bayonets) sharpened or semi-sharpened edges. Tips of blades are typically pointed to give a blade piercing power, but some wide-bladed knives, like Ontario's SP-8 Survival Machete and "abalone"-type divers' knives, have flattened ends, sharpened for scraping, digging, and for chisel duty. Cleavers made for kitchen use are flat-faced, but usually do not have sharpened forward ends, because their only functions are chopping and slicing.

There are several edge configurations or "grinds." Some are sharper or stronger, or hold an edge better. These will be described in detail later. Suffice it to say that in the New Millennium, with the abundance of materials that can be and are used in the manufacture of every part of a knife, there is a cornucopia of possibilities for knife design—and for you to tailor the knife you use to match your precise desires, without having it specially made.

Clip-point: A clip-point is one of the most common blade styles, and it is the most common for classic folding-knife patterns. A traditional clip-point angles down from about midway up its spine to terminate in a very sharp point. Usually, the clip is straight, looking as if were clipped off from the blade, but on modern designs, the plane is often curved inward, making a blade look even more Bowie-like.

A standard clip-point is un-sharpened, because most of the knives it is used on are lightly built, with slender blades. As such, they are prone to breaking if used for heavy prying, chipping, or

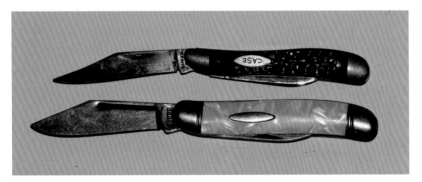

Despite minor differences, both of these folders have a main blade with a clip-point configuration, as do most classic slip-joint pocket knives.

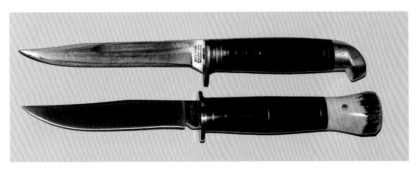

This pair of clip-point Bird & Trout knives, the top with a "swedge" (a swaged or angled false edge), the lower with a plain, straight clip, are examples of clip-point fixed blades.

stabbing jobs, so their spines are left at full thickness to provide maximum strength. But if a variation is possible, it exists, and some clip-points have false edges, or even serrations.

Bowie-point: If you were to bevel the clip, giving it a usually dull "false" edge, the blade becomes a Bowie style. Bowie blades are better for drilling, stabbing, and survival uses.

If a clip-point is left un-sharpened to maximize its shear (prying) strength, then you may extrapolate that taking off the metal necessary to create a bevel there does nothing to make a Bowie knife's tip stronger. For that reason, a Bowie is traditionally robust, a large and strong knife built to take whatever hard uses might be required of it.

Choil: A choil is the usually, but not always, square-shaped, full-thickness (and therefore un-sharpened) portion of a blade just ahead of its handle. A few modern knives have taken to leaving off the choil, and sharpening a blade all the way back to a knife's hilt (this sharpened portion of a choil-less blade, common to chef's knives, is called a heel). Deleting a blade's choil is a relatively new practice, brought about by complaints from users who feel that a choil deprives them of getting as much cutting edge as possible from their blade.

In fact, feeling that a choil is unnecessary illustrates that knives have not only become ultra-specialized, but that they are no longer used for the multitude of sometimes rugged chores that this original multi-tool might once have been expected to perform. The purpose of a choil is to add strength to a blade at one of its two weakest points. Besides its tip, the juncture where a knife is most likely to fail from stress is the forward-most point where its handle ends, and where the cutting portion of the blade begins.

By pinioning a blade between two handle scales, a fulcrum is created at the place where they meet, causing that juncture to be the weak spot when a blade is used for prying—if you were trying to snap something in twain, fixturing it thus would be the best strategy for doing that. Adding

Credited to Jim Bowie, but probably conceived by his brother Rezin, the design we have come to recognize as a Bowie Knife is a superbly multi-functional configuration that has proven itself from farms and frontiers to battlefields.

a full-thickness choil there reinforces that critical area, and maximizes lateral strength.

A choil is a classic, and I think still necessary, reinforcement at the weak point where blade meets hilt, protecting it from breaking there should a knife have to be used for prying.

Cutting Edge: The lowermost portion of a blade that is actually sharpened, and which does the cutting. This is not always the same as the ground edge—e.g., Bowie, hollow-ground, sabre-ground, etc. In those cases, where the sharpened cutting edge is below the ground edge, at a steeper angle, the cutting edge is known as a secondary edge. On most knives, the cutting edge is a secondary edge.

Drop-point: A drop-point knife curves down to its tip, usually less than a third of the way up its spine, terminating at a point above its center line. This downward curve is un-sharpened to maintain strength, and is stronger than a clip point because its design retains more material in a blade.

   One advantage of a drop-point configuration is that it puts a knife's point on its blade's center line, which better concentrates the power of a user's thrust than a knife whose point is offset. Just as a shovel's blade is offset to make it gouge (dig) rather than just penetrate, so is a drop-point's tip in line with the entire knife's center line to give it maximum penetrating force. A drop-point is a strong point, because a minimum of metal is removed from its tip.

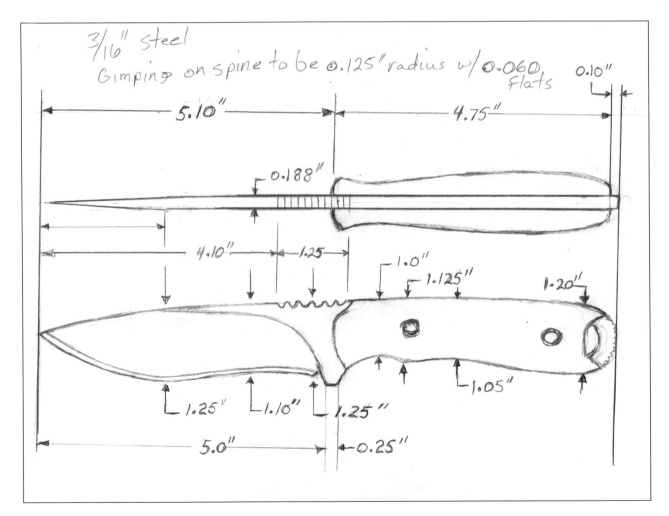

An original drawing from designer Brian Griffin depicts the Schrade SCHF42 while it was still in its concept stage.

Ground Edge: This is the edge that most often determines what a knife is called—i.e., hollow-ground, flat-ground. The configuration of a knife's ground-edge has a lot to do with how sharp it can be made, and how easily it sharpens.

Fuller: A fuller, known colloquially as a "blood groove," is a channel ground lengthwise into a blade between its cutting edge and spine. Similar grooves are used extensively by the metal stamping industry (where they are called "strongbacks") to add stiffness to flat parts, and make them difficult to bend. A fuller works the same on a knife blade, giving it enhanced power to stab without flexing. This was important in the days when a blade might be called on to pierce an armored breastplate. Today, a decreased call for such uses, and improved alloys, have made fullers unnecessary for most knives.

This Boker-made, Martin-designed survival knife boasts an oversized fuller in its heavy 440C blade, not to stiffen it in this instance, but merely as a purely aesthetic fashion statement.

Fuller Spine: Not all stiffening fullers are of a groove type. On double-edge blades that need strength as well as mass, a fuller might be an extra-thick ridge that runs lengthwise down the center of a blade. This type of stiffener is especially popular on double-edge swords, which benefit from maximum strength and power when hacking through an opponent's armor.

This Schrade spear head exhibits two types of stiffening/strengthening features: a groove-type fuller in the blade's center stiffens it, while a spine-type stiffener at the tip adds more metal to strengthen this naturally weaker area.

Hilt: A hilt is a name for the entire handle of any sword or knife. When a Shakespearean villain was run through "up to the hilt," that meant the full length of a blade had been inserted into his body, and could penetrate no deeper. In most of its applications, the term "hilt" includes the entire handle, the pommel, and the hand or finger guard.

Pommel: A pommel is the butt-end of a hilt. Often ornamental, or entirely non-functional, a hilt is sometimes contoured to keep a handle from slipping forward out of its wielder's hand when a blade is used with a slashing or chopping motion, and this usually hooked end is called its pommel. On a purebred survival knife, like Schrade's legendary, and long-gone, M7-S, the pinned-on solid-steel pommel incorporated a nail-puller/ice claw on one side and a flat hammer on the other. On a few of the more tactical-type knives, the pommel terminates in a sharp cone that some call a "skull crusher," but works just as well for breaking a car window. On some other knives, like KaBar's USMC Combat Knife, a pommel is a piece of shaped steel that is pinned to the tang to hold its handle in place, and to serve as a light hammer.

In today's world of inexpensive, mass-produced molded knife handles, the pommel has largely been relegated to just being the butt of a knife hilt, but the Tak-Ri fighting knife from TOPS (which also proved very handy as a field and, especially, hunting knife) has a simple tang-pommel which can dig or chip ice, or inflict crushing wounds to an adversary's skull.

False Edge: A beveled portion of a blade, usually along its spine, an inch or so from its point, that is not typically meant for cutting, but as an aid in penetration when a knife is used for stabbing or drilling.

Finger Choil: The feature commonly known as a finger choil is a finger-size indentation in the underside of a blade or handle, immediately ahead of a knife's handle, where the choil would normally be. Sometimes the finger choil is part of the handle, a crosswise groove located directly behind a conventional choil. The

The two arc-shaped indentations in the blade and handle of this big Armageddon knife from TOPS are known in tactical vernacular as "finger choils," with the rearmost of the two in the handle's "subhilt." Finger choils ostensibly provide enhance user control, but were seldom seen before the latter twentieth century.

reason for a finger choil's existence is a belief that it gives a long-bladed knife better point control in a knife fight. In fact, a finger choil seems to be more of a contemporary design, and was seldom seen on knives that were designed for fighting before the twentieth century.

Gimping: Also sometimes known as jimping (spelled the way it's pronounced), gimping is an inch or so of machined striations cut into the spine of a knife's blade, usually just ahead of the handle and atop the choil. Gimping is there to accommodate the way hunters who skin and process their own game have always lain a forefinger lengthwise along the top of their knife's blade to gain better tip control for fine cutting tasks.

Gimping—traction grooves for an extended forefinger—are a necessity for any knife intended to work as a hunting knife.

Sawteeth: To many a veteran of wilderness skills, a row of coarse sawteeth along a blade's spine is a large part of why it's a survival knife—a blade that doesn't have them is some other kind of knife. Sawteeth were what made the GI-issue USAF Pilot's Knife a survival knife, while the KaBar Marine Corps Combat Knife was not.

Today, the reason for sawteeth is virtually forgotten. I recall a review of survival knives in *Blade* magazine in the early nineties that downgraded a knife's value because its sawteeth didn't work well for sawing a branch in half. The truth is that sawteeth on a survival knife's spine are not meant for sawing wood; ever notice that actual saws have thin blades? A survival knife's are for making the squared notches necessary to construct snares and other wooden tools of wilderness survival. And in a pinch, sawteeth have proved adequate for ripping through the thin sheet metal of an airplane or helicopter fuselage, *a la* the New Millennium Aircrew Survival and Egress Knife (ASEK) that is issued to military pilots.

Serration: A serrated edge is comprised of a series of sharpened recesses—short, narrow grooves—that are ground into a blade adjacent to its cutting edge, reaching back to the choil, but almost never to the tip, except in the instances of some bread and steak knives. Individual serration grooves may vary in size and shape, depending on the manufacturer, but tend to alternate between a wide groove and a narrow one. In action, the grooves act like a very sharp saw, ripping away pieces of material as they cut into it. This is not the action you want for skinning or filleting a fish, or for most cutting tasks, but material that defies the sharpest edges, like rubber hose, wet hemp rope, or tire sidewalls are most easily cut with a serrated edge. This explains why serrations are always located rearward on the blade, nearest the handle, where the greatest force can be exerted. Individual serrations are sharpened with rod-type hones, and companies like Smith's Edgesport make tapered diamond hones especially for that task.

Solid Spine: A solid spine is a characteristic of single-edged knives. Theoretically, a double-edged knife, which has a cutting edge on both sides of its blade, is superior, because it has twice the cutting surface and twice the longevity. But in real life, those advantages are more than offset by their disadvantages. Foremost is the detraction in strength that results from literally removing half the steel (and strength) from a blade in order to apply the second cutting edge.

The head of this Schrade spear has both a fuller (groove) type stiffener, and a ridge type to give its tip maximum strength.

Spear-point: Sharpen the upper spine radius of a drop-point and it becomes a spear point. As the name implies, this configuration endows a knife blade with maximum penetrating power, making it very effective as a jabbing or stabbing tool. Having only a minimal amount of the spine beveled at its tip allows it to retain most of its strength, so it takes a good deal of abuse to snap or bend its tip.

A spear-point is one of my favorite survival patterns. It has sufficient belly—the sharpened radius that extends from the straight portion of a cutting edge to the knife's tip—to make it suitable for skinning, butchering, and filleting. And it's a perfect choice for knife fishing (described in my survival manuals), a technique that I have often used in my younger, more outlaw-oriented days, to procure large food fish so stealthily that fish and game officers had virtually no chance of apprehending me.

A spear-point knife is designed for stabbing penetration, much like a dagger, except with a much stronger build to make it functional for prying and other rugged uses.

Tang: A tang is the portion of a knife, machete, or sword blade that extends into its handle. The best and strongest knives are "full tang," and the blade extends in one solid piece to the butt of the handle, even contoured with the handle, so that its slab sides, called "scales," sandwich the tang from either side. Slabs are typically secured to the tang using Chicago screws, sometimes conventional screws, or rivets. Screws allow a knife to be disassembled and cleaned, and are often preferred in a corrosive (saltwater) environment.

Some knives have a "three-quarter" tang, which, as its name implies, extends roughly three-quarters into its handle. This tang is most often seen on kitchen knives that are not intended for rugged, often abusive field use, but some tactical-style knives also have three-quarter tangs. One of the toughest knives I own, a D2-bladed Outcast machete from Kershaw, had to be re-handled after its Kraton rubber handle, molded over its three-quarter tang, split across where the tang ended, but the handle did not.

Another type of tang is the "rat-tail" tang. This is essentially a tang that has been reduced enough for a hollow handle to slide over it. The US Navy Pilot's Survival Knife, the original survival knife, had a handle made from leather washers slid over its narrow rat-tail tang and stacked atop one another, then held in place by a nut-shaped steel pommel, pinned securely to its tang.

Beware of some rat-tail tangs, because on at least a few traditional Scagel-type hunting knives—the traditional bone- or antler-handled hunting knives with solid buttcaps (pommels)—the rat-tail is just a rod that has been brazed to the blade, and threaded on the pommel end. A handle of usually faux bone or antler is then slid over the tang, and held there by a screw-on butt cap. This type of knife is often poorly made, and the brazed-on tang on many of them is notorious for breaking off, leaving its blade without a handle or a tang to put it on.

Spine: The spine of a blade, as its title infers, is its backbone. It is the strongest, thickest portion of the blade. On a double-edge knife, or dagger, which has both sides of its blade sharpened, the spine runs lengthwise down the center of the blade. A single-edged knife has its spine on top, on the opposite side of the sharpened edge.

A spine is the reason that the best survival and hunting knives are single-edged, because laying the heel of a hand across a knife's spine and pressing down to increase its shearing force is a commonly used and often needed cutting technique. That is of course impossible with a double-edge knife, and with many of the newer experiments in survival knife designs, like Buck's original Intrepid and Gerber's Silver Trident, both of which had largely unusable sharpened sections along their spines that were more dangerous than useful to their users.

Sawteeth are less hazardous and more useful. With gloves, maybe a little padding over them, sawteeth still permit you to press down hard on a knife's spine to shear through material—like rubber garden hose—that is difficult to slice through. Be aware that the sawteeth commonly found on a survival knife's blade are *not* intended to actually saw wood, but rather to rip nice sharp notches that are a mainstay of survival snares and traps, and to rend the sheet metal of an airplane fuselage. Remember, the first purpose-built survival knife with sawteeth along its spine was the United States Army Air Force's Pilot's Survival Knife.

Blade Coatings: Before the advent of knife-quality stainless-steel alloys, it was necessary to protect a field-grade knife's blade from rust and corrosion. Sport-hunting knives typically went bare, because a deer hunter's knife was part of his identity, and it was meticulously cleaned. The "natural patina," a blackish oxidation caused instantly by contact with animal fats and other acidic foods—the same corrosive discoloration known as "bluing" when applied to firearms—was acceptable, even unavoidable. But red rust can create permanent pits in a polished blade overnight. Every experienced gun owner can confirm that neither bluing nor the "natural patina" of frontier-era guns like the Brown Bess does anything to ward off red rust.

For that reason, the US military long ago applied a phosphate-based coating known as Parkerizing to field utility knives like the USMC Combat Knife and the USAF Pilot's Survival Knife, as well as to the legendary M1911 Colt Pistol. Parkerizing was great if an item was kept in storage, but it wore off easily and quickly in field, and exposed areas rusted.

Anyone who spends more than a few hours at a time in the outdoors will realize the importance of a protective coating that permits knives, guns, axes, and any other gear to endure the same conditions as their owners. As a boy, my friends and I experimented with combination layers of Rust-Oleum® primer, acrylic floor wax, smeared-on epoxy resin, even tape. Anything that might help to keep our valued knives and guns from becoming pitted scrap metal during a week-long backpacking trip when it was impossible to come in out of the rain.

After a few very expensive, initially aftermarket, attempts at Teflon®, baked-on epoxy powder-coat, and other protective finishes, most of which performed little better that our home-brewed coatings, knife and gun makers made protective layering standard for at least some of their products. Today, there are multitudes of finishes available, from sand-blasting and jeweling on stainless blades that are corrosion resistant, to standard black, gray, and even pink or green. Whatever its color, be assured that every blade's factory-applied protective coating has been approved by government authorities to be non-toxic and safe for use on food.

A pet peeve is that it has become stylish to sand a knife's protective coating off, leaving bare metal, usually with just a hint of the coating left around the edges. This is done for the same reason that a friend of mine was hired by wealthy tourists to brush-paint a brand-new oak dining set, then scuff the dried paint around the furniture's edges using sandpaper. It's also the same reason that "stone-washed," even holed "distressed" blue jeans became fashionable after manufacturers learned that consumers were dragging new jeans down the road, tied to their cars' bumpers, before wearing them. These seemingly illogical practices supposedly create an illusion of use and experience, two characteristics that cannot be purchased. The process of "antiquing" is dumb, but harmless, when applied to furniture and clothing, but removing a working knife's protection is akin to riding a dirt bike without a helmet. If the folks who created the knife thought that a protective coating was necessary, consider that they might be correct—unless your knife is no more than a fashion statement.

Blade Grinds: A knife's ground edge describes the way the length of a knife's blade is shaped from its spine to its sharpened cutting edge. This configuration has a very real effect on how well or how poorly a given alloy and hardness performs for different jobs.

Following are the most basic grinds. Bear in mind that none of these designs are written in stone, and there exists a lot of latitude for variations. For example, the saber grind, a classic edge grind, might be made so that its bevels extend higher up a blade toward its spine, thereby making a

Considering steel alloys, hardening processes, blade designs, and other variable factors, along with the abundance of edge options—most of which are shown here—it's no wonder that there exists such a variety of specialized knives today, many of which were not even possible a generation ago.

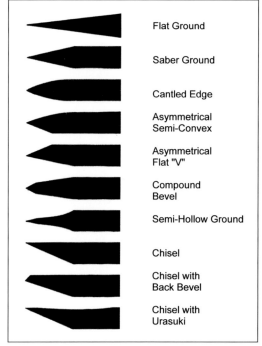

Flat Ground

Saber Ground

Cantled Edge

Asymmetrical Semi-Convex

Asymmetrical Flat "V"

Compound Bevel

Semi-Hollow Ground

Chisel

Chisel with Back Bevel

Chisel with Urasuki

cutting edge both sharper and more able to remain that way longer. Variation is the stuff of creativity, and technology, tools, and materials make possible blades that Jim Bowie could have only wished for.

Saber Ground: The first knives and, as the name implies, swords, were made with a saber grind that sharpened only the bottom of a blade in a broad V. This removed a minimum of metal, and strength, from a blade, which was crucial in an era when a sword or knife could serve as both tool and weapon in a single day.

In its most basic form, the short-sided V leaves a functionally sharp, but very strong edge that is hard to chip or dent. The sharper the V of the cutting edge—the higher up a blade the bevels reach—the sharper the knife can be, so blades that are saber-ground generally have a grind that extends about halfway up the blade, leaving half its width at full thickness. For field and survival knives, a saber grind is ideal, and preferred.

The saber grind's greatest downfall is that it dulls comparatively quickly. This is less of an inconvenience with today's wide range of steel alloys, and it has never been a deal-killer with woodsmen who could sharpen their own blades well, but needed a tough, dependable blade.

Hollow Ground: This grind consists of a broad radius ground into both sides of a typically very hard blade, extending from the spine down to its cutting edge. This results in a thin, fragile, but extremely sharp edge, too easily chipped or broken to be used for a general duty or field knife, and usually restricted to straight razors.

For reasons of fragility, a straight razor is most assuredly not the awesome street weapon depicted in novels and movies. Sure, it can seriously, even fatally, lacerate a victim, but aside from being as dangerous to its wielder as to its victim, and decidedly hard to hang onto, it cannot stab, and it's likely to just break in half during a struggle. Against an adversary armed with a knife, or one who is actively fighting back, it's a poor choice. I've actually seen a few posts on social media sites where tactical-types claim to favor a straight razor as an urban self-defense weapon, but, in fact, the choice is a poor one. A nasty slash from a straight razor is always trumped by a stab through the heart.

Semi-hollow Ground: Knives that are advertised as being hollow ground are actually semi-hollow ground. They have a radius ground into either side of their blades, like a full hollow ground, but in this case, the radius begins about halfway down from the spine. This configuration is a happy medium between the brute strength of a solid bar and the ultra-keenness of a full hollow ground, and this is the most common hunting knife design of all time.

Semi-hollow ground edges are a trademark of Skagel-type hunting knives, and today they're found on many survival and outdoor utility knives, as well. My own first hunting knives were semi-hollow ground. The then newly designed Buck Bearclaw-style lockback folder—arguably the first dedicated all-game hunting folder—that I got for my fourteenth birthday was a semi-hollow ground, as was my favorite deer hunting blade, a faux mother-of-pearl type that was simply marked Solingen, Germany on its choil. Because of its ease of sharpening and a decreased tendency to chip or sustain damage provided by today's alloys, semi-hollow ground blades are now found on military and utility knives, even small "war" axes that used to be saber-ground.

This new Spyderco Chef's knife exemplifies why the flat-ground pattern (usually with a secondary edge) is preferred for razor-edged kitchen cutlery.

Flat Ground: As an outdoor knife, flat-ground was simply not feasible until the turn of the century, because steel alloys and heat treating technologies at the time wouldn't allow it. Because of its "geometry," a generic term that's used these days to describe a blade's configuration, a flat-ground blade is potentially extremely sharp. Its bevel extends in a single plane all the way from its spine, down to its cutting edge, so it has the triangularity to not only be keen, but to retain that sharpness for a maximum time through hard use.

Inherent weaknesses in the flat-ground design include a lack of strength that, before the creation of stronger, tougher steel alloys, required that knives have a fuller or "strongback" ground into their sides to stiffen them so they didn't flex when used to stab. A blade that bends during frontal penetration is sacrificing stabbing power.

The cutting edge of a flat-ground design is inherently weak. Too hard, and it will chip when used to chop with; too soft, and it will dent. Thus, any knife that sports a flat-ground blade has to be made from exceptionally strong, exceptionally tough alloy that has been precisely hardened to optimize both those qualities.

While maybe most kitchen knives are of a flat-ground design, only outdoor-purposed knives made from the best alloys with the best hardening can pull off being flat-ground. When Ontario Knife Company first introduced its 1095 flat-ground RTAK (Randall's Training and Adventure Knife) —under license from a Randall's company that really doesn't want to talk about that collaboration anymore—its advertising inferred that the big knife was virtually indestructible. It was not; while I was teaching a week-long survival class in temperatures that ranged from -8 to -25 degrees Fahrenheit, the job of trimming a pine shelter support proved too much, and two half-dollar-size chips broke out of the edge. The failure seemed only logical to me under such harsh conditions (but not acceptable for any knife that wants to be classed as a survival tool), but it sure caused a stir between the two companies, and now Randall makes its own knives under the ESEE brand, ESEE being an acronym for Escuela de Supervivencia (School of Survival), Escape and Evasion.

In comparison, a flat-ground D2-alloy RAT-7 from the same company (Ontario) has proved to be unreasonably tough. The downside is that my own eyes have shown me that there are few people in the world who can coax a shaving-sharp edge from D2 steel, a reminder that there are numerous attributes to consider when shopping for the ideal knife.

Sheepsfoot Blade: A sheepsfoot blade has no upward sweep, or belly, at the end of its blade. It extends straight from the choil, and the tip radius is from the top, rather than the bottom. Its cutting edge is therefore ruler straight, giving it superior performance for tasks such as slicing, and a very sharp, very controllable point for cutting out shapes from paper, or as a crafts or utility knife. In a bygone era, it was the most preferred blade for cleaning a horse's hooves.

Karambit Blade: Popular with some in the tactical set, probably because it resembles a steel claw, most handymen and do-it-yourselfers will recognize the karambit, or hawksbill, style of blade as a linoleum and vinyl flooring cutter. The curved blade is hook-shaped, but instead of being sharpened on its outer radius, or "belly," like a skinning knife, a karambit's cutting edge is only along its inside radius.

The claw-like design of a karambit blade, like the seat-belt cutter or gut hook that it resembles, is ideal for long, continuous slicing jobs in sheet materials like leather, tarpaper, or carpet. The reverse hook is best for keeping its blade engaged, so it doesn't slip free while making a cut that must be straight and even.

As a weapon, the karambit design is like a straight-razor, in that it's more formidable looking than it truly is. In the hands of someone bent on doing harm, it can inflict nasty lacerations, but it doesn't stab well—the most common cause of death with knife wounds—and it's generally clumsy and too limited for martial applications. The original idea of the karambit-style blade as a tactical knife most likely originated with wind-driven sailors who carried one religiously for slicing and

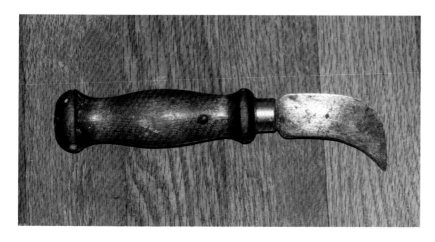

Originally a sailor's knife, made especially for cutting straight lines over large areas of canvas sailcloth, the karambit design is most recognized today as a flooring knife.

mending sails, so it was inevitable that a few of the wave warriors, inebriated at a port-of-call, might grab the nearest thing that resembled a weapon during a dark alley confrontation. But the karambit sailors' knife was seldom employed as an intentional weapon until recent years.

Double Edge: For specialized uses—primarily as a lethal weapon—where penetration is the overriding factor, a double-edge knife, with a cutting edge beveled into both sides of a blade, has been a knife of choice since Roman times. The double edge's most obvious weakness is that removing the metal necessary to create a second edge also removes a significant portion of the knife's strength. For that reason, double-edged knives that were carried as weapons or for general utility uses were necessarily heavy and strong.

After stronger, more refined mass-produced steels became a reality, small, strong daggers became common enough to be issued by militaries. By 1918, during World War One, the M17 Trench Knife had become standard issue. It's a testament to that knife's deadly effectiveness that soldiers who were captured by the enemy while carrying a trench knife were often executed on the spot.

The lethality of a slim, strong dagger continued to make it a favorite into WWII, when British commandos, especially, made a legend of the Sykes-Fairbairn knife, designed by British

policemen and soldiers Eric Sykes and William Fairbairn. Fairbairn pioneered a combat philosophy that he called "gutter fighting," in which he endorsed the idea of winning by any means possible, no matter how low-down. To that end, the knife designed by these men proved to be utterly effective for inflicting stab wounds that were swiftly or instantly fatal. The knife was good for little else, but it excelled at killing.

A double-edged knife has been used since before Biblical times as the weapon of choice against human flesh. It is inherently weak, but capable of inflicting massive wounds.

Stiletto Ground: A stiletto edge is probably best described as a dagger whose bottom edge has been sharpened conventionally—the entire length of the blade—but whose upper sharpened edge extends back from its point only a short distance. This gives a stiletto the piercing power of a dagger, but with the shear (bending) strength of a full-thickness spine. It is especially preferred for slender blades that are intended to stab as well as cut, but lack the metallic beef to withstand much abuse.

The killing power of the aforementioned Sykes-Fairbairn commando dagger is a historical fact. The scope of the Sykes-Fairbairn's utility was too narrow, however, and the Army needed a blade that incorporated more usefulness. Thus was born the M7 Bayonet. Engineered to be a little wider, less tapered, and given a stiletto edge that retained most of its spine, the M7 Bayonet worn by the M-16 rifle of the Vietnam conflict kept the lethality of the Sykes-Fairbairn dagger, but with the strength and utility to serve as a field knife.

That was proved when Schrade turned the M7 bayonet into the M7-S Survival Knife, one of the finest and most iconic belt-worn survival systems ever created. (If I sound a little prejudiced for this particular knife, I am, because the M7-S served me exceptionally well in all types of weather and environments for a dozen years, and probably was responsible for keeping me alive on more than one occasion.) For some reason, the M7-S, and its Schrade successors, the Bomb Tech-01 and the Double Eagle, never caught the collective eye of the survival crowd. Nonetheless, the BT-01 stands as my favorite survival knife. I just wish that this discontinued knife had been made with a better alloy than 420HC.

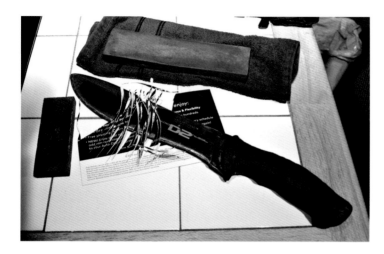

A stiletto point has the penetrating power of a dagger, but without the blade weaknesses inherent to a double-edge design.

Cantled Edge: Sometimes referred to as a convex edge, the term cantled edge derives from the rounded seat of a saddle, called its cantle. Instead of having flat sides that meet in a sharp point, the way the nearly universal beveled edge does, a cantled edge has rounded sides that meet in a slightly less pointed apex. This edge configuration—seen often on axes—gives an edge maximum strength against damage and wear during hard uses (like chopping) by removing a minimal amount of metal. A cantled edge can still be made quite sharp, and it retains a moderately sharp edge through a good deal of work.

Cantled edges, as mentioned above, are probably most often found on axes. Lumberjacks, and folks with wood stoves—before the era of splitting mauls—often kept a double-edge axe, with a very keen beveled edge on one side, for chopping, and a cantled edge on the other for splitting. That isn't such a common practice now, but the heavy machetes of today often wear a cantled edge.

Combination Edge: Combination edges are often found on knives and other cutting tools that have thick blades—including some cantled edges. The simplest description of this edge is that it is actually comprised of two edges—two bevels—that work together to form a blade's cutting edge. The primary, wider bevel is at a steeper angle, but its sides do not quite meet to form a pointed apex at the bottom of the cutting edge. That apex is achieved by applying two additional bevels at shallower angles along the bottom until they meet at a point, which is then polished to a cutting edge.

The purpose of this method is most often simply to save the work that it would take to hone away the steel sufficient to attain a sharp apex from the primary bevels. You'll see this often on a new, never-sharpened axe or big knife (my own included), just because its owner got tired of honing before a proper edge had been formed. By applying a secondary "cheater's" edge, he or she gets an acceptably keen working edge that will improve over time, with every subsequent sharpening, until it has become a single, very sharp edge.

Recurve Blade: A recurve blade, also called a bolo blade, is characterized by the fact that it flares outward at one end, with a rounded belly toward its tip that is wider than the rest of the blade. This makes its blade end-heavy and amplifies the inertial force of whatever amount of muscle a user puts into a swing. The result is that a shorter blade—preferred in thick bush where foliage restricts the length of a swinging blade—has greater chopping power than its mass would permit if the blade were straight. The outward flare of a bolo blade detracts from its stabbing ability, however.

I once dispatched a white-tailed deer that had been seriously injured by a car, using a KaBar Black Camp Knife—it was the only knife I had in the truck. The method I used was one that I'd used successfully dozens of times in the past thirty-five years: a hard point-first thrust up through the lower jaw, through the upper palate, and into the brain pan. The normal result is instant death, but I knew that I was going to have a problem with the two-inch-wide bellied-out bolo point. And I did; the hardest part of this killing thrust is penetrating the bony upper palate, and this knife simply stopped just before reaching the apogee of its belly. Fortunately, I knew how to resolve that problem from past unpleasant experience. Bolo blades are superior choppers, but they are poor stabbing weapons.

The recurve, or Bolo, type blade artificially increases the length of a blade's cutting edge without increasing the blade's length.

Tanto Blade: Tanto blades have been around since roughly the tenth century but, aside from the occasional katana (samurai sword), they were rarely seen in the United States before the 1980s. The dual cutting edges that define the tanto point are on two abrupt and separate planes, not the single, sweeping, bellied plane of the multi-function skinning, cutting, chopping, and fighting blades that made the American frontier into places that families could settle and live. The tanto knife, so good for penetrating armor and dispatching enemies, was little good to an American hunter or trapper who needed his knife do a multitude of things that didn't usually involve killing human beings.

Ironically, tanto-style knives didn't find much of a market in America until knives in general began to lose their value among residents there. The guys I worked with, who almost daily tried (the operative word is tried) to borrow my knife because they, in their own words, didn't have use for one, began to show off cheaply made (that is my opinion), partial-tang tanto knives that were reputed to be capable of punching through a car door. The logic in that ability was lost on an old deer-skinner like myself, but I do believe that stabbing holes in car doors suggests that too many Americans had indeed lost the genuine need for a belt knife in their daily lives. To this day, more than thirty years later, I've never found a need to punch a hole through a car door with a knife.

Today, there is an Americanized version of the tanto that's available. It sports a sweeping belly, rather than the two adjoining edge bevels of a true tanto. This design change does little to detract from blades in terms of strength and all-round efficacy, but it does add to the usefulness of the blade.

The two-plane tanto design is intended to deliver the penetrating power to pierce armor, with maximum tip strength to resist breaking.

Kukri Blade: This knife first gained notoriety as a warrior's weapon in 1814 when it was used against British troops who tried to invade Nepal. The mountain tribes, known as Gurkhas, used the long, inwardly curved shortsword to ambush brightly uniformed troops at every turn as they tried to maintain their trademark appearance of a disciplined rank-and-file army while marching through untracked jungle. So impressed were the British that they hired the Gurkhas to work for them—an alliance that continues to this day.

During WWII, British Gurkhas, themselves masters of the bush, wrought tremendous harm on supposedly unbeatable Japanese jungle fighters. The configuration of the kukris blade causes it to cut deeper and harder as it reaches the end of its slashing arc. The Gurkha strategy of simply running out of the jungle, delivering one hard, slashing blow across an enemy's neck, then disappearing back into shadowed foliage, left a good many sentries silently decapitated, and definitely instilled a sense of fear into the pride of the Japanese army.

Like the tanto, this specialized knife has had a limited following among northern outdoorsmen from Norway and Siberia to Canada and America. The kukri's acutely angled blade, so effectual for dismembering enemies in close combat, is quite cumbersome for most everyday camp chores.

Some authors have pointed out how Ghurkha troops have learned to employ their issue kukris for all types of survival tasks, but that demonstrates how adaptable the soldiers are more than it does the utility of this design. My own experience with them during week-long outings in wilderness have been less than impressive.

Scagel Type Knives: William Scagel was the father of the twentieth-century hunting knife. By the time of his death in 1963, Scagel-style knives, typically with a full-length, rat-tail tang, a handle made from stacked leather washers slid over the tang and held in place with a screw-on (sometimes pinned) pommel cap, and a simple brass fingerguard, had become the deer hunter's knife.

Scagel-style blades are typically clip-point, semi-hollow ground, and made from traditional 1095. Handles are typically simple, roundish, and swelled outward at their centers, and with a high polish. Sheaths are generally simple leather affairs with stitched seams, belt loops, and snap-down leather retaining straps. Some handles are hollow tubes made from faux mother-of-pearl, charred bone, or antler. Many are made military-style, and are comprised of stacked leather washers, sanded smooth and polished.

In all instances, Scagel knives are attractive, ergonomically nimble in every position and, providing they are made from quality materials (cheap knock-offs do exist), they perform well for all types of hunting and camping jobs. Nothing speaks to the truth of that claim so well as a century in the hands of American and Canadian meat hunters.

Although Bill Scagel can no longer be at the helm of a company that makes knives bearing his name, the company that picked up that mantle in the twenty-first century promises to remain true to Scagel's vision. You can see the new Scagel knives at: www.scagelknives.com

This classic Scagel-type hunting knife, with its thoroughly modern blade of A1 steel, is a creation of Northwoods Knives, operating out of Michigan's Upper Peninsula until the death of company founder Dave Shirley, whose artistic genius will be forever missed.

CHAPTER THREE
BLADE MATERIALS

It was the summer of my twelfth year on Earth, and as I usually was whenever I could be, I was back in the woods where nobody could find me, enjoying the freedom and seclusion that can only be had in a wilderness.

I was tying off a tarpaulin roof over the frame of my shelter, and I reached a point where I needed both hands. As I've always done in such situations, I flipped my prized Western Bowie knife downward by its handle, causing it to stick, hilt-upward, into the earth.

This time, however, the blade struck, not with the smooth, quiet thud that I'd been anticipating, but with a "clink" that sounded disturbingly like breaking glass. The blade had hit a rock, and it had snapped in twain as cleanly as if it had been a shard of window pane. Now I stood with the two halves of what had been my most prized possession on a personal level, and my most crucial wilderness tool.

My heart was as broken as that knife. That wasn't the last time a knife would fail me, and every such incident has been awful. Like having your car's engine suddenly die while you are far off the beaten track on a cold and stormy night, having your knife break in the woods is a profound, wrenching loss. And I personally have seen situations where a failed knife can be life-threatening.

The cause of this particular tragedy was poor alloy composition, poor heat treatment, and generally poor production quality. There's a lot of romantic talk about the good old days, the grand ethos of generations past, and products of old that were manufactured using arcane secrets of craftsmanship that have somehow been lost. In truth, the metal-folding forging secrets used to make the samurais' katanas of old, and the blacksmithing sorcery used to hammer out Jim Bowie's Iron Maiden, were neither unknown nor even impressive by today's knife-making standards. When every chunk of steel was hand-crafted, a good blacksmith, like a skilled grandma, could be graded by the quality of the knife blades or oatmeal cookies, respectively. But these days, recipes for steel and dough can be precisely duplicated in massive quantities, and every characteristic that once made a thing the best of its kind has been identified, and can be mass produced in great numbers.

The Bronze Age

Tools and weapons made of smelted metal first appeared during the third phase of mankind's rise to dominance, following the Paleolithic and Neolithic Stone Ages. It began with the smelting of bronze, an alloy of copper and tin, which appeared in Greece and China about 3000 BC, and in Europe around 1900 BC. The temperature required to smelt (melt and mix together) bronze from copper and tin is 913 degrees Centigrade (1,675 Fahrenheit).

Soft copper, pure deposits of which occur naturally, had already been in use for centuries as jewelry, and even as tools and weapons, although it was too soft to be of much use for cutting tools. Then, probably by accident, copper and tin were melted together in the relatively low heat of a wood fire, producing bronze.

The discovery of bronze changed everything. Individually, both tin and copper were so soft as to be nearly useless, but smelted together as brass, they formed a hard, yet flexible, corrosion-resistant alloy, with nearly the strength and toughness of a mild steel. Bronze was easy to smelt at the attainable (wood-fired) temperatures of the day, and it produced very functional plows for farming, swords, and spearheads for doing battle, and armor for protecting oneself from those weapons. It was used to make buckles and buttons, for efficiently processing fish and meat, and for wire to bind, make rivets, craft hinges, and other, more complex machines. Bronze represents a huge step in the creation of civilization.

So important was bronze that it is still used today, and for many of the same implements, although its primary uses today are ornamental.

Some confusion exists over the differences between bronze and brass. Fundamentally, whereas bronze is a blend of tin and copper, which has the flexibility to be shaped through hammering, brass is a mix of copper and zinc, which is hard and strong but brittle. Brass items are usually cast in a mold made from two halves of wet sand into which mirror-opposite cavities have been impressed. These halves are mated and bound together, then the molten brass is poured through a knock-out hole, filling the cavities inside the mold.

When cool, the mold is broken apart, often destroying it, and the hard metal, sometimes quite sophisticated item inside is removed. After grinding and smoothing away the "flashing" that naturally occurs where the two halves of a mold are mated, the spigot, handle, or whatever is ready for use. This is an oversimplification of the process, and there are innumerable variables which can make a casting better suited to specific purposes, but that's it in a nutshell.

The Iron Age

Iron was a rare, difficult to smelt, and apparently little-valued metal in the Middle East as far back as 3000 BC. Egyptians who sometimes extracted it from meteorites called it "black copper." But iron remained unknown, or at least unused, to most of the civilized world until centuries later.

Extracting it from rocky ore demands higher heat than is possible with a simple wood fire —1,204 Centigrade (2,200 Fahrenheit) —which meant that more sophisticated blacksmithing techniques, involving coke-fired forges, bellows, and tools were required.

Iron was the next great leap forward for humankind. It was harder, stronger, and heavier than bronze or brass, and those qualities made it superior as axe heads, plows, and shovels. Depending on how it was created, how much heat was used, and, most important, the type and quantity of its carbon content, it could become white iron or gray iron—generally just lumped together as brittle cast irons—good for woodstoves and the cheap "trade knives" that trappers bartered to Indian tribes. Or it might be made into malleable iron, which was softer and would bend, making it generally more suitable for chain links, nails, and horseshoes.

Even within just the area of malleable iron, there are different grades with different characteristics, like black-heart iron, white-heart iron, and pearlitic iron, to demonstrate just a little how complicated this most basic of metals can get in today's world. The following sections will further help to explain and simplify the nuts-and-bolts of metal alloys.

Cast Iron: Cast iron is the oldest ferrous metal. It is primarily composed of iron (Fe), carbon (C), and silicon (Si), with traces of sulfur (S), manganese (Mn), and phosphorus (P). It has a high carbon content of 2 percent to 5 percent, making it hard and brittle. Its structure is crystalline, evident when the metal is viewed in cross section. The composition of cast iron, and what applications it is best suited for, are determined by the methods used to manufacture it.

Common gray cast iron is easily cast in a mold, but it cannot be forged or machined without chipping or breaking, whether hot or cold. Gray cast iron has its carbon content distributed as flakes throughout the metal, and when the material is broken, it appears as bright, reflective speckles along the broken surface.

For centuries, gray cast iron was used to make "trade knives" and axes that were bartered to natives by immigrants from the Old World. Cast iron was inexpensive, it could be honed extremely sharp, and it held an edge well. Gray iron knives were, of course, superior to flint and obsidian, but they were broken often enough to keep them in demand. Gray iron, being able to take repeated heating and cooling, was an invaluable material to pioneers who needed wood-burning stoves, and is still preferred for that application today, as well as for casting the ever-popular cast-iron cookware.

In white cast iron, the carbon content is combined chemically as carbide of iron, and is distributed more homogenously throughout. This isn't so obvious, because you can't easily break white cast iron. It has excellent tensile strength and malleability, which is why it is also known as "malleable" (or "spheroidal graphite") iron.

Both types of cast iron are still manufactured by much the same process as it was by our ancestors: Iron ore is heated in a blast furnace with coke and limestone (about 2,100 degrees Fahrenheit for gray iron, about 2,800 degrees for white, or wrought iron). These temperatures liquefy ore, deoxidizing it and eliminating impurities. The molten iron is poured into molds of the desired shape, then allowed to cool and re-harden.

Hard gray cast iron develops a protective scale on the surface, which makes it initially more resistant to corrosion than wrought iron or mild steel. Protective finishes include bituminous (essentially, coal dust) coatings, waxes, paints, galvanizing, and plating. Unprotected iron of either type can oxidize (rust) within hours in the presence of humidity and oxygen in the air.

Wrought Iron: Wrought iron is in reality a white iron alloy which has a very low carbon content of less than 0.08 percent, in contrast to cast iron (2.1 to 4 percent). It is semi-fused fibrous slag inclusions (up to 2 percent by weight) which give it a wood-like grain, visible when the iron is sanded, etched, or bent in half. Wrought iron is tough, malleable (form-able), ductile (stretch-able), mildly corrosion-resistant, and easily welded. Before the advent of mass-produced steel in the early 1900s, wrought iron was the most common metal construction material. Prior to the technology that allowed mild steel to be mass-produced, items that were made from wrought iron included rivets, nails, wire, chains, rails, railway couplings, water and steam pipes, nuts, bolts, horseshoes, handrails, wagon tires, straps for timber roof trusses, and ornamental ironwork. Wrought iron built the civilized world.

Today, ornamental rails and other items that are labeled as being made from wrought iron are, in fact, made from mild steel, such as 1010/1008.

Steel: The origin of steel can be traced back to 2,000 years BCE, having replaced bronze as the metal of choice for tools and weapons. The problem was, steel was more specialized, and more complicated to manufacture, and only a skilled blacksmith—the village scientist—had the expertise to create the metal required to craft a high-quality farming plow, or a sword that could defend a home without breaking in two or becoming a pretzel. A blade as fine as those we have come to take for granted in the twenty-first century would have been as prized as fabled Excalibur, if it could have existed at all.

There are recorded instances of great warriors who were forced to withdraw from a battle long enough to step down on the middle of their sword blade, to bend it back straight enough to continue fighting. Conversely, if the sword were tempered too hard, it would break in two, and its wielder would be out of the battle for good—if he was lucky. A skilled blacksmith was as prized by the village in which he lived as anyone there. He was the person who made it possible to plow fields, to shoe horses so that their hooves didn't split, for making the armor that kept village defenders from being skewered, and for forging the knives that were so vital to butchering meat and defending loved ones.

Mass-produced Steel: But steel, the magic recipe of iron with 0.2 to 1.5 percent carbon that's harder than wrought iron, but tougher than cast iron, was only achievable in small quantities by skilled blacksmiths, so all knives and other steel implements were crafted by hand. Then in 1856 a British metallurgist named Henry Bessemer invented a blast furnace that he named the Bessemer converter. Bessemer's converter enabled large quantities of iron to be converted to steel in just minutes by blasting the molten "bloom" with compressed air using a predetermined formula.

Bessemer tried to gain a monopoly on mass-produced steel with more than one hundred patents, but the genie was out of the bottle. The 1860s saw many improvements to Bessemer's process by inventors like Karl Wilhelm Siemens, who developed the open hearth process, which he dubbed the Siemen's Gas Furnace.

The effect of having mass-produced, readily available steel was instantaneous, first in the railroad industry, where rails in high traffic or high stress locations (like curves) had to be replaced every few weeks, or they might fail, causing trains to derail. Later, beams and girders of stronger, lighter steel made construction of high-rise buildings feasible, and city skylines became urban landmarks.

Later, with continuous advances in steel-making sciences, alloys with heretofore unknown qualities emerged, making possible high-stress, heat-resistant, super-strong applications, and leading to advances in cannons and armor, more powerful engines, longer bridges, and of course better knife blades.

As steel recipes, or "alloys," became more numerous and more specialized, it became necessary to catalog them. To begin, they were itemized by the Society of Automotive Engineers (SAE), then by the American Iron and Steel Institute (AISI). Today, most steel alloys are referred to by their AISI designation, which in most cases remains unchanged from the SAE number. For example, SAE 1095 is the same as AISI 1095.

Blade Steels: Even a generation ago, choosing a good knife was a lot simpler, because there were fewer options to select from. The mechanics were less sophisticated, as always, reflecting the technology of the time, and there were relatively few blade alloys to choose from. China wasn't the steel-making juggernaut that it has become, super-hard tool steels were still in the realm of custom knifesmiths, not mass-produced as they are today, and hardening processes hadn't become the fine-tuned exact science that they've become.

As alloys become more sophisticated and metallurgical sciences discover more and better ways to control the properties of a steel down to and beyond molecular levels, it is becoming impossible to speak of knives with the same cocktail party simplicity. For every rule there is an exception, and nothing is absolute. Even so, there are three fundamental qualities that every knife aficionado should know: hardness, toughness, and strength.

Hardness has become the benchmark for assessing overall blade quality, because, generally speaking, the harder the cutting edge, the sharper it can be made, and the longer it will retain its sharpness. In reality, there are other factors—like the configuration ("geometry" in blade vernacular). Hardness is usually stated as a value on the Rockwell Corporation's "C" scale (the C scale is one of several, including other hardness measurements, like the Brinell scale). Hardness is determined by how far a penetrator (a carbide ball or a diamond penetrator called a brale) is driven into a steel under a predetermined amount of pressure. A very good blade will measure around 58 on the C scale—abbreviated as HRC—but in the new millennium, it isn't unusual to see a knife with a Rockwell of 60 or more.

Hardness became the standard for assessing blade quality because it provided an idea of how sharp a knife could be, and because it revealed the homogeneity of a blade. In generations past, it wasn't unusual for different points on a blade to vary by as much as five points, which was indicative of poor quality steel. Better knives today have hardness differentials of one point or less at any place on their blades.

Toughness is a measure of a steel's resistance to abrasion or, in knife terms, the ability of a cutting edge to remain sharp when it is in use. An edge loses its keenness when the polished apex where its sides join becomes rounded through wear. A perfect blade doesn't wear at all, and so remains pointed and sharp, regardless of what it cuts. That, of course, is an impossibility. It also demonstrates why hardness isn't the only measure of blade quality, just the most convenient to measure. Cast iron is very hard, but although a trade knife of the 1700s could be made shaving-sharp, it lost its cutting edge swiftly when skinning a deer, and its blade was easily broken.

Strength is the quality that allows a knife to be used as a prybar. If a blade is meant for nothing more strenuous than slicing an onion, this is not a critical trait. In modern times, it's not even that important for a Ted Nugent-class, steaming gut-pile, sport hunter's knife.

But neither is strength the absolute measure of a knife's quality. During an extreme-cold survival class, I, the instructor, once broke my expensive and supposedly unbreakable 1095 survival knife doing exactly the same tasks as a student who had requested that he be permitted to carry his own 440B flea market-grade Bowie knife. In any other environment I had the superior blade, but in that below-zero forest his scrap-metal fantasy knife, which dulled spreading peanut butter, was better than mine.

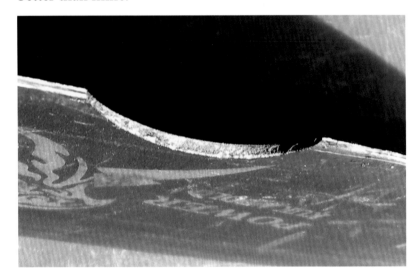

This brutally strong TOPS Power Eagle Machete stands as proof that any knife can be broken after enough abuse (like batoning).

Crucible Particle Metallurgy in Alloys: Another stabilizing factor that makes the steel alloys of today more precise and unvarying than they've ever been is the strategy of blending component ingredients in sintered form, a process called Crucible Particle Metallurgy, after Crucible Industries, where the process was pioneered. An oversimplified explanation of this process is that powdered elements of an alloy are thoroughly blended before being melted—again, much the same as cookbooks recommend that dried ingredients for a cake batter be mixed prior to adding wet ingredients. Doing this better mixes salt, sugar, flour, and so on, and results in a more silky, creamy batter that mixes better, bakes more evenly, and tastes better.

The same strategy makes for a very smooth steel with almost no variation in composition or performance characteristics from one end to the other. A USMC Kabar knife from WWII might exhibit a variation in hardness of more than five points, meaning that one part of a blade is hard enough to break, while another part is just plain soft. In contrast, Benchmade's discontinued RUKUS folder has a CPM S30V blade with a very hard and tight 58–60 HRC; no part of this blade is too soft or too hard, and it possesses the desired qualities throughout.

Blade Steel Characteristics: One nationally televised knife show, called Cutlery Corner (which is, in fact, an hours-long infomercial dedicated to selling knives), routinely claims that its offerings are "Rockwell tested." Some knives even sport a stick-on decal on their blades to prove that they've been Rockwell tested. By itself, that statement is meaningless. It's like saying that there are tires on the car you're buying, but neglecting to mention their brand, type, size, or if they have air in them.

You might have read knife specifications that advertised one factor of a blade using a two-digit numerical factor, followed by the abbreviation "HRC," or just "RC." This is a blade's hardness value, usually measured on the Rockwell Corporation's "C" scale, although there are several yardsticks, like Rockwell's A or B scales, the Brinell scales, or the Vickers scale. Typically, hardness of a material is determined by how far a very hard (carbide steel or diamond) penetrator is driven into it by a predetermined amount of pressure.

Not long ago, knife makers tended to leave this rating off of published specifications about the knives they manufactured, believing that it made little difference to buyers. But a blade's hardness, or "Rockwell," has long been thought to be a measure of its quality, and the best knife makers are again posting that value proudly. Rockwell hardness, measured on that firm's "C" scale (there exist a number of measuring scales from Rockwell and other companies), and usually abbreviated "Hrc," is a pretty fair indicator of how well a knife will retain its keenness. As a rule of thumb, the higher a knife's Hrc value, the harder its blade, and the better it holds an edge. Today, knives range from 50 to a whopping 68 Hrc (the patented DiamondBlade Summit, reviewed later)—that higher value being unheard of just a few years ago.

Generally speaking, but not always, the higher the Rockwell rating—the more an alloy is hardened during heat treatment—the more brittle its metal becomes. Note that most steels can actually be driven to a much higher hardness than their blades indicate—for example, common 1060 "spring" steel can be tempered to 66 Hrc—but are usually intentionally "drawn back" to a softer Hrc to prevent them from becoming too brittle for use as a knife blade. A 1060 blade at that hardness would chip like glass when you used it, and would invariably snap in half at some point.

Hardness variation in a knife blade often indicates the quality of a steel used in its production—not just of an alloy in general, but of a particular batch. When I worked as a quality control manager, every truckload of coiled steel delivered to us was required to be accompanied by "certs" (certifications) that listed each element in that particular batch of steel, and its value in percentage points. These certs were then checked meticulously against the recipe for that alloy as it was listed in the appropriate *SAE Steel Certifications Handbook* (my office held twenty-five of these weighty hardbound tomes in those days). The quality of our stamped and drawn (formed and stretched under immense pressures) manufactured parts simply shot upward when I forced the company comptroller to stop purchasing second-tier steels at cut-rate prices. By making him purchase "number one" steel, I eliminated the tearing and splitting of stamped steel components that couldn't be manufactured using substandard alloys, and our quality rating soared overnight.

Variation in a batch of steel caused by flawed recipes can have a very negative impact on mass-produced knife blades, resulting in cutting edges that can be very sharp and very dull, very brittle and as malleable as clay—all in the same blade. Such extremes are rare, but they have happened.

Better batter makes better pancakes, and steel alloys generally follow the same rule of thumb. Stringently controlled proportions of, for example, Cobalt (Co), Vanadium (V), and Nickel (Ni) can result in very much better or worse steel, just as rigidly followed recipes for amounts of baking powder, salt, and flour can have a real impact of how good a cake turns out. Tightly applied and controlled specifications make the steel alloys of today infinitely better than the same alloy produced just a generation ago.

The "Best" Knife Alloy: What the Experts Have to Say

Which alloy is the best choice for any given task—from kitchen to hunting to wilderness survival—has been a subject of endless argument for as long as there have been choices. Whenever a new steel recipe appears, some expert or another is guaranteed to claim that here, finally, is the Excalibur that we've all been waiting for.

I am not qualified to debate the idiosyncrasies of every knife-grade alloy with the finest blade smiths in the world, but as a knife user, I'll willingly match my mettle against anyone on Earth. I say that anyone who claims that there is a perfect do-it-all knife steel (or design, for that matter) is lacking on the side of hard experience. Just as every superman has his kryptonite, so does every super steel have its weakness.

Having said that, a couple of the knife masters who I respect the most have granted me a small sample of their wisdom:

Blackie Collins: Walter Wells "Blackie" Collins is one of the most innovative knife designers to ever become a legend. He made his name with a number of eye-catching and updated Bowie-design fixed blades under the Smith & Wesson brand. He is best known for his folding knives, primarily assisted-opening designs for Gerber, and for starting a trade magazine titled *American Blade* in 1973, which became *Blade* magazine in 1994. Blackie Collins was taken from us in a motorcycle accident on July 20, 2011, at the age of seventy-two.

Two weeks before his death, I had the privilege of interviewing Mr. Collins for a magazine column that I was writing. In that interview I delved into background information concerning what turned out to be Blackie's last knife design for Meyerco company (a disappointing product that more resembled a paring knife than the survival knife that it was supposed to be).

The new knife was made from 440A, the original stainless-steel alloy. That seemed archaic, in light of newer and arguably much better blade steels like S90V, ATS-34, or even 420HC. When I asked why, Blackie told me, "If I had to choose one knife to do everything for the rest of my life, I'd choose one of the four-forties."

A lot of lesser knife experts than Blackie Collins—myself included—would disagree with his choice, but in fact there are few of us who are qualified to contest his assertion. And whether you personally concur with Blackie's preference or not, his opinion is certainly proof enough that good old fashioned 440 is not obsolete. Having skinned scores of deer with a 440C folding knife, I personally could not debate Blackie's statement without being a hypocrite.

A.G. Russell III (CEO A.G. Russell Knives): This man and I are not friends. He's coarse, he's abrasive, he's ornery—he's just like me.

And like me, he's cursed with unbending honesty and integrity—even when it offends others. A. G. Russell won my admiration (and made some powerful enemies) in 1988, when everyone was fawning over a Cold Steel, Inc. knife called the TrailMaster. The big Bowie-style knife seemed to be quite impressive on its surface—until A. G. called out CEO Lynn Thompson for fudging on some of the "trials" that seemed to make it more impressive than it actually was. Speaking from personal experience with Cold Steel's then-new Kukri, which also did not live up to its hyperbole in the field, A. G. made a probably permanent enemy with his review. But A. G. doesn't lose sleep over repercussions from telling truths that others won't.

When asked to say a few words for this book, eighty-two-year-old A. G. Russell offered this tidbit of personal wisdom: "When I was young I wanted a blade steel and heat treat that would allow me to work a knife hard for a week and have it still sharp enough to continue to work. Now I look for a steel and heat treat combination that will sharpen easily and hold a good edge for a reasonable time."

I interpret that to mean that his years of experience have convinced him that, unless he's skinning buffalo on a daily basis, he'd rather spend an occasional few minutes re-honing an easily sharpened knife than expend the sometimes hard work required to re-establish a good cutting edge on a dulled super-hard knife.

Leo Espinoza (President TOPS Knives): "Over the past twenty years the knife industry in the USA and overseas has grown at a rather accelerated pace. There have been many new designers, intricate gadgets, even plenty of new steel grades that are great for knives. Add to that the sheer number of outdoor personalities, survivalists, preppers, military and security, etc., and it's easy to see that the knife industry has completely exploded."

Chris Hayes (custom knife maker): Chris Hayes is a custom knife maker of the old-fashioned one-at-a-time, hammer-and-anvil blacksmith sort. He prefers to craft his blades from O1 Tool steel. The sharpness and edge retention of this steel have made him a believer in its value as a knife steel. O1 is such a tricky and difficult alloy to work with that most knife makers prefer not to deal with it; if you don't heat treat it exactly right, it can become brittle enough to chip, and the alloy's tendency to discolor from exposure to acids (animal fats, citrus fruits . . .) makes it unpopular with the show-knife set. Chris also works in Damascus, or any other type of steel that you'd prefer, and he's one of the few remaining craftsmen.

Charles T. "Chuck" Buck (past CEO Buck Knives): The passing of this icon of knife design and manufacture in February of 2015 saddened me as if he'd been a member of my family. I never knew the man beyond our telephone conversations, letters, Christmas cards, and emails, but insofar as those communications were concerned, we knew one another for twenty years. One of my most prized possessions is a Buck-made M9 Field Knife with a solid buttcap, instead of the usual bayonet latch plate. It was the last of a production run that was made for shipment to Japan, where it is illegal to own a knife that will mount to a firearm; he saved it for me because he knew that as a survival instructor, I'd prefer a hammer to a bayonet mount. I will always remember Chuck for his sometimes humorous obsession with making an "official SEAL knife" —an impossible undertaking, because that team of specialists carries the knife that suits them, personally. Chuck didn't have a favorite alloy that I knew of, and he was open to trying new materials and new designs as much as any knife expert I've ever encountered.

Ken Onion (knife designer): "Favorite alloy? I have a few. Takefu Super Gold 2 or Super Cobalt are faves if price is no issue. CPM-3V and CPM-4 are favorites for heavy choppers, and BD1N is the best overall bang for the $$$ in the game."

John Moore (late CEO of Mission Knives): This founder of Mission Knives will probably be best known for his creation of the first beta-titanium field knife. This non-magnetic, virtually indestructible metal is the stuff that landing gear struts of Navy carrier jets is made from, and John's titanium knives have long been in service by mine disposal units in the Middle East. John wasn't everyone's cup of tea; he had no reservations about telling people that he was a genius—which he was—and he didn't mind telling someone that they needed more education before they pontificated on a topic. John and I first met, via telephone, when I was assigned to review Mission Knife's Katrina Search-and-Rescue Knife. John had already sent a copy to another knife expert, who told him that his sample had "skinned twenty-four deer without needing to be sharpened." My own experience was that the Katrina was unbreakable by human muscle, but that it didn't hold an edge worth a damn. John already knew that, which is why he wanted the knife evaluated by an honest knife authority.

Knife Alloys: It would be impossible to address every alloy of steel that has been turned into a fine knife, but following are some of the better alloys that have done just that.

Note that many of the alloys mentioned here overlap on every level, just like the sea of firearms calibers that shooters have been arguing about endlessly for fifty years. In fact, some steel alloys are precisely identical to one another, they just have different designations because they're manufactured in countries that do not use American identification systems.

For example, Japanese-made SK-5, so highly touted by some publications for its outstanding characteristics, is exactly the same as AISI (or SAE) 1080, which is not highly regarded at all by some of the same people. In its own turn, the 1080 alloy—which I happen to think makes a fine machete blade—is known by a confusing array of proprietary designations. Cross designations for AISI/SAE 1080-alloy steel include: FED: QQ-S-700, AMS: 5110, AMS: 5110B, ASTM: A29, ASTM: A510, ASTM: A576, ASTM: A682, MIL SPEC: MIL-S-16974, SAE: J403, SAE: J412, SAE: J414, UNS: G10800. And that is just for a single alloy.

Adding to the confusion is the relatively new process of finely powdering the individual elements of an alloy—vanadium, carbon, manganese, etc. —before combining them into a molten blend. This process, pioneered by the Crucible Particulate Metals (CPM) company, has changed the knife industry by creating the most pure, most homogenous alloys ever produced in a steel mill. One analogy would be lumpy pancake batter compared to silky smooth blended batter. Added cost of producing such alloys has not obsoleted conventional alloys in chain-link fencing, railroad components, bridges, and other applications where purity isn't critical, but particulate metals have changed knife blades for the better forever.

Also take into consideration hardening processes. These range from oil-quenching, heating, and then super-freezing in liquid nitrogen, slowly cooling metal while wrapped in a cake of clay . . . and so on. Some blades are zone hardened, also known as differentially hardened. Zone hardening is defined as making a cutting edge alone extra-hard to enhance its edge retention, while the bulk of the blade is left softer, tougher, and less likely to break under stress. Depending on how quickly or slowly an alloy is cooled, and by what medium, for how long, and a bunch of other factors, a steel may take on an almost unlimited variety of characteristics. The real advantage of zone hardening is that a machete can be hard and sharp enough to butcher meat, yet withstand the pounding of being used to prune branches without sustaining permanent damage—like the Vietnam-vintage GI jungle machete, which invariably snapped in two after a short period of chopping anything harder than bamboo and lianas.

So don't get wound up in a confusing spider web of numbers and alloy designations. It is important to know some of the basics for purposes of practicality—like I chipped a high-quality 1095-steel TOPS Armageddon knife while using it to chop frozen venison for our sled dogs; after that, I switched to a softer (lower edge retention) 1075-steel Mah-Chete from CRKT. You should know enough to select the right alloy to suit your intended use, but don't get mired in numbers like a stereo maven, computer geek, or gun nut.

Variations on a theme, the real differences in types, styles, sizes, and materials used for knives in the twenty-first century have become virtually endless. We can only imagine what the lowly knife will have evolved to in the second century of this millennium.

The 10-series: (1095, 1085, 1070, 1060, 1050, etc.) Many of the 10-series steels are used for cutlery, though 1095 is the most popular for knives. When you go in descending order from 1095–1050, you generally go from more carbon to less, from more wear resistance to less wear resistance, and tough to tougher. As such, you'll see 1060 and 1050, used often for swords, machetes, and axe heads that are designed for hard striking against other hard surfaces. For knives, 1095 is the original standard carbon steel, inexpensive, tough, and hard enough to take a remarkably keen edge when tempered well. AISI/SAE 1095 sharpens easily, but it rusts overnight, and so knives made from it usually have a protective coating. Do not remove this coating, as has become popular with dudes who like to give their knives an "experienced" appearance. And if you possess high-carbon cutlery like Ontario Knife's time-tested Old Hickory brand, wash, thoroughly dry, and put away those knives immediately after each use; never leave them in a dish drainer, else they'll be covered in red rust in just hours—and pitted beyond repair not long after that.

1095 was originally developed as a simple tool steel, but it was easier to work than harder and tougher tool steels—like O-1 or A-2—and so proved very effective for mass-produced knife blades. Rough blade blanks could be stamped out swiftly from sheet-metal stock using a flywheel-type punch press (commonly used by metal-stamping companies even before WWI) and ground to desired proportions. After a simple heat-and-quench hardening operation, the blades (unsharpened—soldiers were expected to do that for themselves) were fitted with handles and sheaths, and issued by the million to troops headed off to fight The Big One.

A carbon content of 0.95 allows the steel to be quenched to a hardness of Hrc 66. For knife blades the steel is usually drawn back (tempered down) to 56–58 HRC, which provides an optimum combination of hardness and toughness for that alloy.

Perhaps the best endorsement for 1095 comes from Leo Espinoza, the president of TOPS Knives (www.topsknives.com). "One of our favorite steels is still 1095. We use it for a variety of factors.

While it may not perform in some areas as well as some of the new super steels will, it still makes an excellent knife at an excellent price. The edge retention with 1095 when heat treated properly (the sweet spot for this steel grade is about 57 on the Rockwell C scale) is great. Many people comment on how it amazes them they're able to use a TOPS for so long without needing to re-sharpen it—whether they're processing animals, cutting in the woods, or just using their

One of the original mass-produced knives, made from SAE 1095 alloy, the original mass-produced knife steel, the Kabar USMC Combat Knife proved its worth on the battlefield and in peace time for more than half a century.

knife for everyday cutting tasks. One of the best features of 1095 is how easy it is to re-sharpen, and to go hand-in-hand with that, how well it takes an edge. We pride ourselves at TOPS on our differential heat treat of 1095; that is what sets us apart from many other production knife companies. So between the edge retention, how well it takes an edge, how easy it is to re-sharpen, the differential heat treatment, and the price, 1095 continues to be a favorite steel for TOPS."

Believe me, I'd argue with Mr. Espinoza if it were warranted, but I agree with his assertions. And judging from the popularity of TOPS knives with serious outdoors people, so do a lot of others.

1085: A favorite for heavy-use field knives. With proper hardening, this steel can reach a respectable 52–54 HRC, and still remain tough enough to take the pounding of field use. It can be chipped when used to hack through bone, or if it strikes a nail. Edge retention is marginal, but the steel resharpens easily, it takes a very keen edge, and the toughness has been worth it to me. Kabar's Cutlass Machete is made from 1085.

This Kabar Cutlass Machete has proved that 1085 high carbon steel is a good choice for chopping knives, in which toughness and strength are more important than the ability to retain a keen edge.

1080: As you might extrapolate from its number designation, 1080 isn't a lot removed from 1085. It can be honed to a very sharp edge, which it holds tolerably well—expect to have to resharpen it after a job more demanding than cutting the flaps off of a cardboard box. It can, and has, skinned and butchered deer-size animals, but I've never gotten through the task without withdrawing for a few minutes to stone its blade back to functional sharpness.

So far as toughness in the field, forget about it—1080 is nigh unbreakable. You might (will) nick, roll, bend, and possibly even chip its edge, with common life chores in a wilderness, but there's little chance that the blade will actually break. Very similar to 80CrV2-alloy, 1080 is a "forgiving" steel in that you can make a mistake, then reheat and re-forge it to your intended dimensions without losing any of its inherent qualities. That alone makes it popular with novice knife makers. It is claimed that blades of 1080 *can* be hardened to 66Hrc, but its nominal working hardness should be 55-58Hrc.

This Kharon folder from Kabar's Zombie Knives line, with it's blade of AUS-8 steel, served well under some very demanding conditions for more than half a decade.

SK-5: A Japanese-made high-carbon steel that is the equivalent of AISI 1080.

1075: AISI 1075 provides exceptional strength while resisting wear, making it ideal for the railway industry. A high-carbon steel that can be oil or water hardened, AISI 1075 also performs well in hand and machine tool applications. CRKT's very tough Mah-Chete is made from 1075, with a rather broad hardness range of 50-55Hrc.

1060: The mid-range carbon content and relatively high manganese content of 1060 makes for a tough blade steel that will withstand abusive applications, hold an edge well, and sharpen easily. 0.65C 0.85Mn. I've made knives from this steel myself; it's easy to work, and even my poor hardening skills produced rather good skinning knives.

Carbon V: Carbon V is a copyrighted trademark of Cold Steel, Inc., and as such it has not always been one particular formula of steel. Rather, it describes whatever steel Cold Steel happens to be using. Many knife authorities believe that this company does indeed change steels from time to time, unannounced to their customers, and can legally call whatever the alloy might be by the name Carbon V. Knife designer Joe Talmadge has stated, "Carbon V performs roughly between 1095-ish and O1-ish, in my opinion, and rusts like O1 as well. I've heard rumors that Carbon V is O1 (which I think is unlikely) or 1095." Some industry insiders believe that Carbon V is 0170–6 or 50100-B (both are the same alloy under different proprietary designations). Based on my own experiences with Cold Steel blades, I believe the knives I've used were 1095.

T10: TR10 is basically the Chinese equivalent of our 1095, but it has silicon added as an alloying element to improve the steel's strength and wear-resistance (edge-holding) properties. T10 blades can be tempered to a high hardness and hold an edge well. As with 1095, rust resistance is low, and T10 blades must be religiously maintained

80CrV2: Except for a lower (about half) manganese content, and .01% more carbon, Chinese-made 80CrV2 is identical to 1080

DNH7: DNH7 is a relatively simple high-carbon steel similar in composition to 1075. Differential hardening of DNH7 produces a fine working blade that holds an edge well.

Renowned for its ability to retain a sharp edge, but reviled by most experts for the difficulty that nearly all of them have in achieving such an edge, D2 is the author's preferred survival knife alloy.

1566: A high-carbon and manganese spring steel used by Hanwei in many of their differentially hardened Japanese swords and through-hardened medieval swords. This deep hardening steel provides a consistent microstructure ensuring a long life and excellent edge holding in demanding applications.0.6–0.7C 0.85–1.15Mn

L6: L6 was developed for the manufacture of saw blades, with excellent resilience and impact toughness (provided by the relatively high nickel content) at high hardness levels. The Bainite phase of L6, achieved by careful heat treatment, is much sought-after in sword blades.

D2: This may be the author's favorite all-round survival knife steel. It is very hard, exceptionally strong, and tough enough to hold an edge through what would be abuse to most alloys. That advantage, as well as D2's biggest disadvantage, is made evident by the quote from one magazine knife expert that "D2 takes a lousy edge and holds it forever." As evidenced by my own shaving-sharp D2 blades, that is not true. But it has been said that if you put a hundred-dollar bill next to a D2 knife, and told a roomful of guys that any one of them could have it if they could get the blade sharp, you'd almost always go home with the money and a dull knife.

Classed as a die steel, D2 has been a favorite blade material among knife users for many years. Its high chromium content almost qualifies it as "stainless," and while its stain resistance is good, it does require some maintenance. The very high carbon content allows the steel to be quenched to the mid-60s HRc and drawing back to 58–60 HRC produces a tough blade with superb edge-holding properties.

65Mn: 65Mn is a readily available Chinese steel that is formulated to provide good wear resistance and hardness. The medium-high carbon content makes for a high degree of toughness and resilience, while the manganese, in addition to improving these properties, improves the hot-working characteristics of the steel, making it an excellent candidate for forged sword blades.

50100-B: Sometimes known as 0170–6, which is the steel makers classification, 50100-B is a good chrome-vanadium steel that is somewhat similar to O1, but much less expensive. The now-defunct Blackjack made several knives from O170-6, and Carbon V may be 0170–6. 50100 is basically 52100 with about one third the chromium of 52100, and the B in 50100-B indicates that the steel has been modified with vanadium, making this a chrome-vanadium steel.

52100: 52100 originally developed as a ball-bearing steel, can have an enviable combination of hardness and toughness when correctly heat treated. It's mostly used by custom makers due to a tricky heat treat regimen.

5160: 5160 has achieved a reputation for toughness and resilience, particularly in larger knife and sword blades, where shock absorption is a requirement. Careful heat treating of a 5160 blade can produce a hard edge section and a softer core (differential hardening), a useful characteristic in hacking blades, but hardly a unique one. This is reportedly "the only steel that survival expert Ron Hood trusted," and it was utilized by Buck when the company made its Hoodlum knife. Buck's representatives repeatedly ignored my requests to evaluate the Hoodlum when I was a contributing editor for *Tactical Knives* magazine—and that's all I have to say about that.

DNH7: A relatively simple high carbon steel similar in composition to 1075. Differential hardening of DNH7 produces a fine working blade that holds an edge well.

65Mn: A readily available Chinese steel that is formulated to provide good wear resistance and hardness. The medium-high carbon content makes for a high degree of toughness and resilience, while the manganese, in addition to improving these properties, improves the hot-working characteristics of the steel, making it an excellent candidate for forged sword blades.

W2: Reasonably tough and holds an edge well, due to its .2 percent vanadium content. Most files are made from W-1, which is the same as W-2 except for the vanadium content (W-1 has no vanadium).

O1: This is a steel popular with forgers, but not so much in mass production. O1 isn't the easiest steel to work, but it has the reputation for being "forgiving," meaning that it can be de-tempered, and worked again. Worked properly to maximize its best qualities, O1 is an excellent steel; it takes and holds an edge superbly, and it is tough (although not as tough as, say, 5160). It rusts easily, however, and tarnishes on contact with any vegetable or meat (fat) acids. Randall Knives, Mad Dog Knives, and Chris Hayes Knives use O1.

Although not especially popular with mass producers of knives because it's a difficult alloy to work, custom forgers like O1 because of its toughness and edge retention.

O2: Also known as Böhler Tool Steel K720, O2 is a very tough and strong oil-hardened, high-carbon tool steel. Its chemical composition allows it to be hardened to a high degree while retaining ductility and toughness. O2 is easy to sharpen, but its low chromium content means it tarnishes easily.

A2: An excellent air-hardening tool steel, tougher than D2 and M2, but with less wear resistance (it doesn't keep an edge as well as either of those steels). A2 is not suitable to be differentially tempered, or "zone hardened," so it will be evenly tempered throughout. Its good toughness—ability to absorb abuse —makes it a choice for "combat" knives. Chris Reeve and Phil Hartsfield both use A2.

440A: The 440 series of stainless steels has been used to manufacture outdoor knife blades since the sixties, and they are still the most popular steels in the commercial knife market. The late knife-making legend Blackie Collins (1939–2011) told me in June 2011 that if he had to choose one knife to do everything, it would be made from " . . . one of the four-forties." 440 steel is readily available, inexpensive, and produces very serviceable blades. 440A has the lowest carbon content of the class but can be heat treated to the upper 50's HRc.

440B: With its relatively high carbon content, 440B has the ability to produce tough blades in the 59–60 HRc range. 440B has excellent stain-resisting properties, making it a good choice for fixed blades in harsh environments.

440C: 440C was the top of the line in stainless blade steels until more modern stainless alloys became readily available in the 1980s. 440C is still highly regarded, and used in both custom and commercially produced blades. It can be heat treated to hardnesses as high as HRc61 (although 58–60 is more usual). It takes a good edge and holds it well, although frequent touch-ups are necessary during hard use.

A particularly functional example of 440C, this Boker-made, Newt Martin-designed Apparo-7 survival knife has proved itself to be an outstanding example of what a hollow-handled survival knife can be. (Its sheath, not so much.)

420HC: A popular production blade steel, with low cost, easy machine-ability and high corrosion resistance, 420HC produces affordable blades that satisfy typical knife users. With hardnesses in the low 50s HRC, it requires frequent touch-ups to maintain a satisfactory edge, but sharpens easily.

420J2: A low carbon stainless steel, 420J2 has a high ductility and is resistant to corrosion, but has generally poor edge retention. Its easy machinability makes it a favorite for pots, pans, and tableware, as well as the very cheaply made paring knives that some stores keep in containers near checkouts as impulse items. 420J and 420J2 are also favorites for the sometimes weird fantasy knives designed by Gil Hibben for United Cutlery. The alloy is also used as the outer layer on laminated steels such as San Mai III and the ZDP-189/420J2 knives from

Although generally maligned on Internet knife forums, this Schrade SCHF39 survival knife (which failed because of its poorly designed slingshot sheath, not because of the knife) demonstrates that 420 High-Carbon—the steel used in the original GI-issue M9 Bayonet—is not so bad a choice for a knife blade.

Knives made for commemorative purposes, and intended for display, rather than use, are generally made of 420J, which is soft and easily worked, but will not hold an edge.

Spyderco, and often as the liner lock in folding knives. 420J2 can be buffed to a mirror-like shine, but its softness makes it easy to scratch.

M2: A "high-speed steel," it can hold its temper even at very high temperatures, and as such is used in industry for high-heat cutting jobs (drill bits are often made from M2). It is slightly tougher and more wear resistant than D2. However, M2 rusts easily. Benchmade has started using M2 in one of their AFCK 710 variations.

H1(Myodo): This alloy is the epitome of stainless steel, insofar as rust resistance. Because of this,, it's popular in diving knives. Its carbon content is 0.15 percent, but having 0.10 percent Nitrogen helps its performance. H1 doesn't hold an edge well, similar with Aichi AUS-6 and AUS-8 steel, but has more corrosion resistance. H1 is work-hardening steel, which is said to get harder as it is used, though no one seems to know how to bring out that property in real life.

AUS-6: Part of the AUS family of Japanese steels; the "6" in its designator represents its 0.6 percent carbon content. The steel produces a tough blade with hardnesses typically in the mid-50s HRc. It will take a good edge but requires fairly frequent touch-ups in hard use.

AUS-8: A popular blade steel and used by both custom makers and higher-end knife manufacturers. It is a tough steel, with a hardness in the 58–59 HRc range, takes a fine edge, and holds it well.

8Cr13MoV: A Chinese-made stainless steel alloy that is very similar to Japanese-made AUS8, which is itself identical to the American-made line of 440 steels. Typical hardness is 58–59 HRC.

This discontinued, but extremely useful, Kershaw Carabiner Tool boasted a high-quality Sheepsfoot-design blade made of AUS-6 (note that some tools used different alloys).

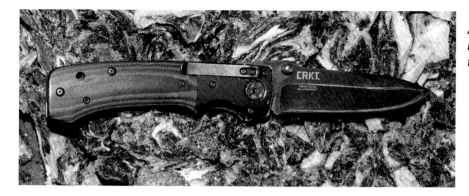

A good example of an 8Cr13MoV blade: the Ruger All-Cylinders knife from CRKT.

AUS-10: With a high carbon content of 1.10 percent, AUS-10 produce a blade hardness in the 60–61 HRC range while maintaining very usable toughness. It will take and maintain an excellent edge, much like 440C. AUS-10 has slightly less corrosion resistance than 440 in harsh environments, but has a slightly tougher blade.

Sized to clean dirty fingernails or be worn around the neck with a pocket compass and a fire striker (a very handy survival outfit, indeed), A. G. Russell's diminutive Hunter's Scalpel has an AUS-10 blade that tells you this is not a toy.

CPM S30V: Created using the Crucible Particle Metallurgy (CPM) process pioneered by Crucible Industries. The CPM process provides a steel with a fine grain structure and very even distribution of carbides. S30V's high vanadium content creates vanadium carbides, which are harder than chromium carbides and produce excellent edge-holding qualities. The steel is expensive to produce, which restricts its use to the high-end knife market. S30V is a martensitic (martensite is a very hard carbon-based outer layer) stainless steel designed to offer the best combination of tough-

Possibly the baddest folder ever made, Benchmade's discontinued RUKUS carries a stout blade of CPM S30V.

ness, wear resistance, and corrosion resistance. S30V offers substantial improvement in toughness over other high hardness steels such as 440C and D2, and its corrosion resistance is equal to or better than 440C in various environments. The CPM process in general produces very homogeneous, high-quality steel characterized by superior dimensional stability, grindability, and toughness compared to steels produced by conventional processes.

CPM S35VN: A martensitic stainless steel designed to offer improved toughness over CPM S30V. It is also easier to machine and polish than S30V. Its chemistry has been rebalanced so that it forms niobium carbides along with vanadium and chromium carbides. Substituting niobium carbides for some of the vanadium carbides makes CPM S35VN about 15 to 20 percent tougher than CPM S30V without any loss of wear resistance. CPM S35VN's improved toughness gives it better resistance to edge chipping. Because both vanadium and niobium carbides are harder and more effective than chromium carbides in providing wear resistance, the CPM stainless-blade steels offer improved edge retention over conventional high chromium steels.

Sharp, tough, and strong, with outstanding edge retention, S35V alloy makes the blade of this SOG Strat Ops auto a good choice as a tool or as a weapon.

CPM S90V: A unique tool steel made by the Crucible Particle Metallurgy process. It is a martensitic stainless steel with a high volume of vanadium carbides for exceptionally good wear resistance. S90V offers substantial improvements in wear resistance over 440C and D2, and other high chromium tool steels, with corrosion resistance equal to or better than 440C. Its high vanadium content forms hard vanadium carbides with chromium carbides for wear resistance, leaving sufficient chromium in the matrix to provide good corrosion resistance. The wear and corrosion resistance of S90V make it an excellent candidate to replace 440C, where increased wear is a primary concern. It can replace D2 or other tool steels in applications where improved corrosion resistance is also of benefit.

154CM: Manufactured in the US by Crucible Industries, 154CM was originally developed as an aerospace steel. Its high molybdenum content affords it an ability to maintain strength and hardness

As this eight-year-old Zero Tolerance knife shows, 154CM is a dependable, hard-working alloy.

at high temperatures. This same property proved to greatly diminish the tendency of the steel to decay in heat treatment of knife blades. This powdered metallurgy steel has more uniform distribution of carbides—so it takes and holds an excellent edge, and provides good corrosion resistance, wear resistance, and toughness.

N690Co: Made by Bohler in Austria, N690Co is their best conventional (non-powder metal) steel. N690Co is stainless and has excellent edge-holding capabilities. The high carbon content allows the steel to be tempered to 60HRc while the Cobalt inhibits cracking (chipping) at this level of hardness. The vanadium contributes to edge-holding by producing a fine grain structure. Bohler's unique cross-rolling technology produces a homogeneous steel sheet with excellent carbide distribution.

ATS 34: Made by Hitachi Metals in Japan, ATS 34 has a long proven record as a high-quality blade steel, used extensively by both custom makers and manufacturers. It has excellent toughness and takes and holds a keen edge. ATS 34 is virtually identical to 154CM in its chemical composition, and is said to have been introduced as a reaction to a shortage (since rectified) of 154 CM in the alloy steel market. ATS 34 has excellent toughness and the ability to take and hold a keen edge, but it is impossibly difficult for probably most honesmen to get keen.

One of the finest field knives to come out of the Buck factory, this Strider has an ATS-34 blade that confounds most honesmen—it is not an alloy for the masses, but if you can sharpen ATS-34, you can sharpen anything.

Sandvik 14C28N: This is Sandvik's most recently developed product in its popular series of knife steel. The optimized composition creates a steel with a unique combination of excellent edge-holding features (stability, sharpenability, and sharpness), high hardness, and high corrosion resistance. This new version of steel has the ability to be heat treated so that the wear resistance is improved over prior steel types without affecting the microstructure. Sharpening the knife is therefore relatively easy, while edge stability in terms of chipping and edge rolling is still very good.

Sandvik 7C27Mo2: This is Sandvik's most corrosion-resistant knife steel. It combines exceptional corrosion resistance with decent edge properties.

Sandvik 12C27: Sandvik's most well-rounded knife steel with excellent edge performance, allowing razor sharpness, high hardness, exceptional toughness, and good corrosion resistance. 12C27 stainless alloy has a fairly straightforward C/Mn/Cr composition but produces tough user blades that sharpen well and have good edge retention.

Sandvik 12C27M: This knife steel was developed for highest possible edge performance while still having good enough corrosion resistance for daily use in a dishwasher.

Sandvik 13C26: This knife steel is developed for razor blade applications, which means a strong focus on hardness, sharpness, and edge stability.

Sandvik 19C27: Sandvik's most wear resistant stainless knife steel, developed specifically for abrasive work. Sandvik 19C27 is the odd grade in the Sandvik knife steel portfolio because it's a coarse carbide grade, unlike the other Sandvik knife steel grades.

VG10 (Takefu): A high-end stainless steel, Japanese-made, and preferred especially for kitchen cutlery and folding knives, although some very nice fixed-blade hunting knives have been made from VG10. The G in the name stands for "gold," meaning premium. VG-10 takes a very good edge and retains it well, especially when given a highly polished, acute edge. Nominal hardness is 60–61 HRC, although some knife makers have pushed it to 62HRC without excessive edge brittleness. Sometimes called V-Kin-10, VG-10 possesses a high carbon content containing 1 percent carbon, 15 percent chromium, 1 percent molybdenum, 0.2 percent vanadium, 1.5 percent cobalt, and 0.5 percent manganese. To put it in personal terms, based on my own experience, VG-10 makes for one hell of a good kitchen knife.

A prime example of premium kitchen cutlery, this simply named Cook's Knife from Spyderco has a VG-10 blade that will surpass most of the pricey cutlery advertised only as "fine German Steel."

Shoki 390: This is one of the newer "super steels" that sets new standards for edge retention and toughness. Essentially identical to CPM 20CV, M390 is a PM (particulate metal) stainless steel that offers outstanding wear resistance with excellent corrosion resistance through the use of high chromium and vanadium content. The PM process combined with the high chromium content imparts M390/CPM 20CV with good grindability and excellent polishability. Its high austenizing temperature imparts M390 with a high attainable hardness of RC 58–62.

MBS-26: The MBS-26 stainless steel is treated by three stages of quenching, sub-zero treating, and tempering until the steel reaches a hardness of 58–60 HRC. Masahiro believes this is the ideal hardness for a kitchen knife with the features of the MV-H range. Spyderco uses this steel in their outstanding Santoku chef's knife.

These are facial whiskers on the MBS-26 blade of this Spyderco Santoku knife.

MV-H: Made from MBS-26 high-carbon stainless steel. This MBS-26 is proprietary to Masahiro; however, it comes from the VG family like the VG-10 that the Kasumi Damascus knives first used. It is important to point out that these knives are solid MBS-26 stainless steel, and not just a thin layer clad with layers of inexpensive stainless steel.

CTS-BD1N: As a knife steel, this proprietary alloy of Carpenter Industries is pretty incredible. It is a high carbon, high chromium, nitrogen-hardened martensitic (a concentration of hard carbon atoms) stainless steel that can be hardened in oil or air. CTS-BD1N has an extremely high working hardness, up to 63HRC, with excellent edge retention, and great corrosion resistance. This alloy was developed to be an improvement over Carpenter's existing CTS-BD1 steel, in which vanadium was replaced with nitrogen, producing almost four times more carbon atoms, with a smaller molar (concentration of atoms) mass. Also known as Carpenter-BD1N, this alloy is described by world-class knife designer Ken Onion as "the best bang for the $$$ in the game."

Ceramic: Ceramic blades are made out of very hard and tough stone-like material, often zirconium dioxide ($ZrO2$; also known as zirconia). These knives are usually produced by dry-pressing zirconia powder and firing them through solid-state sintering, which melts the powder into a dense, homogenous solid. Blades are sharpened by grinding the edges with a diamond-dust-coated grinding wheel. Ceramic blades are typically 50 percent as heavy as their similar-sized steel counterparts, and retain their sharpness up to ten times as long.

If you're accustomed to a hair-splitting steel blade, you're likely to be a little disappointed in the sharpness of a ceramic knife. On the plus side, a ceramic blade remains at maximum sharpness for an extremely long time—long enough to be advertised as "never needs sharpening." However, there is no such thing as an ever-sharp knife (yet), and a big downside with ceramic blades is that they're very hard to re-sharpen, in every sense of that word. I've achieved good results with a diamond-coated bench stone, but the same keenness of a good steel blade has been beyond reach.

Ceramic blades are also brittle. Tests have shown that they aren't actually fragile, and will probably not break if dropped onto a hard floor, but you should absolutely not use them for prying, as a screwdriver, or for any of the other abuses that are common to kitchen cutlery. A ceramic blade will chip if you attempt to re-sharpen it using a pull-through carbide sharpener, so be warned.

Ceramic is just the ticket for part-time gourmets who might be lacking the skill set to re-sharpen a knife; ceramic blades are hard and very slow to dull, but they are easily broken and should not be exposed to even modest prying or other abuse.

Beta Titanium: With the exception of new controlled-dispersion B2 particulate steel alloys, titanium is, at first glance, the outdoor knife user's dream come true. When I was assigned to write up the new and, sadly, short-lived Katrina Search-and-Rescue Knife (a slightly modified version of that manufacturer's standard MPK-10 Utility Knife) for my survival column in *Tactical Knives* magazine, the late John Moore, father of the titanium knife, invited me to "try to break" the sample he sent for review.

To issue such a challenge is generally a mistake. I refuse to participate in such ridiculous activities as "batoning" (I defy you to find any reference to beating a knife blade through a chunk of wood prior to the mid-1990s—the mountain men and frontiersman who built civilization never considered doing such a foolish thing), but I routinely refrain from doing unnecessary tasks with a knife on an almost daily basis, because there has never been a knife that I couldn't break, or at least severely damage. And I never want to break a knife—every one of the numerous occurrences when that has happened has been unintentional.

But now, I had actually been given permission. I hammered the knife through 2x4s by its molded Hytrel (R) hilt, and actually did "baton" its blade repeatedly through the longitudinal grains of several types of hardwood and softwood. I even stood on the handle, with the blade firmly fixtured two inches from its tip, and bounced up and down. I could not break it, not by subjecting it to the most outlandish abuse that any woodsman might ever need a knife to withstand. The titanium refused to oxidize or tarnish when subjected to water, salt, even corrosive caustics and acids, and, except for a little white powder on its normally battleship-gray exterior, it exhibited no sign of wear, regardless of neglect or abuse.

The Katrina's only failure came from its unacceptably soft blade of HRC47. I skinned and butchered thirteen white-tailed deer with it (we raised pureblood gray, or timber, wolves, under license for eighteen years, and meat processing was a daily chore), and the knife failed to skin even one deer without needing to be re-sharpened. (John Moore told me personally that one rather well-known knife expert told him that his sample of the same knife " . . . skinned twenty deer, without needing to be re-sharpened." Be wary of accepting expert reviews at face value). My knife's edge rolled, dented, and blunted with maddening regularity. Re-sharpening on an aluminum-oxide stone took only a minute, though, and the edge honed to surprising sharpness.

The Future of Steel: In February 2015, researchers at Pohang University of Science and Technology in South Korea announced what was perhaps the greatest breakthrough in steel-making since stainless steel was created. Building on a 1970s discovery by Soviet scientists, which revealed that adding aluminum to steel resulted in a lighter and stronger final product, Korean researchers created a steel alloy that offers more strength than the beta-titanium used in the landing struts of aircraft carrier jets, and at least 13 percent more strength against breaking than the same weight of conventional steel alloys.

Blades made of beta-titanium, like this "Katrina" search-and-rescue knife are soft and do not hold an edge well, but they are easy to re-sharpen, impervious to corrosive agents, and virtually impossible to break.

The problem that plagued Soviet scientists was that, although adding aluminum to the mix increased strength, it decreased ductility and brittleness, meaning that once enough force was applied, the metal would suddenly snap in two. In regard to knife blades, that means that an edge would chip under stress, and possibly break in two when used as a prybar—tasks that outdoor and survival knives routinely encounter.

The problem is caused by very tiny, nanometer-sized B2 particles, themselves comprised of super-hard intermetallic compounds of aluminum and iron. In the Soviet trials, B2 particles tended to be clustered, but chief researcher Hansoo Kim's team found a way to intersperse the particles in small groups throughout the steel, making it very hard, strong, with unmatched sharpened edge retention, while still retaining the ductility—resistance to breaking—that might have changed the nature of the knives we use forever.

Unfortunately, that did not come to pass (although, with rapid advances in Ni-Ti-B4C technology, it might by the time this book goes to press). The "pickled and oiled" silicate-coating process that is currently used to de-scale and protect mass-produced steel from oxidation "compromises" the surface integrity of finished super-steel. Precisely how it does that is not being disclosed at this point but, according to Kim, just discovering the process of controlled B2 dispersion is the most important aspect, and he expects that scientists will use that discovery as a springboard to create new and previously impossible alloys.

Effects of Elemental Additives on Steel Properties

Knife makers (usually the village blacksmiths) of yesteryear knew the empirical rules of thumb, like harder steel is usually more brittle, and softer blades won't hold an edge as long. But knives of today are vastly better on all fronts because knife makers have many times the knowledge available to their forebears. Contemporary bladesmiths can have, and must have, at least a rudimentary understanding of how individual elements work to give steels the different properties that make them unique. Steel is far from being just steel, and much of the magic that once made a master blacksmith stand out from his peers has been laid out for anyone who wants to learn it.

Following are some of the more important elements of steel, and how they interact with it to give blades the properties desired by their makers:

- *Carbon (C):* Increases strength but decreases toughness and weldability (most common and important).
- *Manganese (Mn):* Similar, though lesser, effect as carbon.
- *Silicon (Si):* Similar to carbon but with a lesser effect than manganese (important for castability).
- *Nickel (Ni):* Improves toughness.
- *Chromium (Cr):* Improves oxidation resistance.
- *Molybdenum (Mo):* Improves hardenability and high temperature strength.
- *Vanadium (V):* Improves high temperature strength.
- *Tungsten (W):* Improves high temperature strength.
- *Aluminum (Al):* Reduces the oxygen or nitrogen in the molten steel.
- *Titanium (Ti):* Reduces the oxygen or nitrogen in the molten steel.
- *Zirconium (Zi):* Reduces the oxygen or nitrogen in the molten steel.
- *Oxygen (O):* Negative effect by forming gas porosity.
- *Nitrogen (N):* Negative effect by forming gas porosity.
- *Hydrogen (H):* In high quantities, results in poor ductility.
- *Phosphorus (P):* Can increase strength but drastically reduces toughness and ductility.
- *Sulfur (S):* Reduces toughness and ductility.

CHAPTER FOUR
HANDLES AND HILTS

As important as it is to have a strong, sharp blade, it is just as essential to have a grip that feels good and secure in your hand—like a worn-in pair of boots, or a sweater that's stretched out just the way you like it. I once gave away a Gerber BMF (basic multi-function) knife because, although it was a top-of-the-line knife, with a blade that simply could not be beaten by production knives of its time, the girth and contour of its handle made it feel uncontrollable in my grip. That BMF was just too big a knife to feel that way, and it was a danger to its user. I generally prefer a larger blade, and I use larger knives (ten- to twelve-inch blades) quite comfortably, which is a testament to how critically important it is that a knife fit its user's hand.

Handle Styles

A knife without a handle is like a car without a steering wheel—it's pretty hard to steer either one the way that you want it to go without a proper handle. Ask an Indy car driver how important he feels his steering wheel is.

Most knife handles are on the same plane as their blade, because that is the orientation that best suits our human arm design for most cutting and stabbing tasks. Some, like the Nepalese kukri, have their handles at an angle to the blade. In the case of the kukri, this pattern is to get maximum efficiency as a lopper from a blade by artificially increasing a blade's length (the kukri is legendary for beheading Japanese sentries with a single blow during WWII).

Other special-purpose knives with handles that reflect their intended use are the pendulum-like Ulu, the famed Eskimo knife. An Ulu's handle and cutting edge are parallel to one another, specifically for use in skinning large animals and cutting off strips of blubber from seals and whales.

Then there's the push dagger, whose blade is mounted perpendicular to its palm handle, so that its point can be pushed into a target with its wielder's palm. This T-shaped, purpose-made weapon is best known as a favored hideout knife for Mississippi riverboat gamblers, but has also earned distinction in war time, because it is easy to use and difficult to lose in a scuffle. In the movie *Platoon*, Tom Berenger used a push dagger to teach young Charlie Sheen a memorable lesson.

Molded Handles

A majority of knife handles today are molded onto a blade's tang. Molded handles are less expensive to install, but that in no way infers that it's "cheap plastic," to use an idiom of 1960s speech. With the vast array of synthetic formulas available today, the term plastic isn't even applicable.

Petroleum-based polymers still constitute the basis of most synthetic knife hilts, but beyond the old standbys like polyethylene and polystyrene, there have in recent years emerged Lexan, Hypalon, Zytel, and a universe of other recipes. Some have resulted from strengthening the polymer with fibers, others from molding a material under immense pressure to make it denser. Still others are composed of layers, and a few use all of the above, and more.

The Hypalon hilt on this knife demonstrates that an over-molded one-piece handle isn't necessarily weak or vulnerable; this handle repeatedly drove 8D nails through a 2x4 with only superficial damage to itself.

Today, it has become difficult to tell molded polymer products from the materials that they're meant to emulate. Some resins look just like antlers, and so a knife with a trophy-class antler as its hilt is reproducible indefinitely, without ever taking a buck's rack.

Some over-molded hilts appear to be just what they are, but are formed to match a human hand precisely, and some are virtually indestructible.

Slab Scales

Slab scales, as the name implies, are made by mounting two slabs of handle material, cut to the contours of the blade's tang, to either side of the tang. These scales can be shaped to their users' tastes, and today they're made from any number of materials—wood, plastic, rubber, Micarta (essentially layers of resin-bonded fabric that were in use by good old boys half a century ago, long before Micarta was a brand name), bone, antler—anything that can be made to serve the purpose.

Scale handles are used on both folding and fixed-blade knives, but are especially popular on fixed blades because they can be mounted with inset Chicago Screws that permit handles to be removed for cleaning.

Stacked Washers

Stacked washer handles have been in use for at least a century. The legendary KaBar USMC Fighting Knife and the USAF Survival Knife, both of which were military-issue from WWII to Vietnam, used stacked leather washers over narrow rat-tail tangs, as did most of the original Scagel-style hunting knives. As the name implies, this handle consists of a series of flat leather washers stacked atop one another over the tang, then the end of the tang is capped with a usually metal pommel (that can be used for hammering), and pinned to or screwed onto the tang.

Although rat-tail tangs have taken an unmerited bad rap for not being strong enough (they've served well enough through two world and numerous smaller wars), it's usually the handle that fails. Leather tends to dry and shrink with age, leaving gaps between the washers, taking a good deal of strength out of the tang. After years of neglect, the leather finally crumbles and falls away entirely. In recent decades, Marines taking mountain survival training are reputed to have broken the knives their forefathers used to beat Hitler and Hirohito, but I believe that if they did, the reason has less to do with the knife's quality than with the trainees' knowledge of how to use a knife (most of these kids grew up in a world where carrying a knife is regarded with contempt). As I've said, *any* knife *can* be broken.

One time-honored method of preserving knife handles made of stacked leather washers is to soak the hilt of a new knife in a jar of motor oil—or cooking oil, any type of oil will do—for several days. This causes the washers to become saturated and swell. Handles are a bit oily at first, but when the excess is blotted out with an old towel, or just worn and clogged with dirt, they will last virtually forever. Experiments with acrylic floor wax, polyurethane, even car wax soaked into leather have also worked well, but the messy oil treatment endures longest. A representative from Ontario Knife was once intrigued by the hard camouflage shell on the handle of my USAF Survival Knife; he was surprised that the now-indestructible hilt had been formed by thoroughly saturating the new handle with ordinary enamel paint.

Knife hilts made from stacked leather washers can be beautiful.

Hollow Handles

When I was a boy of sixteen, I started grinding my own fixed-blade knives from worn-out mill files. Essentially, a knife is a simple thing to manufacture, if you're willing to put the labor into it that is necessary to make it sharp and (maybe) presentable. And if you follow simple rules like never grinding a blade until it gets hot, or you'll change its temper. It isn't until you get into heat-treating that knife making gets too complex for the good old boy with a bench grinder.

In 1978 it occurred to me that putting a hollow handle made of pipe, sealed with a threaded pipe cap, would make an ideal survival knife, because fishing gear, sewing needles, and other small survival items could be stored in its handle. The problem was to affix handle to blade strongly enough for it not to break off.

And that was always the problem with hollow-handle knives, even after designer Jimmy Lile (who passed away in 1991) introduced us to the first Rambo knife used in the movie *First Blood* in 1982. The Lile pattern used a pinned hollow handle, and it was solid enough if you didn't expect the knife to pry open car doors, but more than a few imitators were just awful.

One of the worst, in my opinion, is the Rothco-brand Deluxe Adventurer Survival Kit Knife, which is still being sold (https://www.rothco.com/product/rothco-deluxe-adventurer-survival-kit-knife), priced at $34 at the time of this writing. This knife, and a few others like it, have blades that are affixed to their handles with a single hollow roll-pin, and some have hollow plastic handles. These knives are unfit for any field use beyond a state park Cub Scout jamboree.

One classic hollow handle knife that was worth carrying is the BuckMaster from Buck Knives—another of Chuck Buck's never-ending attempts to make an official SEAL Team knife for that fickle special forces group (the knife was actually designed by Chuck's son and successor, CJ).

This monster Bowie-type knife is all stainless. Mine came from Chuck, made from 420HC, and like most BuckMaster knives, it had a massively strong handle bolted to an equally robust blade whose spine had heavy sawteeth, with sharp serrations along its false edge, nearer the point. It was even designed to serve as a grappling hook for the hazardous practice of climbing with 550 parachute cord. The BuckMaster's downfall was that it accomplished strength at the cost of weight. The knife alone weighed one and a half pounds, without sheath and gear, and its allsteel construction, with knurled hilt, made it less than a pleasure to handle, even less fun to carry all day.

Then the Chris Reeve Company came up with a cool, but very labor-intensive hollowhandle design that didn't have to worry about mounting blade to handle, because it was all one piece, with the entire knife machined

This Schrade SCHF1 is an all-one-piece hollow handle survival knife that avoids the weakness inherent in hollow-handle knives that are joined together.

from a solid block of steel. This type of knife had been mechanically or financially impossible to manufacture a generation ago, until modern CNC (computerized numerically controlled) mills that enabled a single machine with integral tool-changing capabilities to transform a chunk of steel into a virtually completed knife in a single process, without a hand ever touching it. With this hollow handle knife there were no weak spots, because it was a single piece of steel.

But the Reeve knife was exorbitantly priced. Before long, Schrade Knives, which had been taken over by Taylor Brands, and was being operated under the metalworking genius of Morgan Taylor, began turning out virtually the same knives, using less expensive alloys. The Taylor/Schrade one-piece hollow-handle knives were priced at a fraction (sometimes a mere tenth) of the Reeve knives, which allowed a great many more people to get one into their hands. The Schrade's popularity has caused prices of these knives to increase, but it's probably no coincidence that Reeve has discontinued the line, while the number of single-piece hollow-handle models offered by Schrade has more than tripled. Like the BuckMaster, its knurled handle is cold in the winter, and less than comfortable at any time, but it's just the right size to accept a covering made from a length of bicycle innertube, held in place by a couple of drops of Gorilla Glue®.

Wrapped Handles

In times past, many a stacked-leather handle dried out and disintegrated, leaving a blade and tang, with pommel and fingerguard still attached, that was so unwieldy as to be useless. It was usually impractical to replace the original handle, so we rectified the problem with wraps of cloth or vinyl electrician's tape. Not spiral wraps, but individual turns of tape, each layered over itself, sometimes over a wooden core, shaped and glued to the tang. A similar wrap next to it, and another next to that—until the individual wraps had spanned the entire length of exposed tang between fingerguard and pommel—creates a new, unbreakable hilt. By alternating the number of wraps to create a larger diameter next to a smaller diameter (more and fewer layers of tape), you can create ridges in the finished handle, for added grip.

The blade from a cheap folder, pinned inside a steel pipe with a nail, filled with molten plastic, wrapped with fabric friction tape impregnated with epoxy resin, capped by a dime for good luck. This re-made knife is thirty-four years old.

This type of replacement handle, while virtually impervious to everything except fire, takes a lot of tape to create, so shortcuts were often taken by coating the tang with epoxy resin (or, today, the versatile Gorilla Glue), then two handle halves, shaped to your preference. Taping over this core saved on tape, and still resulted in a virtually indestructible handle. If you used a cloth tape, like electrician's friction tape, or the extremely versatile Gauztex Safety Tape, a handle can be hardened with any acrylic or polyurethane sealer, from floor wax to deck stain, or even impregnated with oil-based paint. I stumped friends, even the guys at Ontario Knives, when they couldn't figure out the hard, flexible camouflage shell that I'd applied by over the leather handle of a USAF Survival Knife.

Or, as with the skeleton knives (put simply, one-piece knives with no handle at all) that have become popular, tangs can be wrapped with parachute cord, clothesline, string, or even a combination, to create a super-versatile survival handle. Some handles are wrapped with a combination of cord, flammable waxed cotton string, and even fishing line, providing cordage for many types of survival needs. There is no wrong or right way to craft a new handle, just designs that do or don't work. So use your imagination.

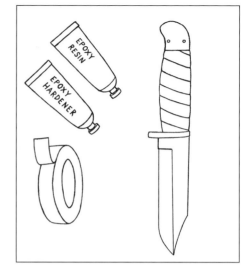

Handles have needed to be replaced for as long as knives have worn them, but twentieth- and twenty-first-century innovations and materials have made it easier to do than ever.

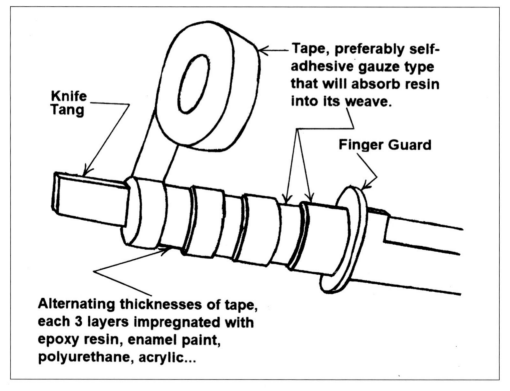

Knife Tang

Tape, preferably self-adhesive gauze type that will absorb resin into its weave.

Finger Guard

Alternating thicknesses of tape, each 3 layers impregnated with epoxy resin, enamel paint, polyurethane, acrylic...

A picture is worth a thousand words; replacing a broken knife handle is a simple task today.

CHAPTER FIVE:
SHEATHS

Let me start right off by saying that this is one of the most irritating aspects of modern knives to me, personally. That's because while knife makers in the twenty-first century are turning out some of the finest, most aesthetically pleasing, most ergonomic, most precision-made knives in all of history, designing the scabbards that encase them is apparently little more than an interruption in the day for many manufacturers. I find that utterly infuriating, because to a woodsman like myself, a sheath is an inseparable part of the system that we call "survival knife." This is where I show my age—and my experience; half a century of frequently hair-raising narrow escapes in the wilderness has taught me how precious a knife can be in a thousand ways, and how easily it can be lost in a hundred different ways. The original Schrade M7-S was one of the first and greatest pure-blooded survival knives not just because of the tools that were incorporated into the knife itself, but because nearly everything else a person might need to stay alive until safety could be reached was contained in two large cargo pockets in the sheath.

Fixed-blade knives of every size need to be carried with their blades safely encased in a protective holster. Not for the same reasons that a rifle or a custom-made pool cue needs a case, but for the same reason that every rifle has a safety catch.

The original pedigreed survival knife (left), the Imperial Schrade M7-S Survival Knife, and its successor the BT (Bomb Tech) Model 01 on the right. Both knives are sadly discontinued now.

A dirk stuck in a waistband, a la Tarzan, is incredibly dangerous to its owner—or at least it should be, because if its owner has the slightest idea of how valuable his knife is, it will be sharp enough to remove whatever appendages might get in the way of its naked blade.

But at the time this is being written, knife sheaths are clearly under-appreciated by both manufacturers and the knife buyers who could force them to make better ones. Many are mostly, if not entirely, inadequate to safeguard the tool that I promise you is going to prove indispensable in any real-life survival, search-and-rescue, or combat scenario. And few do anything more than contain a blade. To put it in my usual gauche terms, almost all of the finest knives ever created are today sold with the most flimsy, unusable, unfieldworthy sheaths ever manufactured. Some of them have been so bad that they literally keep a good knife grounded and out of the field until they can be made useful. By that, I mean that they do not hold a knife securely enough to ensure that it will be there when you reach for it, especially if you're wearing it in rugged conditions, like search-and-rescue operations, where low-crawling through rubble can pull an unsecured knife right out of its holster. And some are so poorly designed that I guarantee that you will lose your knife just doing normal things, like sitting or crouching.

Forgive me for harping on this, but you can prove how precious a knife might be with just a length of clothesline; now, using only your teeth and hands, turn that length of light rope into two lengths of rope. You *need* your knife, and you *need* your sheath to lock it vault-tight to your hip.

Sheath materials have historically incorporated whatever was available. Leather is classic, but wood, and metal sheets, whittled or hammered into shape, tied, wired, riveted, or any other means were common in Europe. Other sheaths have been made from bamboo, whose naturally tough exterior and hollow interior lends itself to being an ideal material. Wrapped in its own fibers, with leather thongs, or glued together with pitch, bamboo has been transformed into some beautifully ornate, lacquered blade covers for Asian swords and knives since the beginning of sword smithing.

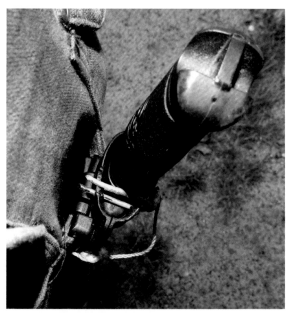

The Ruger Muzzle Brake is a truly superb knife, but its sheath failed to hold it securely; we fixed that problem with a heavy wire clip that inserted through holes in the sheath, preventing the knife from coming out of the sheath until the pin was removed.

The most common traditional sheath is made from heavy leather, folded around a blade, and stitched together at its edges, opposite the cased knife's sharpened edge. To prevent the cutting edge from severing its stitching, better sheaths have brass or steel rivets staked into seams at strategic points.

Some sheaths do not have these essential cut-guards. I have a hard-used and much-loved Kabar Cutlass Machete, with a bolo-type blade, and form-fitted Cordura sheath. When new, this knife's AISI 1085 blade was pretty dull, and, to be honest, Kabar probably presumed that it was likely to stay that way. As soon as I sharpened it, the bolo section severed its stitching, lacerating my palm in the process. I resolved this problem forever by driving several heavy fencing staples, like those used to hang barbed wire on wooden posts, through the stitching, and hammering them flat.

Another problem for me, personally, is the location of the belt loop and retaining strap. I may draw and re-sheath my belt knife thirty times a day, so it's important to me that it hangs right where I can get it when I need it. The hilt needs to stick out slightly, with a couple of inches between it and my hip socket, so I can grab it, quickly and without looking, and re-insert the blade in the same manner.

Velcro-type hook-and-loop straps have become very popular for keeping retaining straps, if they are used at all, closed around the hilt, but they are immediately replaced on any sheath that's going to carry a working knife for me. My complaint, legitimized three decades ago, is that Velcro-type fasteners have no place on most outdoor gear, and particularly not for any application where the two parts of the fastener must be separated with any frequency. The hook side quickly and inevitably fills with dirt and debris, until it no longer holds, and using hook-and-loop fasteners is anything but stealthy. As a hunter, I immediately hated the tearing noise that inescapably accompanies undoing any hook-and-loop hold-down of any type. On any piece of equipment that must hold securely and open quietly, I completely remove the hook-and-loop fastener, and replace it with a snap (example: General Tools Snap-Fastener Kit, six dollars from amazon.com). Alternately, a good old button with a sewn-on loop made of parachute cord (in lieu of a buttonhole) holds securely, and is easy to unfasten.

The retaining strap should also be located low on the hilt, just above its finger guard, directly opposite your hip joint, so that it "breaks" naturally there when you walk. If you draw your knife many times a day, you'll find that it's a good idea to tie down its sheath's lower end to your thigh. That's why many knives are sold with a length of cord already attached there—not to make its wearer look like a gunfighter, but to ensure that a hilt is predictably stationary, easy to grab, and, with practice, can be resheathed without looking at it.

The more modern and stylish looking thigh strap with its quick-release buckle has proved itself in the field to be neither as comfortable nor as effective as a simple, old-fashioned cord-type tie-down. A tied-down knife is easier to draw and re-sheath, and it further illustrates retaining straps need to be mounted low on the handle, at the articular capsule of the hip joint—where your hip moves, the knife should be free to follow. If the handle's retaining strap is mounted high up—as with the famed Kabar USMC knife—a tied-down knife spans across its wearer's hip joint, bridging it, and the sheathed knife rides stiffly, uncomfortably. A lot of highly touted tactical knife sheaths and pistol holsters have proved to be as comfortable as wearing a plaster cast.

Molded Sheaths

Easily heated, molded, and shaped, sheaths made from sheets of Kydex plastic sheets have become the rage for making friction-fit scabbards that often have no retaining straps at all. At first glance, this might seem like a good idea: because there's nothing to unsnap, a knife can be freed with just a good yank. A friction-fit sheath is almost a natural for concealed wear at cocktail parties and social functions, where the most strenuous activity will be a fast waltz, and it is very popular with plain-clothes security types who want a backup weapon that is quickly available.

But be wary of friction-fit molded sheaths in the out-of-doors, because field trials have revealed that almost none of them hold a knife securely enough to keep it from falling out during normal use. And none of them have proved trustworthy for search and rescue or any rough activity that might require belly crawling through culverts, rubble, and climbing over obstacles. Moreover, friction-fit sheaths tend to wear at contact points, becoming looser and less secure with use. And, annoyingly, nearly all give out a resounding "click" when their knives are shoved home, which is hardly stealthy.

If you elect to use a friction-fit sheath, it should keep its knife deeply, with as little of its handle exposed as possible, while still allowing for easy withdrawal. A sheath should have a tensioning screw, if possible, to re-tighten its grip as it loosens with wear. Best of all, it should be augmented by a retaining strap.

A growing majority of molded sheaths also come with a one-piece spring clip that is designed to fit over a buckled belt without the need to unfasten it. Once again, this seems like a desirable feature, because it ideally allows you to put on and take off your knife without the inconvenience of unbuckling your trousers belt.

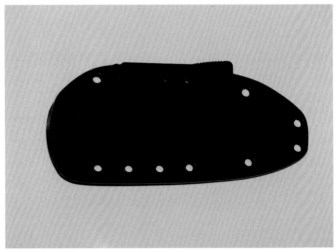

Most molded friction-fit sheaths are woefully inadequate at retaining both their grip on your belt and the knife they contain, but the Red Hill company (www.redhillsheaths.com) manufactures custom aftermarket sheaths that have proven themselves in the field.

The spring-clip is only the latest in a series of mostly failed attempts to make wearing a belt knife as effortless as possible. In my past books, I've decried the problem that many a needed outdoor item is left behind because it is too inconvenient to tote, and so is not there when you need it. But making something easy to carry, without also making it hard to lose, isn't resolving the issue, either. I've had every one of the spring-clip sheaths twist free and fall from my belt during normal activities, like kneeling, sitting, and climbing. That problem can be circumvented usually by taping or tying down the bottom of the spring clip with a loop of stout cord, but having to do that negates the convenience factor that a clip-on sheath is supposed to provide in the first place.

The best, most positive method of guaranteeing that a belt-clip-type sheath cannot fall free of your trousers belt is to simply give it a belt loop, like sheaths have had since biblical times. This is childishly easy: All you need is a six- to eight-inch length of seat belt strap. Fold the length of nylon webbing (the strap) double, so that it forms a loop. Then, using an extremely sharp knife, make a perpendicular buttonhole-like incision through the center of both straps, about an inch from their bottoms. Buttonhole incisions should be no wider than the metal spring clip on the sheath, leaving as much seat belt material on either side of them as possible. Finally, with the newly formed belt

The ESEE Knives company makes some of the best knives in the world, but this ostensibly field-ready knife—the CM-6 model—is virtually guaranteed to fall off your belt just from bending, kneeling, or sitting, and the knife is far from secure in its scabbard.

The same ESEE Knives Model CM-6 fitted with a homemade seat-belt belt loop and a snap-shut leather retaining strap will remain on your hip, come what may.

loop still held in a folded position, insert the sheath's metal spring clip through both buttonhole slots. What you have now is a solid belt loop that cannot slip free of your trousers belt, even though you need to unbuckle your pants to wear it. Cauterizing loose threads around the cuts helps to keep them from unraveling. Or you can harden them with carpenter's glue, which is usually sufficient. The rip-stop weave of seat belt material assures that it will not unravel.

Some other quick-attach systems have included the Velcro-type flap arrangement found on Schrade's SCHF-1 Extreme Survival Knife; the flap has proved itself bulletproof in the field, and it makes the knife easy to detach from your belt, but not one of these have been mount-able without first unbuckling your belt. A successful quick-mount/quick-detach system is the spring wire-clip type found on the back of Smith & Wesson's SW1B M-9 Bayonet scabbard (which mirrors the original GI-issue sheath); I have found it useful to tightly wrap the rounded hooks at the bottom of the clips with vinyl electrical tape to keep them from snagging on the belt loops of BDU trousers, though. And the winner, hands-down, is the hinged dual spring-loaded belt clip on CRKT's Ruger-licensed Muzzle Brake knife, which, judging by the popularity it has already attained with other manufacturers (including Red Hill Sheaths, below), is probably the next benchmark in quick-release systems.

Although no molded, friction-fit scabbard without a retaining strap has my absolute trust, there is a company named Red Hill Sheaths (www.redhillsheaths.com) in Idaho that can make a molded scabbard suited to search-and-rescue or other rough-and-tumble environments. I have

The hinged, snap-shut belt retainer on the CRKT-licensed Ruger Muzzle Brake knife is an example of some of the few secure clips that do not require unfastening your belt to put them on or off.

Even the Muzzle Brake's molded hard scabbard, with its marginally inconvenient slotted blade pocket, required a retaining pin to keep the knife securely in its sheath.

two of his custom sheaths, and they easily out-perform almost all factory-molded scabbards on every level. Owner Chris Maris custom-fits his Kydex sheaths to any knife, custom or manufactured, per your needs and specifications. Prices start at $30.

Specialty Sheaths

A problem with friction-fit sheaths, especially, is that they generally lack the means to carry anything but a knife, and that makes them too limited for survival or outdoor use. For the past several generations, since Schrade introduced their revolutionary M7-S Survival Knife, working survival

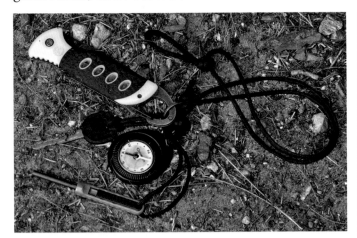

This is a very functional real-life survival kit that has proved its value many times over; not only does it carry The Basic Three, but also a spare car key, a five-foot length of genuine paracord, plus it carries around its owner's neck in a near-impossible-to-lose configuration.

Arguably the premier survival knife in the world today, the XcEST (Cross-country Emergency Support Tool—Bravo configuration shown) from TOPS Knives retails for $230. And, yes, all that stuff does fit onto the knife securely enough for field wear.

knives have been stand-alone survival kits, carrying compass, fire starter, fishing kit, needle and thread, cordage, and whatever other useful items might fit into sometimes sizable gear pockets.

Many knives are sold with survival sheaths, because the baseline for any survival kit in any environment is The Basic Three—knife, compass, and fire maker—and a knife is not a survival knife if it doesn't, at minimum, carry these items on board. Kabar's Zombie line included several different knife models, fitted into a Cordura sheath with a stout plastic blade liner, and an oversized gear pouch. The Armageddon from TOPS Knives is an aptly named knife, fitted into a lined nylon sheath with two quick-release, buckle-down pockets.

If your knife didn't come with a survival-type sheath, or if you want to keep your most valued tool in a top-quality carrier that can turn it into an apocalypse-ready survival system, consider one of the aftermarket offerings from Lost Mountain Iron Works (www.lostmountainironworks.us). If you can overlook the company's penchant for applying none-too-subtle pornographic monikers to its products, this manufacturer offers the most functional and durable sheaths made, bar none, for every size knife, as well as an assortment of add-on gear pouches. Prices average around $100. That ain't cheap, there's no argument about that, but every LMIW sheath that I've seen has been built to last a through a lifetime of rugged use, and it will accommodate any knife that fits into it as if it were made for it. Retaining straps are heavy and logically mounted, belt loops are strong enough to pull a truck, cargo pouches are generously sized, and the entire sheath is built like the serious piece of equipment that it is.

Lost Mountain Iron Works, an aftermarket manufacturer of perhaps the finest no-bull sheaths made, nicely fills the niche being left by the substandard sheaths that so many of today's outdoors knives are sold with.

Sheath Modifications

Velcro-type containment flaps are okay for cargo pouches, because few people will be in stealth mode when they're rigging a field-expedient fishing pole or going for fingernail clippers, and hook-and-loop fasteners have proved adequate for this job in all but the roughest environments. The over-sized quick-release plastic buckles that have become so popular also work but seem a bit over-much for a task that I still like to see done by an old-fashioned snap. A broken or otherwise non-functional cargo-flap hold-down can be expediently replaced by sewing a button onto the pouch, near its opening, then sewing a loop of elastic shock cord onto the flap—just stretch the elastic loop over the button, and your cargo pouch flap will never come open accidentally.

Another necessary but overlooked add-on is an easily grasped extension on the retaining strap that wraps around a sheathed knife's hilt—and if you've spent enough time in the field, you know exactly what I mean. If you're wearing gloves, as you must for about half the year where I live, trying to unfasten the strap so that you can draw your knife, and then re-fastening it after you've re-sheathed it, is virtually impossible with probably most sheath designs. Any way that you can make the strap easier to grasp is correct, but some of the methods that have worked for me is to melt a hole through the end of a nylon strap with a hot nail, then insert a four-inch length of heavy cord (parachute cord or shoelace), and tie it into a simple loop. Alternately, a six-inch length of cord can be tied with a series of square knots, forming a braided tail of sorts.

Each of these working knives has had a "tail" added to its retaining strap to enable it to be unsnapped and re-snapped while wearing heavy gloves in the very cold winters where this book's author calls home.

Many sheathed blades rattle noisily in their sheaths (ironically, many of these knives purport to be for tactical uses), and you don't need to be a combat soldier or deer hunter to become quickly annoyed by the steady "click-click-click" of a blade hitting against its sheath liner as you walk. One of the best solutions I've found is a piece of ordinary braided clothesline, equal to the length of the sheath liner, inserted snugly inside the narrow, folded end of its liner, and held in place at either end with a drop or two of Gorilla Glue. It doesn't matter if the sharpened edge of a blade cuts a crease into the cord; in fact, this may be preferable. Just be careful when sheathing and drawing your knife the first time or two, until it cuts itself a custom fit, because it may require extra effort to do either. As with everything, use your imagination; I've also had good luck at inserting a piece of folded polyethylene plastic, cut from a plastic jug using metal shears, into a sheath liner to take up extra space.

Making Replacement Sheaths

To reiterate the warning about how vital it is to carry a fixed blade knife in a proper sheath, for reasons of safety if nothing else, it's imperative that a sharp blade be secured in a cut-proof, portable container. It's also possible to lose a sheath, and it's so simple to replace it that everyone should know how.

First, think outside the box. There are many materials that may be utilized in the construction of a field-expedient knife sheath. I've used strips of polyethylene plastic cut from gallon-size tea and juice jugs using metal shears, and even folded-over pieces of sheet metal. This type of innovation is a fundamental of real-world survival; a helpless victim sees only what is, while a survivor sees what could be.

The simplest knife sheath is made from automobile seat belt strapping. Junk-yard employees have always thought me to be a little off plumb for paying them a few bucks to scrounge among the derelicts in their yard to cut out lengths of this super-heavy, seemingly worthless nylon strapping.

But, considering the multitude of valuable uses that old seat belts have had for me, it's almost criminal to send them to the crusher.

Making a sheath for a fixed-blade knife from seat belt strapping can be almost childishly simple. In its most fundamental form, begin by laying the knife onto a length of seat belt that's about three times as long as the knife. Fold the bottom (blade tip) end of the belt up, over the knife's blade, until it reaches the finger guard, where handle meets blade. At this point, you'll see that the blade is now encased in a pouch. Leaving about half an inch of free space between the bottom of the pouch and the blade's point, secure both sides of the pouch by driving a small fencing staple (like the kind used to string barbed wire across wooden fence posts) entirely through both sides of the pouch, then bend the ends of the staples inward using a pair of pliers, and hammer the ends down flat —so they won't snag on clothing or skin—using a claw hammer. Be sure to leave enough space for the blade to slide freely, but not so much that it will wobble excessively when sheathed.

Next, the belt loop. Fold the long end of the strap over, behind the pouch, making a loop that's about the same size (a little bigger is recommended) as the width of your belt. After adjusting the loop's size to suit your preference—again, too large is better than too small—cut the end off even with the cut-off end of the blade pouch on the opposite side. Secure the end of the belt loop with three staples across.

To keep your sheathed knife from falling out, use a nail heated over a burner, or an electrically-heated soldering iron, to melt two holes through the center of the outside belt loop strap, about an inch apart from one another, then thread six inches of parachute cord (or old boot lace) through the holes so that the free ends face outward, where they can be tied around the knife's hilt with an easily tied and untied square knot.

Another three-foot length of parachute cord threaded crosswise through the tunnel formed at the bottom of the sheath, where the two sides of the blade pouch are formed, serves as a tie-down for securing the bottom around its wearer's thigh, making it more stable when the knife is drawn and re-sheathed.

This is the replacement sheath's most fundamental form. It will serve its purpose for years to come, but it can be improved upon. Stitching, regular in-and-out, sine-wave-type stitches, applied with heavy sail-cloth (canvas) needles and super-strong carpet thread helps to make the sides

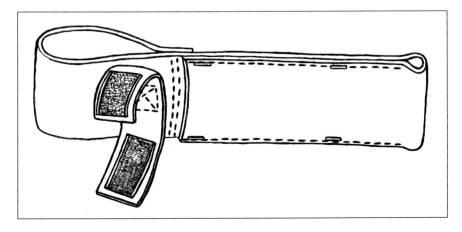

It's inevitable that sometimes a knife loses its sheath, and a fixed-blade knife sans sheath is akin to a firearm with no safety catch. This simple sheath is made from an automobile seat belt—available by the mile at junk yards. Note that stitching along the blade pocket is protected by steel staples.

neater. Dental floss is a terrific thread, too. A second row of stitches along the opposite length adds to the integrity of the seam.

The steel staples help to keep razor-edges from cutting through the stitching. I like to further protect threads by dribbling a strip of carpenter's (Elmer's®) glue along the length of each inside seam to harden them against cutting.

An added step that makes the process a bit more complicated is a liner layer, also made of seat belt strapping that runs the length of the blade pouch, between the two layers of either side. This center layer is sited so that the cutting edge makes contact with it when the knife is sheathed, actually cutting its own custom fit and, I think, making the sheath more attractive.

To make the liner layer, lay the blade on top of a length of strap, and trace around its outline with a permanent marker. Then, using a sheet-metal shear or a very sharp knife, cut out the shape of the blade, leaving a half inch of material at the point end. The liner layer should be precisely the length of the blade pouch.

Insert the liner layer between the two sides of the blade pocket, and as previously described, line up the edges at the sides, and staple them together. Complete the sheath as previously instructed.

If you so desire, the short lanyard that ties a knife's hilt to the sheath may be replaced with a retaining strap of the desired width, sewn to the outside of the belt loop where the lanyard would be. A snap kit, available at most arts-and-crafts stores or online (like the OUTUS 20-snap set from amazon.com, $10) completes the sheath to a professional level. Sew another folded-over (C-shaped) pouch to the front of the sheath, and it becomes a survival knife with a gear pouch. You can attach pieces of Velcro-type material to hold

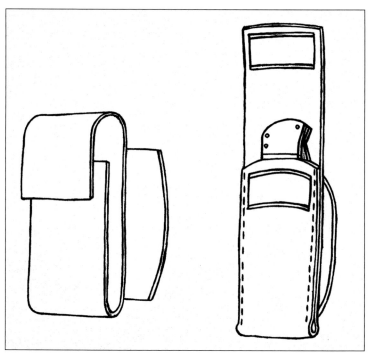

A belt sheath for your favorite folder is especially simple to make. By making the belt loop long enough to be loose-fitting, you can leave off the sheath's top flap, and the knife it holds will never fall out.

its flap closed. A strip of folded-over plastic, cut from a gallon-size plastic container with sheet-metal shears, serves as a hard liner for the sheath, stiffening it so that a blade slides in and out more smoothly.

Likewise, a replacement sheath can be made for a folding knife in a similar manner. An open top sheath, which I carried a folding knife in for more than a dozen years, can be constructed from a single foot-long piece of belt, folded S-fashion. Properly adjusted, this type of sheath will not permit a knife to fall out, because it will fold over on itself first.

The Perfect Sheath

To say that my childhood was dysfunctional is like saying that Michael Jordan was pretty good at basketball. Living in the North Woods, my coping mechanism against an abusive and alcoholic home life became the millions of acres of public forests in northern Michigan. At twelve years of age, my first after-school and weekend job was trapping fur-bearing mammals for the cash their pelts brought from local furriers. Except for my illegal (because I'm Caucasian) commercial gill-netting forays on the Great Lakes with local Indians—who still prefer to be known as *American Indians*, not *Native Americans*—I was always alone. No one ever knew my location (I was, and am, the only woodsman in my family), and frequently I'd be gone for a week at a time.

A knife was as essential to my life as a pair of boots. It would be impossible to say how many times I drew and re-sheathed the tool in a day, but I can state unequivocally that life would not have been possible without a sharp blade at the ready. It is really not possible to say that a thing saved your life—you can only make such an assertion if it *did not* save your life—but I'm pretty sure that my continued breathing would have been a lot more difficult had it not been for having a good knife.

And like any implement that is used repeatedly and often, the convenience with which I could grab, use, and replace that most invaluable of tools was a primary concern. A knife that was difficult to use in any respect was simply not acceptable. Some limitations I just had to live with. Steels weren't nearly as good in those days, and neither was edge retention, but if I could make any aspect of blade utilization easier for myself, I sure did.

A good sheath was critical, no less than the holster that held a gunslinger's tools of his trade. Yet this integral part of a knife system—the knife itself is just one component of that system—has been almost entirely overlooked by many knife manufacturers at the time this book is being written. It's an irony that some of the finest knives ever made are being sold with some of the most God-awful sheaths ever created.

A knife scabbard needs to be too stiff to flex when the blade it contains is drawn or replaced. A flimsy sheath will bind against a blade, slowing it, and a sharp edge will inevitably cut a sheath that bends. A few mountain man re-enactors have argued that a floppy rawhide sheath is more historically accurate, but a sheath that is cut to shreds by its own knife is useless.

In that vein, a sheath needs to be as cut-proof as possible. More than one hand (my own included) has been cut by an edge that severed the stitching that held it together. Other cut points include around the mouth of a sheath, making a sheath liner of hard plastic or metal more than a little desirable. Both of these traits help to explain why molded hard-scabbard sheaths would seem to be a good idea on the surface.

When I evaluated the titanium-blade Katrina search-and-rescue knife for the late John Moore, founder of Mission Knives, my field trials simulated as closely as possible the conditions that a rescue worker might subject his or her knife to as they crawled over rubble, squeezed their bodies through partially crushed doorframes, climbed atop collapsed buildings, and wriggled into twisted vehicle wreckage. It came as no surprise to me that John already had doubts about the "tactical" sheath that had been recommended to him by experts. Specifically, he questioned the ability of the molded friction-fit Kydex sheath to hold his knife securely enough to be considered reliable, and my field trials showed indisputably that it did not.

The company responsible for designing and manufacturing the sheath of course disputed my findings rather vehemently, but John Moore knew the man he'd tasked with evaluating his knife system. John also realized the importance of a knife—especially one that might be called on to break safety glass or hack through an apartment wall.

John's presumption that the simplest sheath design might not be the best sheath design was correct. The knife repeatedly fell free of the Kydex sheath during low-crawl exercises through rubble, and my sample, at least, was replaced with a conventional nylon-and-liner sheath with a retaining strap before I finished my review of it for *Tactical Knives* magazine. I did not make friends at Blade Tech Industries, the maker of the failed sheath, but facts based on actual experience are hard to disprove. Some molded scabbard designs are better than others, but be very wary of any sheath that lacks a time-honored and field-proven snap-down retaining strap. I repeat once again: a knife is too valuable a tool to simply lose it.

The retainer strap, which is necessary, regardless of claims to the contrary, should be positioned so that it holds a knife secure in its sheath, but is not exposed to the cutting edge; a good many of them have been and are severed by the knives they are supposed to restrain—yet another indication of the lack of real field testing that goes into knife designs these days. Whether this can be done depends largely on the pattern of the knife, but the strap should be as heavy and as cut-proof as possible. It should be sited low on the hilt, just above where the fingerguard would be on a conventional knife (many contemporary knives lack this feature), and should ideally encircle the hilt. Diagonal straps which cross over a hilt at an angle to snap onto the blade pocket may be adequate, but they ideally should cross from the unsharpened side of a blade, and should hold the knife so securely that it cannot be pulled out until you release it.

A common problem with diagonal retaining straps is that they're positioned on the same side as the knife's cutting edge, which of course causes a sharp edge to cut the strap each time a blade is drawn, causing a problem like the one in this photo.

How a knife is carried determines how well it performs—it has to be accessible and immediately deployable. I've carried a blade upside down, taped to combat (a.k.a. survival) suspenders, ready to cross-draw, even under an armpit from a shoulder rig. Based on two-score years, thousands of days and nights in a wilderness (I am not exaggerating), and countless cutting, whittling, and chopping chores perhaps dozens of times a day, the best way to carry a knife is the conventional way, hanging from your waist belt under your master hand. With your arm hanging loosely at your side, the hilt should be directly under your palm. This carry configuration was almost universal around the world for thousands of years, in war and in peace, and it isn't likely that we are going improve on it unless we reconfigure our bodies.

CHAPTER SIX
SPECIALTY KNIVES

A knife can be defined as any tool having a sharpened edge that is intended to cut apart materials of one sort or another. Beyond that, all bets are off, and a knife can take the form of a star-shaped blade at the bottom of a Vita-Mix electric blender, the twisted-steel blades of an agricultural hay-mower, or the ultra-thin strips of steel in your Gillette facial razor.

Of course, our main concern in this book is with the tools that are held in human hands and used to remove, separate, cleave, or otherwise rend materials into smaller pieces of themselves. As mentioned elsewhere in these pages, that sort of tool is supplied by nature to every "lower" animal, and it represents the single most defining tool of humankind; without it, we would never have surpassed the status of prey, and would in fact very probably be long extinct.

This chapter cannot hope to cover all of the specialized cutting tools in today's world (even though so many people need to borrow one to open packages), but presented here are some of the most historically popular.

Fighting Knives

Let's face it, this is the type of hand-held blade that readers of books such as this find most interesting. There is no cause for embarrassment in feeling that way, and the truth is that weapons made for killing living creatures similar or dissimilar to ourselves played a crucial role in elevating Homo Sapiens to its present state. To deny having an attraction to this oldest of combat weapons would be to deny one's own instincts.

The term fighting knife is vastly over-used these days. Throughout history, almost any knife can serve, has served, and will continue to serve as a fighting knife. Some of the deadliest, in terms of being used to injure and kill other human beings in everyday life, have been knives that are regarded as kitchen cutlery. The classic chef's knife, with its long blade, sharp point, almost effortless penetration into flesh, and a nimble, ergonomic design has shown itself time and again to be a superbly effective murder weapon. The same can be said for carving knives, boning knives, and most kitchen knives. This would not have been true in eras when anyone who might harm you would also probably have been wearing light armor, like a leather or heavy fabric jerkin, but today almost no one goes about their daily business while wearing even minimal protection against a knife attack.

Curiously, in a world where adding the word "tactical" to a knife's name has actually revived failing designs, this pure-blooded fighter, an aptly named Armageddon made by TOPS Knives, is being marketed under the guise of a machete. The company figures that those who need one will know what it is.

A Rugged Past

Skin color has nothing to do with the fact that life in poor communities is hard, and that kind of life can make some hard people. So it was with the friends I grew up with in "Indian Town." There's no racial slur in the term, unless one chooses to make it a racial slur, as the Odawa, Ojibwa, and Pottawatomie people generally referred to themselves as American Indians, and most still do today.

Every small northern Michigan town in the sixties and seventies had a sub-community known as Indian Town, a place where some of the most downtrodden people in America's history lived, often without electricity and utilities, usually without governmental assistance—hell, some of them didn't even have a birth certificate, let alone a social security number. But I remember them as being most of the best, most trustworthy friends I've ever had, and it is my blessing that a few of those friends are still alive today.

And those *Nish-na-Bee* (Indians) were as rugged as the lives they lived, as hard as the northern Michigan winters they endured, and as tough as the gill nets they set and pulled by hand for the pittance they earned from selling lake trout. Both men and women came to blows easily and often—not love-tap, slap-fighting, but broken-nose, busted-ribs poundings that literally resulted in teeth being swept up, and a few guys being blinded in one eye. As a kid, I got quick at disappearing through the nearest window or door.

It was late summer in 1967, and we'd just returned to our homes in Charlevoix from the annual "Pow-wow" in Cross Village. It might be politically incorrect today, but I would be lying if I claimed that any of the six adults in our packed '61 Buick were less than inebriated. Ducky (the only name I'd ever known her by) and her husband Pete had already begun bickering on the forty-mile trip home, and as they walked down the dirt trail leading from our driveway to their tarpaper shack, their mutual retorts were growing louder, as if entering their dismal abode were a hated end to one of the few tolerable days in their lives. The rest of us, even the five kids, remained ominously, expectantly silent.

Sure enough, barely twenty minutes passed before one of those old panel-van ambulances pulled down the gravel alley that served as a street, and stopped at the shack belonging to Pete and Ducky. Two white-clad attendants wheeled out Pete on an old fashioned gurney, his hands clutching at the blood-stained white sheet they'd draped across his torso.

As she'd done roughly a half-dozen times previously, Ducky had flipped-out, grabbed a dull butcher's knife—it was probably no coincidence that none of Pete's knives were ever keen—and proceeded to slash at his ample belly like she had a starring role in a Halloween movie. The poorly made, lightweight knife, its choil stamped Made in Japan—in an era when that was synonymous with low quality—had barely penetrated his flabby abdominal muscles, but three or four superficial wounds had felled him quickly. As always, Ducky wept and apologized profusely to her husband as a police officer waited to click handcuffs onto her wrists, and Pete patted her hand, saying (as always), "That's okay, Honey, I know you didn't mean it."

Then there was Jackrabbit, another Indian woman who got her moniker by being lightning fast with the razor-edged paring knife that she carried somewhere on her person at all times. This once-attractive (before the alcohol got her) woman's story was that she'd been gang-raped as a teenager; that never happened again, and she was good at inflicting just enough injury to let a guy know that there was plenty more where that came from, but not enough to go whining to the authorities. Even prepubescent boys (like myself) feared her, although I never knew her to cut anyone not asking for it.

That a knife is far from being obsolete as a lethal weapon has been proved so many times, over so many decades, from barrooms in Manila to battlefields in Afghanistan, that one might presume that no intelligent person would actually believe that a gun automatically gave its wielder the upper hand. That that is not the case says a great deal about the mindset of today's people.

The ultimate fighting knife in most environments is a sword. On a battlefield, against armored opponents, a sharp blade that was heavy enough to batter through even metal breastplates, and long enough to reach adversaries beyond arm's length, was one of the best assault weapons of its day. In some instances, one might prefer a stout, heavily tipped short spear. For every instance, the professional soldier was never without a foot-long dirk, even in bed. It was a truism of the day that every Samurai carried two swords—his four-foot Katana and a slightly shorter Wakisashi, not counting the Tanto that accompanied him to the privy. The variations in death-dealing edged weapons is endless.

But just as handguns became the everyday defensive weapons of choice after the firearm era had begun, because a long gun was just too heavy and unwieldy, swords shrank in size and weight to accommodate the needs of their owners. Broadswords, even the shorter Roman Gladius, could hammer a fully armored enemy to the ground on a field of war. But war swords were too heavy and too large to wear in a civilized setting, with small doorways, furniture, and—God forbid—knick-knacks and ornamental displays. The broadsword turned into a more portable and genteel rapier and saber. But even a slender rapier was too long to be worn full-time, and the reach advantage was offset by quarters that were too close to permit free movement of a long blade.

By the nineteenth century, longswords were all but gone, worn only by full-time men-at-arms. In the general population swords had been supplanted by the more user friendly, more versatile dirk. Dirks had been around for as long as there had been swords, and in the era of the rapier, a dirk had accompanied that slender sword as a component of the deadly elegant art of sword-and-dagger fencing—which has been likened to fighting a lawnmower.

You see it sometimes in martial arts-type movies, but in real life, rapier-and-dirk fighting, though it took a lifetime to master, was decidedly lethal, and has been likened to fighting against a lawnmower.

The invention of firearms provided their owners with more reach than the longest sword, and the role of edged sidearms took on a more secondary, close-quarters nature. The ideal choice for that job was a dirk, with an eight- to twelve-inch blade, short enough to be worn everywhere, stout enough to be depended on not to break—even when pitted against a full-length sword, and long enough to reach a foe's vitals with a single thrust. The earliest pistols offered the enormous advantage of making it possible to remove a threat from a dozen paces, but if successive strikes were necessary, defenders had best be armed with a dirk.

By the twentieth century, repeating handguns, social mores, and too many incidents like Jim Bowie's Natchez Sandbar Fight in 1827 had caused the edged sidearm to be banned throughout much of the United States. Texas was one of the first and most stringent to ban, by name, Bowie knives and dirks. (An aside, which might be pertinent: On May 25, 2017, The Texas Knife Law Reform Bill [HB 1935], which relaxed laws against owning proscribed knives, was passed. When it was placed on the docket, almost on cue, May 1, 2017, one person was murdered and three wounded by a knife-wielding sociopath at Texas University).

By WWI, punks, thugs, and railroad hobos were concealing folding knives and small fixed blades on their bodies, while rural farmers and ranchers were still packing the working-belt knives that their forebears had always needed to go about their daily lives. If a law-abiding person carried a weapon for self-defense, it was probably a firearm. Except for criminal uses, knives were relegated to the status of tools, or as backup weapons to a gun.

For centuries, a favorite concealed edged weapon has been the push dagger. It's designed with a blade that extends perpendicularly from a palm-handle, so that the usually double-edged blade protrudes point first from between the fingers. To employ this compact, easily concealed and decidedly lethal icon of professional card sharks, you simply grip the handle against your palm and punch. Even a light blow can inflict a potentially fatal stab wound.

In warfare, the effectiveness of a sharp blade as a weapon has never been forgotten. Trench knives of WWI were renowned for their lethality, so much so that soldiers on both sides often arbitrarily executed prisoners just for possessing one. In WWII, British commandos and US Marine marauders dispatched many a German and Japanese soldier with their knives. In Korea and Vietnam, soldiers' knives accounted for deaths on both sides.

Even in today's technical world, after American GIs in Afghanistan and Iraq found that going house-to-house, from bright sunlight into a dark dwelling, put them at a decided disadvantage, it was decided that a long blade engineered to spill blood was a desirable backup. Troops bursting into a darkened room were temporarily blind, while insurgents armed with long-bladed knives could inflict severe damage with a wild swing. With that in mind, the US Army commissioned James Williams, probably the most dangerous close-quarters fighter in the world, and Columbia River Knife & Tool, a world-class knife maker, to create a close-combat dirk of YK-30 Japanese steel. (Its maker, Daido, likens YK-30 alloy to air-hardened AISI 02 tool steel). The Hisshou is but one extraordinary example of why the knife is far from obsolete as a weapon.

Sadly discontinued, this Schrade Double Eagle field knife is a very effective combat weapon.

Characteristics that make a knife a preferred weapon include ease of handling. It must feel comfortable in the hand. It must be secure in a hand that's wet with perspiration, water, animal fat, or even blood. Its handle must feel adroit enough to transition between every position so a hand can grip it as swiftly and smoothly as possible.

A fighting knife's blade needs to be long enough to reach a vital organ or blood vessel, which is at least three inches. It needs to be slender enough to penetrate, with a point that is on its blade's center axis to most efficiently transfer thrusting (stabbing) force.

Sharp, slender, and built to be injurious to flesh, these knives may peel an apple or open an envelope, but they were engineered to be weapons.

A fighting knife *must* be sharp. A sharp blade is superior to a dull one simply because it cuts more easily and more deeply. All things considered, the fighter with the sharpest knife is most likely to emerge victorious, which is bad news indeed for whomever is the loser of a knife fight. If you intend to use a knife as a weapon, you need to know how to sharpen its blade or be close friends with someone who can do it for you.

Finally, you need to be smart. Take no chances, and do not reveal yourself to be armed (this of course presumes that you are a defensive fighter and not a mugger or robber). I once had a disagreement with Steven Dick, editor of the defunct *Tactical Knives* magazine, about the president of a knife company that I take a bit less than seriously, who has for decades represented himself to be a D'Artagnan of sorts, despite appearing to be somewhat less than fit. Mr. Dick insisted that the fellow was a knife-fighting expert, and seemed a bit perturbed when I asserted that the victor in a cut-and-slash melee was typically the combatant who embedded the pointy end of his blade into his adversary. In the real world, on real streets—or real dark alleys, as the case may be—it doesn't matter how you do it, so long as you get it done, and many a martial arts master of any stripe can attest that the only sure way of winning a fight is to avoid it altogether.

Just as a person intending to use a gun for self-defense needs to know how to load it, so too does a knife fighter need to know how to sharpen his weapon.

James Williams, probably the most dangerous close-quarters fighter on the planet, demonstrates the weapon that he designed at the behest of the United States Army, the CRKT-made Hisshou dirk.

The Axe as a Weapon

Knives aside, every lumberjack can tell you (although most will choose not to) that an axe is the most dangerous close-quarters weapon ever designed. A three-and-one-half- to five-pound head of modern steel alloy—like the razor-sharp 420HC used by Fiskars/Gerber in their carbon-fiber hafted splitting axe —can pierce the skull of a grizzly bear with one strike. When I was eight years old (1964, for those who are interested), it became my job to fill the half-cord woodbox that heated our house every night when I came home from school, homework be damned. I could barely lift that old double-bit timbercruiser axe my stepfather foisted on me. A year later, I had become more than a little adept with it. By the time I'd decided to chuck it all and go into a wilderness for the next year and a half to build a log cabin homestead in 2001, I was forty-four years old and pretty comfortable at taking large chips from tree trunks until they fell over.

Of late, axes have been used several times as weapons of mass murder. Even in the hands of someone who doesn't have the skills of a lumberjack, an axe is capable of taking down anyone with a single blow. Farmers of old used one for thousands of years to mercifully kill half-ton bulls for meat. An axe has no respect for body armor, Bowflex bodies, or firearms if a shooter is within its reach. It never runs out of ammunition, it can strike repeatedly and swiftly, and

While it might seem distasteful to some, the frozen rabbits constitute a welcome and much relished summer meal for the author's gray wolves and sled dogs, while incontrovertibly demonstrating the power that a sharp axe can exert against flesh.

every strike is potentially lethal. Short of a large-caliber gun, it is the most lethal weapon you can carry, and in skilled hands it is very, very dangerous.

An axe might not be the first choice as an everyday-carry self-defense weapon, but you need to know how dangerous it can be, whether in the right or the wrong hands. You wouldn't want to carry one when you're out clubbing, but should zombies ever take over Earth or, more realistically, if EMF radiation prompts widespread riots after the panic of nationwide or global blackouts, an axe is both the edged weapon to avoid, and maybe the first choice for your own protection.

Hunting Knives

Almost every boy from my rapidly disappearing generation knew what a hunting knife was, and he lusted after one of these magnificent tools. A hunting knife meant that you had achieved manhood. Most of us already had folding knives and .22 rimfire rifles (it was a different time with very different children), but a fixed-blade, usually Scagel-modeled sheath knife meant that you had reached a level of maturity where you could handle a deer-class centerfire rifle and hunt with the men. This was long before the "Motor City Madman" had anointed himself as a master deer-slayer who marketed T-shirts that extoll the joys of leaving a steaming pile of deer guts in a cornfield. When you got your first hunting knife for Christmas, only threats from your mom would make you stop sleeping with it each night while you dreamed of the next deer season.

Any knife that could be used to process a deer from animal carcass to some of the most delicious red meat an American boy could fry, barbecue, or jerk could be used as a hunting knife. But the dream of most was a rat-tail tanged, steel pommeled, stacked-leather-washer model with a Bowie-type, semi-hollow ground five-inch blade. Sheaths were always stitched-and-riveted leather affairs with snap-down retaining straps, right-hand only, and with pointed tips that invariably developed a permanent bend.

Blades were labeled (if they were labeled at all) with the words "High Carbon Steel" on the choil. That was usually SAE 1095, but sometimes 1085, or some other softer alloy, but they were virtually never made from stainless. Blades were sharply pointed to make precise incisions in a deer's hide, without severing the all-important Gambrels tendon (the equivalent of a human's Achilles tendon). The Gambrels tendon was essential to keeping the animal securely suspended from steel tenterhooks inserted in a slice in its hide between that tendon and the ankle bone, and it could not be severed or the animal would fall.

This Scagel-type "Buffalo Skinner," from the defunct Northwoods Knives Company of Gladstone, Michigan, is a beautiful example of the kind of knife that every sporting deer hunter would be proud to have on his or her hip.

The radius of the blade, called the "belly," was large, even exaggerated, to increase the amount of cutting edge that could be stroked between skin and muscle, effectively increasing the amount of time it could be worked between sharpenings.

There is nothing as fine as a beautifully crafted hunting knife. Unlike a survival knife, or any other working knife, some of which are pretty plain, or even homely, a hunting knife is intended to flatter its user, to make a hunter proud to wear it as if it were a finely worked piece of jewelry. It is an icon of a sport that should be the most noble, and perhaps last, bond between this planet's apex predator and his canniest and most challenging prey. Deer hunting is a religious experience, and a superbly made fixed-blade hunting knife is the artful nimrod's crucifix, never more so than with today's almost science fiction metals and materials. We would have thought ourselves in heaven.

This modernized eye-catching alternative to a conventional deer hunter's knife is the Redi-Axe, from Rapid River Knifeworks, in Rapid River, Michigan. Its field trials are explained in detail in Chapter 10.

Fishing Knives

The activity was a bit less than legal for me because, ironically, I was of Caucasian blood, but fishing on the Great Lakes with my Indian friends was a good job for a teenager with the North Woods in his blood.

But when it came to delivering and getting paid for our night's catch, which had to be cleaned before they were weighed, I was expected to stand off to one side. My Ojibwa partners needed no help, and were in fact slowed down by my attempts to assist them. I just stood there and watched in awe as they removed entrails and gills from our catch of lake trout with a few movements that were almost too fast to follow.

Anglers prize a good fishing knife as much as a hunter values his hunting knife, and no tackle box is complete without a sharp, flexible, thin-bladed knife. Long fixed-blade fillet knives, typically car-

Removing the top, boneless fillet from a fish demands a very sharp, preferably thin-bladed knife.

ried in open-top leather sheaths, are favorites, even to the point of being displayed as decorations on rustic cabin walls.

A more portable long-time classic that has been found in almost every tackle box for more than half a century is the French-made Opinel folding knife. Designed by Marcel Opinel in 1955, this inexpensive little folder was found in most tackle boxes that I can recall, and in a Great Lakes state with one thousand more lakes than Minnesota—whose license plate boasts that it encompasses ten thousand lakes—you can bet that there were a whole lot of anglers. The French-made knife

When the author was a boy, the French-made Opinel folder was as common to tackle boxes as fishing hooks and split-shot sinkers; it was a locking-blade knife, when lock blades were not common, and it could fillet a fish nearly as well as a dedicated fillet knife.

The Opinel fishing knife employs a strong, ingeniously simple blade lock comprised of a rotating ring that blocks an opened blade from closing on fingers—an ideal knife for young anglers.

boasted an INOX (inoxidizable) stainless blade, and was the first successful stainless-bladed folder. The knife employed a unique and clever "Virobloc" locking system that consisted of a rotating steel ring that blocked its blade from closing. That alone made it a favorite for everything from cutting an anchor rope to filleting a bass. That knife is still made today, in several variations that range from traditional to all-modern materials—even a poly-handled survival version with a molded-in whistle.

CHAPTER SEVEN
USING THE KNIFE AS A WEAPON

A knife is the original multi-tool. The specialty knives described earlier are just some of the designs that have been created to exploit the versatility of this simple, magical implement. There are few things, from the meat in the hamburger you had for lunch, to the car you're driving, to the house you live in, that are not a direct result of a sharpened edge being used to process raw materials into something useful for a given purpose. Upholstery that covers furniture must be cut, as does the material for clothes and shoes. The coffee you drank for breakfast was ground up by rotating steel blades, as was the wheat used in the flour of your pancakes, and the skillet they were fried in was blanked from a flat sheet of steel before being "drawn" in a press and formed into a pan by a die.

But the knife, unfortunately, is most notoriously famous for being employed as a weapon, used to cut living flesh. Firearms and explosives have shaped the courses of humanity for only a relatively short while in our history, while edged weapons have established, built, and felled the mightiest empires for millennia.

This lightweight saber embedded in a block of frozen meat is visual proof to how deadly a weapon a cutting edge can be.

I do not at all like to write about methods and strategies for using a knife as a weapon. That people with no knowledge of the techniques covered in the following pages have recently begun to make the most heinous uses of knives an almost daily occurrence is more than enough testimony to the deadly effectiveness this most original icon of humankind as a tool of death. You don't need to be martial artist to kill or maim with even a dull paring knife. To impart to the general public information that informs them how to kill and maim even better and more effectively feels to me like a whole lot responsibility. The last thing that any conscionable writer wants to do is to even inadvertently teach a psychotic individual improved methods of murdering someone.

At the same time, the world in which we live is in no way becoming a safer place for us or our loved ones. It has been proven time and again that just going to a movie theater with your loved ones, dining out at a favorite restaurant, or even walking a boulevard could, and does every day, cost innocent people their lives. The "hood," to use the vernacular of people who believe that killing children as collateral damage is just a part of the romantic criminal lifestyle of their hip neighborhoods, has for decades been a site of so-called drive-by shootings—the definition of which is just to wildly empty a gun's magazine at everything before speeding away to hide. I once dated the sister of a civil rights lawyer who hated me for what he called my violent philosophies—until the night he was beaten and robbed in front of his wife and children in the parking lot of a "nice" Detroit restaurant (that lawyer now carries a .380 automatic pistol).

Nor does the ever-tightening noose of legal restrictions against firearms ownership by any but select American citizens (if you've had the least problem with authorities, you are not entitled to self-protection) do the least good to make citizens safer,

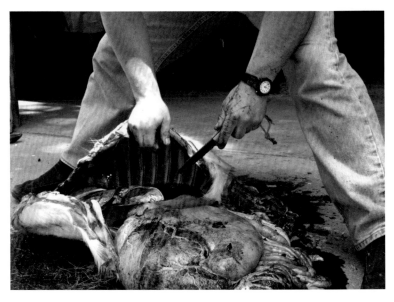

Anyone who has ever butchered an animal knows fully well how easily a sharp knife rends through flesh.

which has been historically proven. The most obvious result that prohibition of gun ownership has had is to make homicidal sociopaths turn to knives, machetes, and axes as weapons of mass murder. Now there is a push by Utopian politicians to outlaw knives, as well —and the rise of the American Knife and Tool Institute (AKTI) as the knife counterpart of the National Rifle Association—is a worrisome result of this latest attempt to make the world safer by taking away anything that might be used as a weapon.

Street Smarts

The public high school that the redneck boy attended for a year as a ward of the state in Holly, Michigan was far from being the quaint little farm-community institution that it was supposed to be. Even by the early 1970s it had been tainted by the proximity of the city of Flint, twenty-five miles away, which even today is considered one of the most violent cities in the nation.

Kids were still more naive than they've become, and generally less sociopathic, but if you wanted mescaline, acid (LSD), reds, yellows, poppers, horse (heroin), or just plain old weed, it was available to anyone who could come up with the cash.

Perhaps ironically, kids in that generation were more educated about life and death in the real world. Almost everyone knew how to shoot, most boys hunted small game, at least (most girls simply weren't interested). And every boy carried, at minimum, a pocket knife—schools had no opinion on that, and a small cutting tool was not considered to be a weapon.

Even in those relatively innocent days there were a few "jitterbugs," as we called them, future residents of one of the infamous prisons that Michigan operates as a major business. After classes had ended one autumn day, a prime representative of this illustrious social category was waiting for the redneck boy's companion in the school parking lot. He was puffed up about some imagined slight, obviously stoned, and accompanied by the usual gallery of underlings who needed to be impressed regularly by the toughness of their leader.

This cross between James Dean and Scarface sauntered up to his intended victim, and snapped open a long-bladed florist's knife whose spring cam had been worn off to produce what was known as a "gravity blade."

"What's up?" the assailant said in a menacing tone.

Without thought, because he was scared, but clearly to the assailant's surprise, the redneck boy drew his own Buck Bearclaw-style lockback, and snapped open the heavy blade.

In response, the thug slashed at him, and the redneck boy turned his right shoulder into the blade. The dull, never-sharpened blade zipped harmlessly across the heavy nylon fabric of his snowmobile jacket. Automatically, the big hunting folder in redneck boy's left hand slashed across the back of his assailant's right hand.

"Aaaaahhhhhh . . . !!!!!," the thwarted

Despite its tongue-in-cheek moniker (it's actually a dirk), this Death Dagger from Kabar's line of zombie-fighting knives is an ideal fighting knife, well suited to saber-and-dirk combat.

would-be attacker screamed in a voice several octaves higher than normal. His mother-of-pearl handled knife clattered across the asphalt as he pressed his lacerated right hand hard against his abdomen. Epithets spewed from his mouth as his buddies gathered around, helping their bleeding captain toward the school doors.

As redneck boy and his companion hurried away from the school, they heard an ambulance scream past. The boys waited for a policeman to knock on the door for several days, but nothing ever came of the incident—"snitches get stitches," to use a common street-ism of the day.

Knife fights tend not to unfold the way many a high-rise-dwelling novelist depicts them. In real life, most are over as soon as first blood is drawn, because being sliced open holds an instinct-deep revulsion. It's a rare person who can resist slapping a hand over a gaping, bleeding wound in an attempt to staunch the flow.

When you hear a person spouting that old saw about the foolishness of bringing a knife to a gunfight, what the speaker is telling you is that he does not understand the lethality of a knife as weapon. He, like probably most people, overrates the superiority of a firearm over a knife in a fight, especially at close quarters.

To demonstrate, consider the following scenarios: First, an assailant armed with a knife, fifteen feet away across a room. You have a pistol, out of its holster, in your hand, at the ready. The knife wielder moves toward you with earnest intent to do harm. His first stride narrows the gap by six feet, and in one second he's close enough to reach you with a slash that extends four feet from his body. You are very fast, but your bullet is only a third of an inch across, and you must land it on a fast-moving target that measures less than three feet across. Regardless of magazine capacity, your best chance of success lies with the first, aimed shot. His wild, un-aimed slash covers an arc with a radius of at least four feet. If it is the middle of the night, in your home, you're probably lightly clad in light clothing. Even a relatively dull knife parts your abdominal muscles, maybe cuts deeply into your extended arm, maybe severs a tendon—or an artery—causing you to lose your weapon, or instinctively clap a hand over your wound. A second slash, half a second later . . .

Seldom seen working together these days, dirk-and-saber fighting—a long sword in one hand and a dirk in the other— was once a greatly feared combination, likened to fighting a lawnmower.

Equally disingenuous is anyone who purports to be expert at knife fighting. Becoming that means regularly engaging in a level of violence that cage-fighters want nothing to do with. Examples of true experts include rare examples like Miyamoto Musashi (1584–1645), who was undefeated in sixty duels, where losing the contest almost always meant losing your life. True expertise is derived from the word "experience," and there were never many fighters who were expert with sword or knife fighting, particularly after the nineteenth century. Many were well-practiced, but actual experience was just too dangerous, even when it wasn't illegal.

Steven Dick, past editor of *Tactical Knives* magazine, and a special forces combat veteran of the Vietnam War—a man I genuinely admire, even if we don't personally like one another—once spoke with me about the president of a knife-making company who was considered to be an edged weapons expert. Personally, I consider the man to be a blowhard. I said as much, arguing that the winner of any knife fight was determined by which contestant got the pointy end of a blade into his opponent first. That's an oversimplification, and there's always a rare exception—like the tough-as-iron Jim Bowie, who won a knife fight against multiple opponents with a sword-cane protruding from his chest—but it's nonetheless true.

Knife fighting is a very old and much studied form of martial art.

Knife Grips

The grip with which you hold a knife with should match the task at hand. The name of different grips changes with who is describing them, but for our purposes, what a particular grip is called will be less important than what it enables a wielder to do with it.

Forward Overhand Grip: This grip is probably the most natural, in the sense that when a person takes a knife in hand, it is the most common. With this grip, the upper (back) part of a knife's handle is held between the thumb and forefinger, the finger guard against that forefinger. The four fingers are wrapped around the lower, cutting edge, side of the hilt, with the blade pointed forward.

This grip is limited in that is indelicate and cumbersome, not permitting fine tasks that require point control. Its advantage is that it permits powerful forward thrusts from waist-high: an underhand thrust to the kidneys or groin, for example. If a knife is held cutting edge facing up, the thrust is followed by a slash that exploits its cutting potential, and the blade is pulled upward while it is embedded in flesh. If the grip holds the blade cutting-edge down, the slash is of course downward, against the edge.

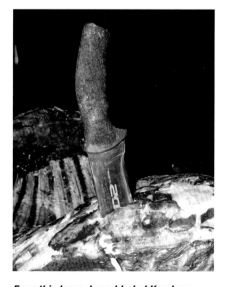

Even this large, long-bladed Kershaw Outcast had no problem punching through the bones of this ribcage, leaving a wound that would have been no less than horrendously lethal on a living being.

Modified Overhand Grip: This grip enables a user to have finer tip and blade control. The grip is essentially the same, except that the forefinger usually extends parallel along the blade's spine—which is why many knives have a row of gimping (traction grooves) there to provide more secure control. The remaining three fingers wrap around the hilt. The forefinger provides amplified control over a knife's tip and belly, essential for delicate tasks.

Reverse Overhand Grip: This grip is the same as the forward overhand grip, except instead of the blade facing forward, a blade faces reverse, pointing away from the rear (pinky-finger side) of the hand. For most people, this grip is the most powerful, insofar as delivering a stab, and perhaps especially with the follow-up slash. Again, the direction of the slash is determined by which direction the cutting edge faces. Like the stabs delivered with this grip, follow-up slashes from either direction, so long as they're with a blade's cutting edge, are especially powerful for most people.

Changing Grips

The ability to manipulate your grip on a knife with one hand, without laying it down or relinquishing your grip, is essential. You don't have to learn fancy carnival-quality edged acrobatics, like those seen in so many movies, from *Young Guns* to *Blade*, but it is critical that you can change the orientation of a knife in your hand as needed to derive maximum efficiency from the tool.

For example, I was once at the home of an acquaintance who, in spite of his reputation as a sport hunter, knew very little about butchering meat. It had almost become a tradition among for me to help him process any deer that he'd managed to tag. He seemed surprised when he walked up to me unannounced while I was slicing steaks from a hind quarter, and the blade of the large butcher's knife I'd been using suddenly disappeared from sight—and from potential danger to bystanders—to lay flat against my forearm. There was no conscious thought in the act; it was a reaction that I'd learned long ago when working at crowded workbenches where salmon, deer, and other meat was being processed in quantity. Folding a working-size blade flat against one's forearm kept everyone safe.

No special skill is required to manipulate a knife skillfully in a real-world environment. And it doesn't hurt that with a little practice, you can look pretty cool while practicing safe knife handling.

Most fundamental to shifting your grip on a knife are your thumb and forefinger—or your middle finger, whichever feels most secure to you. Most knife handles are flat-sided, which is conducive, but this method works with every type of handle. Grip the handle on both sides between thumb and forefinger and, using them as pivot points, practice rotating the knife back and forth—blade down, then blade up—between them. When the handle reaches a point where it's perpendicular to your palm, either blade-forward or blade-back, wrap your fingers around it.

Practice this between-forefinger-and-thumb method. You'll be amazed at how much versatility this simple technique offers for shifting a knife in your hand. With a bit of practice, there is little risk of losing grip of your knife while transitioning from a grip that has the delicacy to peel an apple to one with the brute strength needed to penetrate a car door.

Though not as stylish and showy as some of the edged acrobatics that are shown on cinematic productions, the thumb-and-forefinger pivot is a simple to learn fundamental of changing your knife's grip positions.

Most knife hilts are suited to being gripped between a thumb and forefinger, and then rotated between those digits to change the direction their blades face.

The next most important grip-transitioning skill that you need to teach yourself is the two-finger roll. This shift uses the first two fingers to straddle a knife's handle, with the fingers acting as fulcrums to rotate a knife handle over them using pressure from the thumb. This same technique is often seen by office workers who use it to rotate a pen or pencil between their fingers. Using this method to shift a heavier knife requires a bit more strength, and correspondingly more practice, but it is also a necessary grip-shifting skill for anyone who wants to become adept enough with a knife for it to become a useful tool.

Practicing either of these easily learned grip-manipulation techniques is simple enough for a child. You can increase your agility with either of them anytime you have a ruler, any eating utensil, or just a stick in your hand.

You probably won't mind that with a little practice (it really doesn't take a lot of dedication for most people to master these exercises) you can look pretty impressive as you nimbly switch from one grip to another. But there's a real purpose to this, as well. Just days before this writing, one of our sled dogs became snagged by its collar, and was being choked to death. While I gripped the heavy nylon strap with one hand to relieve pressure against my dog's throat, I drew the DiamondBlade fixed-blade knife from its sheath on my hip, flipped the blade to the position I needed, and deftly parted the collar with a single stroke. That was just one example of an experience in which I just didn't have the precious seconds—or an extra hand—to use fumbling with a razor-sharp blade.

Some of the classic practice moves of sword and knife fighting—because no one is in fact an expert at this martial art, merely a polished practitioner.

Knife Wounds

I have often commented in my typically gauche fashion about the foolishness of subscribing to the belief that possession of a firearm automatically endows one with superiority over a knife-wielding adversary. The sole advantage inherent to a gun is that it can theoretically inflict a fatal wound from a long distance. But discharging a firearm, even several times, is no guarantee of actually hitting a target. A wild swing from a sharp blade from four feet can eviscerate through light clothing, and an attacker with intent can close a gap of fifteen feet in a mere second.

According to the FBI's Uniform Crime Reporting (UCR) statistics, deaths by knife have risen steadily by as much as 400 percent since 2010, accounting for at least twice as many homicides as all firearms combined. Ever-stricter anti-gun laws are directly responsible, because as legislation restricting new gun sales become more stringent, that segment of the populace that has always meant harm to others is finding new weapons with which to do it.

The most common cause of death from a knife is repeated stabbing. In most instances, a killer is in no way trained, but rather is in a manic state, usually enraged or frightened enough not to remember details of the stabbing. In a local case a few years ago, a man was found guilty of pre-meditated murder, as opposed to a lesser charge, because the man he killed with a knife was killed by a single, perfectly executed stab through his ventricle. The prosecution proved that the wound was not an act of thoughtless passion, but a deliberate assassination.

While an assailant with a knife is rarely a threat at thirty feet, a knife wielder at ten feet should be considered lethally dangerous, regardless of how well armed his opponent might be. A single stab—as described above—can kill as surely as any caliber of bullet, and a slash delivered with force can inflict more tissue damage than any firearm short of a grenade launcher. Following are some common knife wounds that prove cutting weapons are far from outdated.

Punctured Lung (Pneumothorax): Take, as a proven example, the oft-practiced black art of sentry elimination, taught to commandos of World War II. A human's lungs are attached to the spine and back wall of the ribcage by the pleural sac. A short-bladed knife driven into the pectorals of, especially, a heavily muscled man (like James Bowie) is likely to inflict a relatively minor would—literally a "flesh wound," as TV shows have long been fond of calling such injuries.

Contrarily, a three-inch blade punched into the side or back of its victim's ribcage will probably penetrate through to a lung, perforating the air sac, and causing it to collapse. A collapsed lung (*pneumothorax*), even just one of them, all or partially, is sufficient to decrease blood pressure to dangerous levels, and make it difficult or

Professional soldiers have known since Biblical times that a slender blade can easily punch though the protection of a rib cage to almost instantly put an enemy out of commission by disabling his ability to breathe.

impossible to breathe. Air inside the torso, trapped outside the lung, can exert pressure against the heart muscle, as can blood trapped inside the area (*hemothorax*), causing cardiac failure, leading to death. In short, an average-size folding knife can topple the largest man with a single blow over a relatively large area of its victim's upper torso. A strong man who cannot breathe, who loses consciousness from *hypotension* (low blood pressure), or experiences a cardiac event is unlikely to be willing or able to continue to fight.

Arterial Bleeds: Contrary to vampire movies, "cutting the throat" of an enemy—specifically, severing the jugular vein—of a person you mean to kill is an ineffective strategy. Veins, the often-blue blood vessels seen so prominently just below the surface of the skin on workout professionals, are low-pressure return lines in a body's circulatory system. Severing a large vein completely may cause a victim to bleed out slowly, but vein cuts often clot. Arterial blood is brilliant red, the color that corpuscles take on when they're rich with oxygen, on their way to feed muscles and organs with this life-giving gas.

Severed arteries do not clot, and slicing through one of those virtually guarantees that the sufferer will die from blood loss in about four minutes. The only ways to prevent a body from pumping all of its blood out is to apply a very tight tourniquet on the heart side of the wound, thereby restricting all blood flow through the ruptured vessel or, more contemporarily, by bandaging over the wound snugly with an anti-hemorrhagic (clotting) product like battlefield-proven QuikClot® sponges. An option is to clamp a severed artery shut—like a ruptured hose—on its heart side with a hemostat, but that tool is rarely found outside of operating rooms and the living rooms of pot smokers (the latter use them as roach clips, and they generally lack the wherewithal to isolate and clamp a hemorrhaging artery). In every case, failure to stop an arterial bleed will almost always result in death, and staunching blood from an artery is a difficult proposition.

Because of their fragility, nature has placed arteries well inside a body, usually near a bone, where only the deepest and most severe of wounds

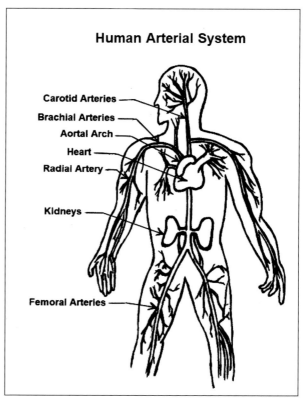

Human Arterial System

Carotid Arteries
Brachial Arteries
Aortal Arch
Heart
Radial Artery
Kidneys
Femoral Arteries

Positioning of the greater and lesser arteries within a human body; note that they are evolved to be deep within, protected by bone and flesh, because severing one is an almost guaranteed fatal wound.

can reach them. There are major arteries, like the renal, radial, and femoral arteries. Major arteries are usually accompanied by corresponding veins; for instance, femoral arteries are paired with femoral veins; subclavian (pectoral) arteries are matched with subclavian veins. This is not always true; sometimes corresponding arteries and veins are named differently, but it is always true that a ruptured artery is more serious than a ruptured vein.

Femoral arteries are prime targets if you want to inflict a fatal wound, because the vessels extend the entire length of either leg, being especially large inside the thighs, then branching into smaller arteries below the knee. A blade-length stab—that is, driving your knife in up to its hilt—followed by a slashing motion, as if you were trying to cut the thigh completely off, anywhere between groin and knee, is usually sufficient to sever a femoral line. And that is sufficient to quickly take the fight out of the strongest man, killing him unless he is just minutes away from an emergency room. If you've seen the movie *Blackhawk Down*, a factual recounting of events in which a young American trooper lost his life in Somalia, when a shrapnel-severed femoral could not be clamped, you've seen a realistic depiction of just how serious a severed artery can be.

Renal Arteries: I've mentioned that my own childhood was far removed from the ideal American upbringing. The same holds true for my siblings. When my oldest sister was sixteen, an unwed new mother, and emancipated (given up on) by the courts, she moved to the small southern Michigan city of Port Huron, hoping to escape the small town poverty of northern Michigan, where she'd grown up.

She took with her a trusting nature and a lack of street-smarts that was to cost her dearly. One morning her neighbor, a young woman about her own age, came to her apartment for a cup of coffee. While my sister was filling the coffee pot with water at her sink, the neighbor plunged a four-inch paring knife into the small of her back.

Instinctively, my sister wheeled and smashed the half-filled coffee pot against the side of her neighbor's head. The neighbor went down, but rage and fear prompted my sister to beat her into unconsciousness with a table lamp. Many people in those days did not have telephone, so she knocked on the doors of several of her neighbors before she found one willing to get involved enough to call an ambulance.

My sister was lucky. With just some minor surgery and a few stitches, she was able to return home (which immediately became northern Michigan again). But doctors told her that if her neighbor (recently released from a mental institution) had struck two inches over, she'd have bled to death from a severed renal artery.

Renal arteries are two large arteries that carry oxygen to the kidneys, located at either side of the lower back, just above the pelvic bone. In the sport of boxing, it is illegal to land a blow to this area, because kidneys are organs of heavy blood flow, and they are relatively easy to damage. A hard punch from a trained fighter can disable, even kill, a strong man.

Kidneys are only lightly protected by thin layers of lateral and lumbar muscles, and are fed oxygen from above by a large diameter renal artery. It is very easy to drive a knife through these muscles, about six inches above the belt line, into the kidney or the artery leading into it. By driving the knife point-first into the lumbar muscle, next to the spine, and drawing the cutting edge across, outward, you create a long, deep gash from which blood flows profusely. If a victim doesn't go into systemic shock immediately, probably losing consciousness as a result, he will within a minute or two. Death results about four minutes later, and unless a victim is placed upon an operating table immediately, it is a certainty.

The aortal arch is a classic death blow. This is an extraordinarily large arch-shaped junction where the left and right carotid and subclavian arteries join above the left ventricle of the heart muscle. This is where the "pig sticker" is driven in and drawn across, at the hollow just above the sternum (breast bone), right below the chin.

A stab wound through the aortal arch, whether the cutting edge of a blade is drawn across to widen it or not, is fatal. This strike has often been used by commandos and covert operatives for sentry elimination, because not only does death come swiftly (faster if a victim is held from behind, and struggles, hastening the loss of blood). And if it was done "correctly" (somehow that doesn't seem an apropos description), a blade also severed the victim's trachea (windpipe), making it impossible to breathe or to scream.

Carotid arteries run the length of the neck along either side. Like all arteries, the carotids are embedded deeply for their protection, next to the cervical spinal column (neck bone). Movies depict a person who's getting his "throat cut" as dying quickly from simply having a knife blade drawn across his Adam's apple (larynx). In fact, cutting the throat of, say, a sentry from behind requires a very sharp knife, and a determined application of muscle.

With this technique, the cutting edge of a blade is driven deeply into the side of the victim's neck, opposite the arm doing the cutting (the left side of a victim's neck if the knife is held in the right hand). The initial penetrating thrust may well sever both carotid arteries. With the knife inserted, its blade is then drawn across in an arc, around the victim's neck spine while maintaining very hard inward pressure on the knife blade to keep it deeply embedded, until it separates the trachea, then reaches and severs the opposite carotid artery. While decidedly effective, cutting a throat is this manner demands a very sharp knife and a person who is inordinately strong of grip, bicep, and upper torso. It is a simple matter of fact that not many people are willing to or capable of killing using this technique.

Personal experience also causes me to cry "BS" on the purported beheading videos that have been shown on the Internet by goatherders turned terrorist. While I don't doubt that the lifestyle of these 140-pound Islamic murderers

Despite amateur-quality videos posted on the Internet, purporting to depict a hostage of some terrorist gang or another being beheaded for imagined crimes, it is not easy to decapitate any animal larger than a goat without chopping through its spine with a large, heavy blade. Note that you never actually see the murderer cutting through his victim's spine.

has been physically demanding, I am a 190-pound lumberjack from the North Woods, where roofs must be shoveled free of snow to keep them from collapsing and felling a dozen twenty-ton trees a day falls under the heading of home insurance. I have personally beheaded a thousand large animals—pigs, deer, goats, sheep, and cattle—because taking off the head is a necessary part of processing a carcass for meat. It is extremely difficult, or plain impossible, to sever the neckbone of a larger animal without chopping through the bone. The way individual vertebrae are interlocked makes working a knife blade to cut the soft tissue between them virtually impossible on all but the largest animals, and cutting through the bone with hand pressure is beyond my above-average capabilities. I suspect that is why I've never seen the actual beheading in these heavily edited videos, just a victim laid down so his head is out of the camera's eye, followed the purported headsman holding the severed head up like he's seen in movies, and wailing that silly ululation that has become a trademark of some Middle Eastern cultures.

Finally is the brachial artery, which extends across the shoulders, then branches into the arms. A downward stab, into the hollow between the trapezius (shoulder muscle) and the clavicle (collar bone), followed by a hard prying motion against the handle of the embedded blade severs that artery, which leads directly to the aortic arch.

Alternately, a stab, especially a wrenching, slashing stab that opens the wound wider into the upper arm or forearm may sever the lower end of the brachial arteries.

In every instance, an arterial bleed is marked by copious amounts of bright red, oxygen-rich blood pulsing under pressure from the wound. Even if an arterial wound isn't sufficiently debilitating to bring down an adversary immediately, a minute of high pressure blood loss will usually bring down the toughest, most determined foe.

Brain Wounds: The *LRRP* (long range reconnaissance patrol) Ranger was part of a six-man team on a patrol in North Vietnam when his unit encountered a company-strength group of NVA Regulars crossing the same rice paddy that they were. With no chance of winning a firefight, miles behind enemy lines, and outnumbered twenty to one, the Rangers dispersed and went to ground in the tall grass. As luck would have it, the tail NVA trooper, doing his job and wandering back and forth while following the main body, nearly stepped on one of the Rangers. Without a sound, the Ranger rose out of grass, and drove his M7 bayonet up through the NVA trooper's palates and into his brainpan, killing him silently and instantly. By the time the dead NVA's comrades missed him, the Rangers were gone. I have used this same killing stroke subsequently on white-tailed deer and smaller animals. It takes an earnest thrust to penetrate the bony upper palate

There are soft spots on the armored skull—you can find them on your own head by probing with your fingers. Any knife blow that penetrates or otherwise affects the brain is a disabling, probably lethal wound.

that protects the brain case on almost every animal, so a narrow, very pointed blade is the tool for this job.

A human head is a roadmap of veins and arteries, but a laceration of the scalp, despite how profusely it might appear to bleed, is seldom life threatening. Do not, however, overlook the benefit of blinding an enemy with his own blood, should that prove beneficial to you, because scalp lacerations do tend to bleed a lot.

More lethal is a trauma to the internal skull. A "brain bleed," the most common of which is a subdural hematoma, usually caused by blunt force (clubbing) trauma to the outer skull, is exceedingly dangerous. In this instance, blood loss is contained inside the braincase, where it exerts a hydraulic pressure against affected parts of the brain. As Al Capone could personally attest, a plain old baseball bat can kill with a single blow—again, a contradiction to action movies, where victims can absorb bludgeoning that would kill a bull if the script demands.

A knife wound to the head can result in instant death, which is something that every farmer or professional hunter used to be able to confirm from personal experience. I remind the reader of the often-ignored fact that every pork chop, hamburger, and pepperoni slice belonged to the flesh of a living animal that needed to be killed by someone before it was processed into their dinners.

A sharp, hard blow to the forehead, between the eyes, with the butt of knife, particularly one fitted with a variation of the "skullcrusher" pommel, is usually enough to at least cause unconsciousness. Killing is not a fun process for normal human beings, and it is one of the great ironies of life that the persons who most hate to take a life will also become the most efficient at doing so.

You've doubtless heard new mothers chasten people not to impact the "soft spot" in their baby's skull, the point on top of the head where the cranial plates knit together during maturation. Many an adult on the wrong side of an organized crime boss has been murdered by an ice pick driven forcefully into the top of the victim's skull, through the still-soft spot, and into the brain. A knife blow, with its pommel or blade point, can be lethal there, too.

Under-the-Chin: Wounds to the brain are generally fatal, and usually quickly or instantly. A favorite of Hollywood thrill-peddlers is the under-the-chin brain stab, in which a blade is driven point-first upward under the chin, through the soft palate and tongue, through (or past) the bony upper palate, and into the brainpan. Much harder to do than it looks, this blow, if executed successfully, is almost always fatal, because it penetrates into the cerebral cortex.

In fact, if the stab is straight upward, which is a natural orientation, the point is forced against a victim's bony upper palate. This is a formidable obstacle; it requires a narrow, sharply-pointed blade, and considerable muscle to punch through. The most effective strategy—hard to accomplish in the heat of hand-to-hand battle—is to angle a blade back at about forty degrees, so that it misses the bony part of the upper palate, and passes through a soft area into the medulla oblongata, the "old brain" responsible for the involuntary functions of the body, like breathing and heartbeat. The result is immediate death, as all of the autonomic nervous system ceases to operate.

Auditory Canal: An instant-death strike that I have used numerous times, particularly on deer and other long-eared meat animals, is the hollow between the external acoustic meatus (put simply, the ear canal) and the styloid process, a slender projection of bone located directly behind the hinge joint of the lower mandible, opposite the rear molars of the lower jaw.

You can easily find this vulnerable hollow on your own skull by probing with your fingers directly below your own ear lobes. The hollow in that location is easily identified, being just below the ear canal, and you'll note that exerting an inward pressure here with your fingertips is painful. (FYI, the head area is in fact not a good striking point for a punch, because it is generally well-shielded, but impacting this area with a knuckle will probably result in breaking the fragile styloid process.) The hollow located next to the styloid process bone is an easily found place to inflict a stab wound, using a long, slender blade, driven inward with intent.

Likely impact points with this strike are likely to be the medulla, mid-brain, or cerebellum, all of which are fatal, usually instantly.

Cerebellum: The cerebellum is located at the base of the skull, just inside from the medulla oblongata. Driving a knife, tip-first, upward under the base of the skull pierces this critical part of the brain, or damages, maybe severs the cervical spinal cord. Either way, death or paralysis are virtually certain.

This is a difficult blow to strike insofar as driving a blade home into the cerebellum, because it must go up and under the skull's crest. However, a hard strike or stab to any portion of this area is sure to have devastating effects on a victim, because tendons, muscles, arteries, and spinal cord are all located in this area, and knife damage to any of those is almost certainly incapacitating to a victim.

Eye Socket: This is another favorite of movie makers, and this time they're absolutely correct. A stab through the soft eyeball will probably penetrate into the *cerebral cortex* of the brain. The cerebral cortex is a vital message processing center, and damage here will at the very least disable the capacity to think. This strike might not kill its victim instantly, but it will certainly reduce them to non-threat status.

Other Striking Points: Tendons, which will definitely disable whichever limb they control when severed, are also deep in many places on the body, but very close to the surface in many others. Suicides who elect to cut the artery in their wrists must also cut deeply enough to sever the cords controlling their muscles, an indication of how close to the surface and vulnerable these biological pulley cords are.

The Achilles tendon, most known by its location just above the heel of the foot, is one that is naturally vulnerable, and many street-defense classes teach students to sever this large cord with a knife to disable an attacker. Those classes overlook the fact that this location is almost always armored by thick footwear. Instead, slash the Achilles tendon behind a man's knee, and that entire leg becomes unusable.

Sever either the origin (outer deltoid, or shoulder muscle) or the insertion (inside elbow) tendons, and that arm ceases to function. A deep cut across the inside of the wrist leaves the hand it connects to limp. On every limb, and especially vulnerable at skeletal joints, are easily cut cords (tendons and ligaments) that are vital to operation of that limb.

Perhaps the best non-fatal, but disabling, wounds are to the long muscles. A four-inch blade buried into one of the several long, striated muscles that power the thigh takes the desire to perambulate out of the strongest man. A deep slash or stab into the shoulder muscle between neck and deltoid takes, at minimum, that side of the torso out of action. Severing a muscle in the back likewise disables an upper torso on at least one side.

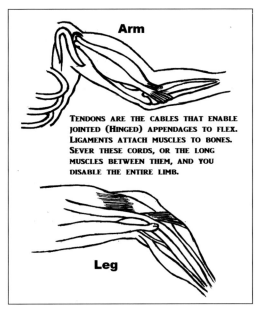

TENDONS ARE THE CABLES THAT ENABLE JOINTED (HINGED) APPENDAGES TO FLEX. LIGAMENTS ATTACH MUSCLES TO BONES. SEVER THESE CORDS, OR THE LONG MUSCLES BETWEEN THEM, AND YOU DISABLE THE ENTIRE LIMB.

Tendons of the arm and leg.

Severing all or part of a muscle is often sufficient to cause that muscle to cease functioning, but a slash is slowed, its force absorbed, by clothing, and few adversaries will be naked. The most guaranteed muscle-disabling strike is to stab point-first deeply into the muscle; this is why it's important to have a blade's tip in line with the center line of a knife's handle, so that the force of a thrusting blow will not be offset in one direction or another. Then, after the blade is inserted, draw it hard crosswise against its cutting edge to widen the wounds.

General Knife Fighting Techniques

A knife whose intended use is as a weapon should be—must be—kept at razor sharpness at all times. Criminals are virtually never proficient gunfighters because they lack the opportunity and the wherewithal to acquire the practice needed to gain expertise. Likewise, a person who has skill sharpening a knife has an upper hand over the majority who can use it only as a blunt stabbing weapon. Using a dull knife as a defensive weapon is akin to using underpowered loads in a firearm intended for defense. If you have need of a knife as a weapon, you need it to be as effective a weapon as it can be.

Since most knives will be carried under the guise of what has become known in survivalist vernacular as "EDC" (Every Day Carry) knives, they are more likely to be used for opening boxes and cleaning under fingernails than as defensive weapons. This means that they will be dulled, and will routinely need resharpening; there is no such thing as a sharpened material that will not dull with use. In fact, many knives will dull in storage, because their polished-keen edges suffer corrosion at a microscopic level. To maintain your advantage over an adversary who will also likely be armed with a knife (or a gun), you simply must have a blade that will cut as easily and as deeply as its design will allow. A sharp knife slashed with purpose across the back of the hand holding a pistol is guaranteed to cause that person to relinquish his grip on it. Sharpening skills are discussed in a later chapter.

Historically, based on actual commando and other real-life combat uses of a knife, from World War One to Afghanistan, a slim, long-bladed dagger type has been the weapon of choice. You cannot argue with the facts, and the Sykes-Fairbairn Dagger, the M7 bayonet, the M1918 Trench Knife, and most other knives meant for fast, clandestine kills have been double-edged or stiletto-edged (i.e., partially double-edged), with a narrow blade that penetrates with little friction, and is long enough to reach vital organs—any length over three inches is sufficient for that. Personally, I'm not a fan of a double-edged knife, because I need a stronger and more versatile tool, but it cannot be disputed that a long dagger has been the edged weapon of clandestine close-quarters battle.

Using a knife as a weapon is pretty terrible, on both ends. If your intent is to disable, then you should try to avoid severing major blood vessels, and concentrate on severing muscles using slashing strikes only. This will inevitably cut veins, but remember that veins are low-pressure return conduits, and they are nearer to the outside, less well protected than high-pressure arteries. Despite vampire tales, cutting a jugular vein will probably not be fatal; severing a carotid, or any other artery, will almost certainly cause a victim to bleed to death in about four minutes.

One of the most aggravating knife exaggerations in cinematic creations is the one where someone receives a slash across his belly that penetrates a T-shirt, to inflict a minor slice across the belly that exudes only a trickle of blood. In a movie, all this does is cause the injured hero to cast a disgusted look at his assailant, wipe some blood on his fingertips, and then taste it before proceeding to win the day. In real-life, a slashing wound across the belly penetrates the clothing there, it will almost certainly part the abdominal wall, literally spilling out the entrails. That sort of injury is a fight-ender, as no one can continue fighting heroically with his intestines spilling out onto his shoes. Clothing usually inhibits the completeness of this wound, making a very keen edge a must if you mean to use it as a defensive weapon.

It is not necessary to kill or to disable with a single blow. Every wound from a knife hurts, and it does real harm, deeper than just pain, in terms of a victim's body realizing at a primitive level that it has been injured. Every wound weakens an opponent, and even the toughest of them cannot absorb many such hurts without collapsing or withdrawing. Most sober, sane people will break off after the first cut, but never count on that.

If you deem it necessary to strike, do not cease until an opponent has stopped moving, or has run away. The objective is not to demonstrate that you are a bad-ass, or that your father can beat up his father, the ultimate goal is to remove an adversary from the fray entirely, and that will normally mean inflicting maximum harm upon an enemy until that enemy is no longer a threat.

Do not stab a hole into an opponent, and then stand back to admire your work. Doing so might very well get you killed—remember, the other guy is fighting for his life, too. A stab to your opponent's ribs must be followed immediately by another stab. And another. And another. You get the idea. When you can no longer easily reach your target because he has fallen to the ground, you might consider stopping your assault.

Likewise, do not leave the blade suck into a victim but pull it free immediately. Paramedics know that an object embedded into a victim's body, be it a knife or a piece of steel from an industrial accident, is best left where it is until a patient is in an emergency room, where there are supplies of whole blood and surgical tools. Pulling free an embedded object often causes blood to pour freely from the wound, and a victim who might not bleed to death were it left in place has often hemorrhaged to death swiftly after the object's removal. If you happen to be the person who put said object into the victim, it behooves you for the patient to hemorrhage, so pull out your blade immediately after inflicting a stab wound.

To help induce bleeding, don't merely pull out your knife after it has been embedded. Give the handle a wrench or a twist as you do so, try to make certain that as much of a blade's cutting edge drags across flesh as possible. The wrenching action uses leverage to maximize whatever tissue damage might have been done to the stab area by widening the wound. Archery hunters know that an arrow lacks the hydrostatic wounding force of an expanding bullet, so increasing an arrow's launching power isn't necessarily advantageous. The ideal, so far as killing force is concerned, is an arrow with a multi-edged razor-sharp head that remains embedded in an animal's vitals as it flees, ripping, cutting, and increasing hemorrhaging with each movement. For that reason, you should exert as much force as possible against a cutting edge as it is withdrawn from a wound channel.

A standard strategy of the Scottish Fencing Masters, many of whom, I'm proud to say, were blood ancestors of mine, was to keep their forward blade, usually a shorter dirk, waving constantly in the face of an opponent, while the longer reach of the sword was held in reserve, ready to strike in an eyeblink. It is instinctive to protect one's eyes, and to have the sharp point of shortsword or dirk hovering menacingly within striking distance of these fragile and invaluable organs of sight is frightening to say the least—so much so that, especially in modern times, drugged-up assailants have actually struck at, even grabbed hold of, a sharp blade—much to their chagrin.

To end this section, I wish to relate an incident that occurred in 1979 in a major Texas city. A young man and his girlfriend were enjoying a nighttime stroll through a city park when they were accosted by a pair of small-time hoods. The apparent leader of the duo pressed a small pistol (which was of course registered and legal for him to carry, right?) to the side of the young man's head and demanded his wallet, while the other made more than suggestive remarks about his girlfriend. The young man reached for his wallet as if to comply, but produced a Gerber Guardian dagger, instead. He grabbed the hand holding the pistol and held it away from himself as he drove the blade repeatedly into his assailant's ribs. The other man fled as his comrade fell to the ground, and the young man walked off with his girlfriend, taking their attacker's pistol with him. Texas police looked earnestly for the young man, whom they dubbed a "criminal," even offering a reward for information leading to his apprehension. For his part, the man told his side of the story—anonymously—in *Soldier of Fortune* magazine, which defied threats of prosecution, and refused to betray the identity of the citizen hero. Because of protections afforded by the First Amendment, the man remains un-prosecuted for that "homicide" to this day.

Fighting versus Sport

In 1521, Ferdinand Magellan made to claim the Philippine islands in the name of Spanish King Charles I, but Raja Lapulapu, ruler of the island kingdom of Mactan, killed the explorer with a Philippine Kampilan single-edged shortsword. Lapulapu, in typical practical Filipino combat fashion, first delivered a low, disabling slash to Magellan's thigh, then finished him with a point-first thrust to the throat. The Spanish won the day, but taken aback by the effective armed combat skills of the natives, they forbade the Filipinos from carrying sword-length blades.

In response, the natives combined their indigenous sword-fighting skills with the Spaniards' own techniques, and applied them to (usually) sword-length sticks, in a style that came to be known as escrima (esk-ree-mah). Filipino escrima is, in fact, stick-fighting, but the term stems from the Spanish "esgrima," which means "fencing."

Today, the word escrima is used interchangeably with the term arnis. When the techniques actually employ bladed weapons, then the art is known as kali. Sometimes all three arts are lumped under the title of escrima.

Escrima differs from other martial arts in that students are encouraged to first learn how to use weapons before learning empty-hand skills. Originally, villagers had little time to learn to protect themselves, so escrima training focused on the practical, using simple, easily learned, and battle-proven fighting skills. Much like American street fighting, or Israeli Krav Maga, the ultimate objective is to disable an opponent swiftly, without sustaining injury to oneself, using whatever objects or means are immediately at hand—no style, no grace, only hard, effective violence.

Knife Throwing

Much of being a successful survival instructor—or a teacher or public orator of any type—is being an entertainer. Sadly, my own classes were lacking in this regard (according to one "professional" student of several courses, "This is the most informative class I've taken, but you're boring"). But even a hard-crusted swamp-tromper like myself had a few tricks. After one hundred classes, I'd learned to predict what most students would ask, how they'd react, and other common idiosyncrasies.

So when the thirty-something client, already a bit adversarial about the low priority I placed on firearms as tools of survival, asked rather antagonistically what I'd do if a bear came into camp, I was ready. I yanked the two-and-one-half-pound, eighteen-inch heavy handmade Bowie that served as my machete from its scabbard that was lashed to the side of my pack, and whipped it by its handle at a dead stump, fifteen feet across the camp. The big blade's point embedded two inches into the wood with a resounding "thunk." He was much impressed, and a bit less sarcastic after that.

In truth, that was a set-up. I'd practiced that particular throw a thousand times, just for guys like him. To him it seemed off-the-cuff and unrehearsed, but as Jeff Randall, president of ESEE Knives, has long pointed out, throwing

The classic by-the-blade knife-throwing position; generally speaking, grasping the blade nearer its tip causes the thrown blade to rotate faster; nearer the blade's center means that it rotates through the air more slowly.

a knife has little value in a real-life survival or self-defense scenario, and it can have dire negative consequences.

The primary disadvantage of throwing a knife is that it is a very difficult skill to master. Those who have mastered the art are in the same category as Olympic floor gymnasts, world-class skeet shooters, and members of the Harlem Globetrotters. These people have talents that folks like you and me can only admire, but few can aspire to. In a real-world mugging or similar situation, throwing your knife at an adversary is about as effective as just handing it to them.

A knife will not fly straight like an arrow. Whether thrown by handle or blade, it will tumble, end-for-end, until it (hopefully) impacts its target point-first—or even at all. The trick is to make it strike tip-first, at precisely the point in its rotation where the blade is perpendicular to its target, and a maximum amount of inertial energy is transferred into the target. And a trick it is; if you were lucky enough to speak at length with a circus knife-thrower, he or she could boggle your mind with all of the variables that must be considered to make a thrown knife stick into its target like a dart.

First, consider the rate of rotation, which is the speed at which a knife turns end over end when it is thrown. This explains the common belief that a knife's balance point should be at its exact physical center. For most all-around uses, from whittling to skinning a hog, I actually prefer that a knife be a bit heavier at its blade than at its handle; a heavier blade feels more nimble in my hand, with better point control. Some people prefer the opposite, with a heavier handle.

Knife throwers always prefer a balanced knife. Any knife can be thrown, but for every knife to throw the same as every other knife, and to be predictable, every knife has to be balanced and exactly like every other knife. That's why purpose-made throwing knives come in sets. A practiced knife thrower who can stick every throwing knife where he wants it every time will not do as well with a Kabar USMC Knife or an average hunting knife.

While no skilled practitioner of the knife-fighting martial arts recommends throwing your weapon at your opponent, the CM6 from ESEE Knives is almost perfectly balanced for throwing.

A few basics to remember are: The closer your grip to the end of the knife, whether throwing it by its blade or its handle, the faster it will rotate. The significance of that to a thrower is that the closer they are to their target, the closer to the end of the blade (or handle) they must grip the knife as they throw it, because that will cause it to rotate faster as it flies through the air. The farther you are from your intended target, the nearer the center of the blade you must grasp it, normally between thumb and forefinger, to make it turn less quickly. In summary, depending on your arm length, a knife's mechanical balance point, the point at which you release, and a host of other, factors—if a target is five feet away, you grasp the knife being thrown closer to its end, so that it spins faster. If a target is fifteen feet away, you grasp it closer to its middle, so that it travels farther with each rotation.

It is essentially as simple as that. But all of these things must be learned by feel and by eye, and they change with each knife. Bearing in mind that ordinary knives not specifically fashioned for throwing are neither built for the task (many will break or be damaged), or balanced for the task, feel free to practice the skill. Throwing a knife is a lot of fun if you do it sensibly, with a mind toward safety, common sense, and protecting your knife from damage. But it is not a realistic component of your knife-fighting strategy; when your life depends on it, keep your knife in your hand.

Fighting Lanyard

That leads us to a very real problem with using a knife as a weapon: keeping possession of it. There are innumerable ways that anyone can lose grasp of a knife.

Hanging a combat knife around your wrist by a lanyard is one answer, which is one of the many reasons that every knife made for use out-of-doors needs a hole at its pommel, to accommodate a length of cord. When skinning and butchering a large hanging animal, it's sometimes necessary to have the fingers of both hands free; in instances like these, a simple loop slung over the wrist is sufficient.

For maximum security when activities might get a little more rough-and-tumble—like a back-alley mugging, or a home intrusion in the middle of the night—you need your knife to be as much an integral part of your body as possible.

This knife is held firmly in its wielder's overhand grip by a combat lanyard made from a precisely adjusted loop of parachute cord.

The greatest danger in a knife fight is losing one's grip on one's weapon, especially if a confrontation degenerates to a dirty scuffle, as is often the case in a genuine battle. The combat lanyard helps greatly in keeping a hilt stuck to your hand.

The fighting (or combat) lanyard is identical to a conventional lanyard, except in this case you begin by laying the lanyard across the back (top) of the handle, so that half of the lanyard loop drapes over either side of the handle. Seen from the side, with the knife held parallel to the earth, the two halves of the lanyard hang down to form a loop. Grip the knife with a normal overhand grip, palm against the upper (spine) side of the handle, opposite the cutting edge. Insert all four fingers through the loops formed by the halves of lanyard hanging down. Slide the cord over your knuckles until it fits snugly.

If the cord does not fit snugly, use the knot that forms the lanyard into a loop to adjust it longer or shorter as needed to make it do so. Getting the length that's best for you is a matter of moving the knot that locks it inward or outward to best suit the size of your hand and your personal preference.

Ultimately, when you achieve the proper fit, your knife will be hard to knock out of your hand, even if you're knocked off your feet. This simple loop of cord might very well be the thing that saves your life in a life or death fight.

On a less mortal note, the fighting lanyard has also earned the status of necessary when I'm skinning an animal or cleaning fish. There are times and tasks when I don't want to relinquish hold of my knife, but I need my fingers, and especially that uniquely human opposable thumb. This lanyard has proven invaluable for enabling me to pinch and pull, or to pick up small objects, without losing grip of my knife.

Batoning

In the past decade or so, there has arisen the apparently previously undiscovered practice of "batoning" a knife blade lengthwise through a piece of wood; using a larger piece of wood as a bludgeon to split it into smaller pieces. Somehow generations of frontiersmen dating back to before John Colter (a guide for the Lewis and Clark Expedition of 1804–06) just never discovered this vital piece of survival information, because it was never used until 1998.

To my shame, the trend was started by Yours Truly while searching for an impressive field trial to demonstrate the amazing strength of Ontario Knife Company's then-new SP-8 Survival Machete in a number of magazine articles, and in my book, *The Outdoors Almanac*. I never dreamed that the next generation of survival experts would try to legitimize "batoning" as a fire-starting technique.

Step 1: Begin with a larger chunk of wood and, using only hand pressure, drive your knife's edge into the wood, lengthwise with the grain, using a rocking, twisting motion. If the chunk is too large to split, as shown, split off just a corner.

Step 2: Using precisely the same technique as in Step 1, split the piece that you split off.

Step 3: Continue using a rocking, twisting motion to split off progressively smaller lengths of wood. There is never, and has never been with any mountain man, trapper, or woodsman, from Neolithic times to the New Millennium, any need to pound on your knife blade with any sort of hammer. Such abuse is not recommended by any knife or even axe manufacturer, and certainly not by any wilderness expert who ever lived.

I mention the practice here for just one reason: to say that it is not only entirely unnecessary, but stupid to hammer the blade of what is perhaps your most vital survival instrument into a chunk of wood. In half a century of living in the wilderness, I have never found occasion to commit this act of abuse, and neither did any of the past masters of woodcraft—including Daniel Boone, Jedediah Smith, and Davy Crockett. Batoning is an invention of the late twentieth century, and used by outdoorsmen who have none of the legitimate uses for their knives, like butchering meat and making tool handles that made blades a part of daily life for our forebears. Some method of determining how good or bad a knife might be had to be created, even if it lacked real legitimacy, so the practice of batoning firewood was invented.

That wouldn't matter, except that driving a knife blade through wood with a heavy club is abusive in the extreme, and the practice *will*—note the absolute lack of uncertainty in this assertion—break its blade. Maybe not the first few times, but no knife alloy can withstand that level of abuse for long without a large, usually half-moon shaped chunk of its blade breaking away. Ironically, the poorer the knife—i.e., the softer and less able to keep a sharp edge—the longer it can typically survive being hammered, so if the practice is supposed to be evidence of good quality, it usually proves the exact opposite.

Manufacturers of working-class Collins-type (single cutting edge with flat hammer-like back) crosscut axes specifically recommend against pounding the tool's head into wood, and if batoning is considered a bad idea for an axe head made from three and one half to five pounds of hammer-forged steel, then it's definitely not a smart thing to do with a knife.

Should it become necessary to split a piece of wood into smaller strips using a knife blade, there is a way to do it that not only won't destroy your knife, but it can be accomplished using the most lightly built folding knife and just hand pressure (and you don't even have to be strong): Simply place the cutting edge atop the end of the wood to be split (it doesn't matter if the end is sawed-off flat or broken jaggedly) and press it down into the grain with a wiggling motion. When it's embedded a quarter inch or so, rocking the blade back and forth while twisting it sideways is sufficient to cause a split to develop in the wood.

Using only hand pressure, push the blade deeper into the split and rock the knife's blade to widen the separation. At this point, the wood will usually split in two. Do not try to split off too large a strip—maximum size is largely dependent on the size of the knife being used and the leverage it provides. When splitting kindling to make a fire, narrower and thinner is always better in any case; it is an axiom of survival fire making that the smaller the tinder or kindling, the more easily it will catch fire. Be especially cautious to not drive the sharp edge down into your skin.

My final argument against the foolishness known as batoning is that not one legitimate knife manufacturer believes that you should hammer their blades through wood. Not one of them. If Ka-bar, Buck, Ontario, and the rest of this world's most credible and knowledgeable manufacturers, who have made knives good enough to serve our troops through a dozen wars, don't think that batoning is a smart thing to do, how many weekend survival experts have the knowledge to refute them?

Butchering

Mike Stewart, the president of a small knife-making concern called Bark River Knives, once wrote on his website that "No knife is made to cut through bone." What he meant was that his company didn't make knives that were capable of chopping through bone. Personally, if I am going to carry a knife on which my life might depend, regardless of environment, in ambient temperatures that may be colder than -40 degrees, Fahrenheit, I want that sucker to be as close to being indestructible as possible.

This Randall Training and Adventure Knife (RTAK) was made under license for Jeff Randall's company (RAT—Randall Adventure Training) in 2006, and advertised as an "unbreakable" survival knife. This one, in fact, broke while trimming jack pine branches from a shelter support during an actual survival class when the ambient temperature was -8 degrees, Fahrenheit.

Beyond that, we raised purebred gray wolves (under license) for eighteen years, and these carnivores demanded meat in their diets. That meant cutting up a lot of large animal carcasses. Being of more or less reasonable intelligence, I matched the tool to the job: If the animal being disassembled was a cow, I used an axe or a wood-splitting maul—wolves and dogs love eating the marrow inside leg bones (my wife called it "wolf candy")— largely because even a broadsword bounces off such a thick osteal obelisk (leg bone). But for separating rib cages from spinal columns, chopping through the pelvis of smaller ungulates like white-tailed deer, even removing a deer's legs—the strongest bones on its body—a large, heavy knife often sufficed.

Chopping through leg bones is, indeed, hard on a knife. After a year of such use, I broke my beloved Power Eagle 12 from TOPS Knives, knocking a silver dollar-size piece from the bolo section of its blade. When I asked TOPS president, Mike Fuller, what he thought had happened, he said "Dunno, we've never had one break before." But Mike understood what a working knife must sometimes do, and he simply replaced it (meanwhile, I reground the broken blade, and it is today one of my favorite field knives).

This 1095-steel, TOPS-made Power Eagle is one of the heaviest, strongest, toughest survival knives ever manufactured by anyone.

The Power Eagle is crafted of 1095 steel, which takes and holds a surgical edge, but tends to chip, even break, when used hard. Knives that have time and again proved Mike Stewart wrong about being quite capable of cutting through bone, while still retaining the qualities to remove skin and cut meat, are the SAE 1085 Cutlass Machete from Kabar (52–54 Hrc), and CRKT's Mah-Chete made from 1075 (50–55 Hrc).

One cold northern Michigan October night, the year-old Power Eagle suffered a half-dollar-size chunk breaking from its blade while chopping venison bones.

I selected these big knives (eleven- and twelve-inch blades, respectively) to be examples here, because the steel of their blades is decidedly less exotic than that used in most contemporary skinning and meat-cutting knives, yet modern heat-treating methods have made these super-tough alloys consistently hard enough to take and hold a good, functional edge. Both need a sharpening before skinning and butchering a deer from start to finish, but that simply gives them the edge retention of the best knives carried by our grandfathers. Their very long cutting edges help to minimize edge loss, and their alloys make them close to unbreakable. If you need to chop through bone, there are indeed knives made for the task, if you look in the right place.

It was a trick, but we posted a photo of the broken Power Eagle onto Internet knife sites, and began to collect excuses for the failure from experts there, all of whom attempted—unsuccessfully—to sound like NASA scientists. Interestingly, Mike Fuller at TOPS just shrugged his shoulders and replaced the knife. Beware advice from experts.

The broken Power Eagle, after being carefully reground ("re-profiled") and its shaving keen edge restored. The knife is actually better than new.

CHAPTER EIGHT
SHARPENING

"Can I borrow your knife?" I hear that request pretty frequently, nearly always from people who tell me that they have no reason to carry a knife of their own.

The answer I give nearly all of them is an unconditional "No."

That's not because I'm mean or selfish: I'll cut, open, or otherwise perform whatever task it is that they need done (providing that it isn't something that'll damage my knife—you wouldn't believe how often that's the case). I just won't let them handle my working knife themselves, not to mention my specialty knives (cooking, hunting . . .), which are off-limits to anyone. Even my axes have a do-not-touch status.

Part of the reason is for the protection of my knife. The knives I choose to rely on for everyday tasks are usually not of low quality, which means that they are not inexpensive (Benchmade, Kershaw, Spyderco . . .). I have innumerable good reasons to carry the finest knife that I can get, and I've learned the hard way that many folks will use them as screwdrivers, prybars, or hammers. I can snap the tip off myself, but it will be in an urgent situation that demands hard use, not while opening a paint can, trying to remove a screw, or hammering on the blade as if it were a splitting wedge.

In truth, my refusal to loan out my knife is based on oft-proven concern for the would-be borrower. I recall one instance, nearly forty years past, when a childhood friend, who I'd have thought would know better, asked to see my rather handsome folding knife. It was a knife that I was proud of, and I regarded him to be of above average intelligence, so I handed the lockblade to him to admire, in closed and safe condition. He opened it, and promptly ran his thumb lengthwise along the edge.

I cringed, even as he did that, knowing what he had done to himself, yet unable to stop him from doing it in time. The highly polished edge, used so many times to split the belly skin of a deer at the merest touch, without cutting through the stomach walls, laid the ball of his thumb open halfway to the bone. Bright blood spurted from the wound as he dropped my knife unceremoniously to the floor and instinctively squeezed the lacerated thumb tightly in his opposite hand.

He gaped at me with a mixed expression of shock and accusation, as if I'd played a dastardly trick on him. Then his father, who'd stood there watching the whole fiasco, turned to me with an equally accusatory grimace, and actually said to me, "You don't need a knife that sharp."

It was my turn to be aghast, because not only was I being blamed for his adult son's foolishness, but the normally intelligent father's remark was one of the dumbest comments I'd ever heard a person utter.

Over several decades, I've found that to be the normal reaction when someone slashes himself with a knife that they've often just sneeringly told me that they know how to handle—to act like I've just pulled a dirty trick on them. As a result, no, you cannot borrow my knife.

Of course I require a knife that sharp—as does everyone who uses a knife in daily life. When I need to strip the insulation from an electrical wire, without severing any of the copper strands within, I need as sharp a cutting edge as I can get. A razor-sharp knife that cuts with only a delicate touch is easier to precisely control, and a whole lot safer to its user—if you don't need to press as hard, you're less likely to slip. Of course, you need

A knife that's sharp enough to do this is necessary for anyone who appreciates the usefulness of a knife. The downside is that it has an edge that's sharp enough to do this.

to be smart enough to comprehend what "that's sharp" means, as much as you do when someone tells you "that's hot."

If you require a more convincing example of how the sharpening techniques that I am earnestly trying to give away in this chapter *can* turn you into a proficient knife sharpener: Just yesterday I ran out of sharp razors, and circumstances demanded that I be clean-shaven. Because we live forty-plus miles from the nearest store where I could purchase a new razor, I fastened an old leather belt that I use for a strop to the towel rack in the bathroom, and— to my wife's dismay—began to polish the edge on the Kershaw Link folder that I pulled from the pocket of my jeans. Then I lathered my face, and proceeded to use the Link to give myself one of the closest shaves I've ever had. My wife hates it when I do that, but she cannot argue with the results— my face was as smooth as a baby's bottom.

Some folks argue that honing to such a polished edge is a waste of time, because the super-sharpness is usually gone with your initial cut in the field. That's a fact, especially with the softer knives of yesteryear, when hardening wasn't the finely tuned art that it is today, and edge retention was accordingly poorer. When we had two or three deer hanging, it wasn't unusual to have more than one knife handy, or to take a break to wash and re-sharpen your blade for the next round.

On the other hand, I recall running up to an overturned Ford LTD, in which a heavy-set lady was hanging upside-down from her shoulder belt, unable to release the catch that her weight was holding fast. We both could smell the gasoline that sizzled while it dripped against the car's hot exhaust, and it was enough to make portions of your anatomy pucker. There was no time to be sawing through a heavy nylon strap with a dull knife. I had no desire to be caught in a gasoline-fueled inferno, and the lifetime of nightmares that would follow watching this lady burn to death while trapped in her seatbelt were more hellish than I could imagine. I had no desire to join her, either.

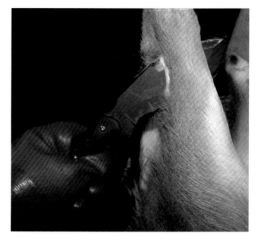

Nothing takes the edge off a sharp knife like skinning a furred animal, and deer hunters need to know how to re-sharpen their knives.

I seldom have a dulled knife for more than a few hours, and it took just one quick stroke of my Buck Crosslock to free her. It might not matter how rapidly a blade gets dull, so long as it's shaving-sharp for that first crucial slash.

The tactical applications of carrying an ever-ready, razor-sharp knife are apparent too. The cutting action of a blunt knife can be impeded, or stopped, by materials that a keen edge slices right though. A dull knife is akin to an unloaded firearm.

Contrarily, a keen edge can transform even a low-quality knife into a fearsome weapon that few handheld firearms can equal, let alone surpass, in terms of delivering horrible wounds. As Weapons Master James Williams, who developed the devastatingly effective Hisshou shortsword at the US Army's request, once observed, a heavy, working-size knife, swung wildly, even blindly, in the confines of a small room can inflict a decisively lethal blow. It doesn't have to be aimed, it doesn't have to be reloaded, and it's as rapid-fire as its wielder's arm. It can slash or stab through most armor, sever whole limbs, or eviscerate an opponent. In a closed environment—like the dark rooms in Afghanistan for which it was designed—it is at least the equal of a firearm.

And that's why you can't borrow my knife. Not only is it an intensely personal possession—like a hairbrush or toenail clipper—it's dangerous to anyone who doesn't presume that it's sharp enough to take off a finger. I'm not kidding: I've very nearly chopped off my own finger at least once, and in one particularly memorable instance, I was forced to contemplate amputation of my own gangrenous finger. In that respect, a knife is indeed a lot like a gun: you don't have to intend harm to yourself or to others, you just have to lose focus for an instant.

But don't take my refusal too personally; you can't borrow my axe, chainsaw, or other power tools, either.

The Skills of Sharpening

My grandpa used to say that he knew six people who could make a knife skinning sharp, and that he'd taught the skill to three of them. He wasn't exaggerating by much; the need for a sharp edge hasn't been a component of most daily lives since a working-size knife was part of every rural American's normal work attire, when meat markets were open-air affairs. If you doubt that a keen edge has become rare in modern America, open your own kitchen drawer or draw a knife from the cutlery block in your kitchen, and see if it will cleanly shave-off strips from a piece of typing paper.

It is a hard, sad fact of life that the hunting knives in nearly every experienced deer hunter's sheath aren't keen enough to part a light rope without sawing through it.

A knife is the original multi-tool, enabling its owner to manipulate materials from an environment into items that couldn't be created using bare hands— or a dull knife—and a keen blade was a prudent sidearm in the days when there was more wilderness than civilization. Before the twentieth century, every good knife was handmade, hand tempered, and the

A knife that isn't sharp is a piece of useless scrap metal.

better ones, made by the experienced blacksmiths, were as prized as any custom rifle of today. It was kept polished, oiled, and honed to a beard-shaving edge, ready to skin an elk, cut loose a rampaging horse, or to dispatch a band of highwaymen.

A dirk like this one was the sidearm of its day, and it was enough to offer effective protection against highwaymen for thousands of years.

As people began moving from farms to towns, and towns evolved into urban centers populated by specialists who could perform ever fewer tasks for themselves, the need for a knife tapered off with each passing generation. Today it's difficult to even find a knife among a group of people, let alone one that is passably keen. As the need to use a knife tapered off, so did the number of persons who could sharpen one, and today you'll find very few people who have a sharp knife. Except for a few slaughterhouses or fish markets—even most restaurants have a guy come in once a week to sharpen their knives—not many humans today have need of honing skills. Like changing the ribbon in a Smith-Corona typewriter or adjusting the horizontal hold control on a television, few people have need of such skills, and almost none have the knowledge to perform them.

That turn of events has led the once universal skill of knife sharpening to become an arcane, even mystical, ability today. Loss of ability is not the worst effect of this problem, because a lack of knowledge is curable; but nature abhors a vacuum, and there are always people willing to exploit even a modicum of personal expertise to profit from the ignorance of others. *That* clouds the water; it behooves such people to present what talent they possess as very complex, and too difficult for mere mortals to achieve.

Writers, because they are writers, sometimes compose whole chapters to impart what is actually very little in the way of useful information, while those who are truly expert at making dull edges into sharp ones are too often unable to convey their expertise in a set of written instructions. The result, predictably, is that there are a lot of written instructions out there, but few sharp knives, axes, and other cutting tools. Like curing diseases and repairing automobiles, there's more money to be milked from instructing hobbyist outdoorsmen and hunters about sharpening a knife than in actually teaching them how to do it. One of the best compliments I've ever received from a survival student has been a perplexed, almost disappointed, look, followed by a remark that went something like, "I thought it'd be a lot more complicated."

In recent decades, it has become as socially unacceptable to possess a knife as it is to light a cigarette, and in a growing number of places, merely possessing a pocketknife is reason to be jailed. In the now-aged Steven Segal movie, *Under Siege 2*, one of a small army of machine-gun-armed terrorists yanks a folding knife from the back pocket of a young hostage and asks accusingly, "What's this?" inferring that the young man was concealing a weapon with which he might disable the gang of heavily armed hoodlums. More recently, I eavesdropped on a social-media website, where there ensued an earnest discussion about why it was smarter to carry a multi-tool, because " . . . a cop is less likely to consider a multi-tool as a weapon." The implications of making it socially embarrassing to possess a tool that has always been, and always will be, necessary to being human are vastly more far reaching, of course, but if just having a knife carries with it such a negative stigma, then it's unreasonable to expect anything but a decrease in numbers of people who can sharpen one.

But the Ginsu advertisements of my boyhood aside, which depicted incredible serrated knives that could cut through a steel can, and then slice paper-thin layers from a tomato, there is no such thing as a knife blade that will not dull with use. Even the much-vaunted ceramics that were once touted to be the next great thing, eventually replacing old-fashioned steel altogether, need to be brought back to near their original sharpness after being dragged across a cutting board a few times. A dull knife is akin to an empty rifle: It doesn't matter which company manufactured it, or how much it cost; if it lacks the ammunition—or a cutting edge—to do its job, the thing is worthless.

Anatomy of an Edge

If you aim to apply, or to restore, a sharp edge to any cutting tool at all, be it a shear die that cuts off lengths of steel thousands of times a day in a metal-stamping shop, a scythe that brings in the sheaves of a grain harvest, or a thin-bladed knife that puts a succulent boneless top fillet of bass into your skillet, you first need to understand the difference between a dull edge and a keen one. Until recently, every set of written instructions for achieving a sharp edge concentrated almost exclusively (and incorrectly) on angles, and many are little more than advertisements for some sort of new sharpening system that claims to enable every housewife, hunter, or amateur gourmet to establish frightfully sharp edges, with no experience at all.

A fundamental secret to honing any type of cutting edge to sharpness is to first understand why an edge is sharp or dull. That means disregarding much, or all, that you've heard or read about maintaining precise angles between edge and hone, using special hones for different alloys, and using special honing oils or solutions. While it is true that you need to maintain a more or less precise angle as you hone, many a shaving edge has been—and still is—derived using a worn, dished-out stone. And, in any case, it's humanly impossible to hold an exact honing angle by visual means alone.

This assortment of handheld knife, axe, and other sharpeners exemplifies the honing options that are available to today's knife owners.

A skilled honesman can sharpen a knife a total darkness, without seeing knife or hone at all. The concept is childishly simple, yet just recently a small knife maker posted on the social media site Facebook that "when sharpening this knife, angle is more important than apex." I just shook my head and ignored replying to a man who clearly knew neither what a sharp edge was, nor the meaning of the word "apex."

On a sharp blade, both sides of its cutting edge meet at a very pointed and highly polished apex (point) that might be just a few molecules wide—narrow enough and hard enough to push between and separate the molecular bonds of less-hard materials. It doesn't matter how, or with what medium you use to attain that state, it only matters that you do achieve it. Steven Dick, the editor at *Tactical Knives* magazine who assigned to me the "Keen Edge" and "Survival" columns for that periodical, once joked to me that it wasn't really fair for either of us to evaluate new sharpening tools, because both of us were capable of achieving a surgical edge on any knife with a chunk of broken concrete.

Many knife-sharpening instructions are mired in talk of angles—which are in fact useless to human beings—but type of grind, blade thickness, and other factors make it necessary for anyone who hones by hand to learn the tactile method described here.

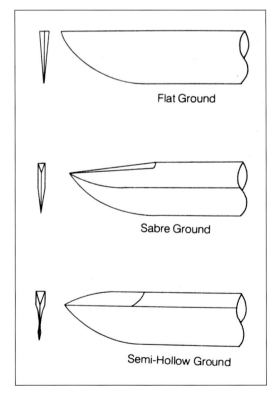

Flat Ground

Sabre Ground

Semi-Hollow Ground

A dulled blade has had the sharply pointed termination of its edge bevels rounded by wear, which translates into trying to drive a broader, blunter surface area into the medium being cut, thus requiring more force to accomplish the same work—essentially the difference between driving a pointed nail and a flat-tipped one. Honing an edge to its original (or sharper) bevel is accomplished by evenly abrading away sub-microns of blade material until the sharpest and most pointed joining of a blade's two sides has been established. It really doesn't matter how that objective is achieved, so long as a cutting edge is even and sharply-terminated.

The traditional sharpener is a flat (-ish) stone, coarse enough to abrade a few molecules at a time from a blade when the two are rubbed against one another. Until the twentieth century, coarse edge-setting hones actually were made from carefully selected natural sandstones, but today's aluminum-oxide hones are manufactured. By keeping the angle between knife and stone constant while smoothly grinding the cutting edge bevels at either side to terminate in an even, flat point from handle to blade tip, you can achieve an edge keen enough to demand

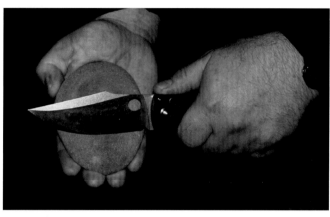

The original sharpener was a hand-picked sandstone, and in the hands of an experienced honesman, a knife, axe, or scythe could be ground to a razor's edge.

respect using only a coarse sandstone. Further polishing those bevels against a harder, less coarse honing surface, like an Arkansas oilstone, reduces burrs to mirror-smoothness, and even an axe can be honed shaving sharp.

Key to becoming an expert honesman is a learned tactile ability to "feel" the edge as it slides against a honing surface. If it slips, catches, or bumps jerkily as you grind the blade against it, then there is not a flat enough mating of blade surface against the stone to drag smoothly, and the edge bevel is either not flat—that is, honed to an even bevel—or it isn't pressing fully flat against the hone's surface. A skilled knife sharpener can restore his or her knife's cutting edge without looking at it just by feeling how smoothly or jerkily a blade drags against it. Many "personalized" knives—most of my own—have had their edges changed through many re-sharpenings, anyway, usually to steeper, sharper angles (exhibited as being wider bevels).

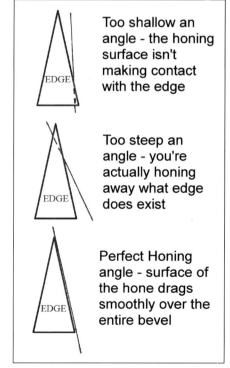

Too shallow an angle - the honing surface isn't making contact with the edge

Too steep an angle - you're actually honing away what edge does exist

Perfect Honing angle - surface of the hone drags smoothly over the entire bevel

It's imperative that a cutting edge match correctly to the surface that it's being honed against, a skill that cannot be seen, but can be felt.

There is no wrong way to create the bevels of a keen edge. The classic honing motion is to begin at the choil (or ricasso), where the sharpened edge ends, closest to the handle. Push the cutting edge into the honing surface, as though you were trying to shave a very thin layer from the hone. Abrade as far along the bevel, from choil to tip, as you can reach with that stroke. Then return your blade to the top of the hone, at its choil, and repeat, honing the entire length of the blade evenly with what will, with practice, almost naturally become a repetitious circular motion. As you rotate the blade in consistently sized circles at a constant speed, draw the knife back from choil to tip, to grind an even, consistent cutting edge with a needle-sharp point. As the ever-circling blade rounds the "belly" that leads to its point, raise the knife's handle slightly to increase the honing angle as cutting angle changes in relation to its radius.

It's usually easier to sharpen an edge by grinding its cutting edge against a hone, but some metals like D2 and ATS-34 tool steels and beta-titanium tend to roll off to one side when they meet at a thin, sharp intersection (the cutting edge). To minimize these burrs, blades are best honed with the edge, with friction applied away from the cutting edge. All edges can be polished sharp in this manner, but they must first have an evenly beveled cutting edge.

For very dull knives, I begin with a coarse aluminum-oxide "stone" (actually man-made), available at hardware stores or online for around $10. A larger stone, three inches by at least six inches, provides a safer and more efficient grinding surface (it's easier to cut yourself using a small honing stone). I wet the stone with water only, then grind a blade hard against it in a back-and-forth motion, toward the edge, then away from it. This maximizes the amount of metal ground off, and quickly sets its edge. I repeat the process up and down both sides of the blade until the beveled cutting edges are even and flat, and the blade feels sharp, but rough. It doesn't matter if the bevels are rough, so long as they're even, because a finer hone can quickly polish a rough edge to sharpness.

If your edge fails to improve (or gets duller), look closely at the areas you're honing, using a magnifying glass if need be. There can be only two problems: the blade's bevels are not flat and even, or the bevels are not being held flat against the stone's surface. By observing your results close-up, and making necessary corrections, you can save yourself a lot of frustration and metal. Bear in mind that the only thing that matters is that you achieve a sharply pointed cutting edge. When you understand that the sides of the blade must meet at a keenly pointed apex, you'll have achieved the most vital knowledge of edge sharpening.

Note that this back-and-forth honing motion generally contradicts what today's sharpening experts say, but the fact is that it works. And it can be accomplished with anything capable of abrading steel from a blade, be it a file, a honing stone, or a concrete sidewalk. With this method alone I can (and have, in one YouTube video) taken a soft 440A steak knife from too blunt to cut my forearm when I sawed against it, to sharp enough to shave off strips of paper. It took about four minutes.

Types of Sharpening Tools

Although it has been the loftiest of goals in the knife industry, and some knife manufacturers—like the serrated Ginsu knives ("They cut a steel can as easily as they cut a tomato . . .") that became an icon of the early 1970s—actually claimed to have achieved it, there is no such thing as a knife that never needs sharpening. To accomplish that Utopian goal, you'd need a knife made of perfect steel that cut without friction and whose perfect blade never wore away. Contrary to advertising claims of knives that "never need sharpening," there has never been such a heavenly gift from the gods. And, ironically, probably most of the knives that claim otherwise are in fact horrible examples; they get away with it by knowing that their target markets are people who cook few of their own meals, and seldom know the difference between a sawing, ripping action of a serrated blade and the fine cutting action of a polished edge. You will not find a Ginsu knife in a chef's kitchen.

To sharpen a cutting tool, you'll need another tool that can create or restore a blunted cutting edge by removing material from the edge, then polishing it. And you'll need the knowledge necessary to make that sharpening tool work for you. Few car buffs would say that having a Lamborghini Diablo is a bad thing, but this prize is entirely wasted on someone who has been deprived of eyesight. Just as a superb knife is shamefully worthless if it lacks a keen cutting edge, so are the greatest sharpening tools worthless if you lack the skills to use them.

The following pages are committed to giving you the ability to whet the blade of any knife into a functional cutting tool. That this author is skilled at doing just that is a matter of history. That's a claim that's easy to prove, and impossible to fake. A sharp knife cuts, a dull one does not, it's as complex as that. Just as Grandpa taught me, my knives are sharp, sharp enough that only a few people are permitted to use, or even to touch, any of them—and our floors have seen enough fools' blood to enforce the sensibility of that rule.

Sharpening a knife is a skill that I sincerely want to give away to others, so please pay attention—this is something that I'm very good at. My own wickedly keen knives are proof enough that these techniques work, as are the thousands of pounds of venison scraps that we have collected for our wolves and sled dogs each autumn for the past twenty-two years is proof that few deer hunters know how to process their own kills. And the fact (prove it for yourself) that you will seldom find a keen knife in any kitchen only further proves it. A hunter, angler, or amateur gourmet with a knife that has to be sawed against an animal's skin to cut it is as embarrassing as a priest with a tarnished crucifix. Both are just unacceptable.

That ends the attention-getting diatribe. Now let's get to the tools you'll need to make your knife into the invaluable tool that it is.

Whet Stones: Whet stones, which aren't called that because you wet them, but because a dated term for honing was "whetting," are my own preferred sharpening medium. Except for the polishing stones known as Arkansas oilstones, whetstones are not natural stones, but are compressed and baked amalgamations of abrasive materials. Man-made stones generally have two sides—one coarse, one fine—to lend them the versatility to take a very dull knife to shaving keenness.

Coarser stones are generally softer, and vice-versa. Coarsest of the man-made honing stones is silicon carbide, also known as crystolon. Medium-coarse stones are aluminum oxide, called an India Stone by Norton Abrasives. Hardest and least abrasive of the coarse man-made stones is novaculite. Sometimes all of these are simply referred to as Carborundum.

All of these can be used dry, or wetted with water, but should be kept clean, or kept wet to maximize abrasiveness. The three synthetic stones mentioned are not recommended for use with any oil. Porosity is a characteristic of coarseness, and the coarser a stone, the greater its porosity. A porous stone that absorbs a lubricating fluid is not a problem when that lubricating fluid is one that evaporates cleanly—like water—or can be washed away with water, like liquid soap. But it has long been a common mistake to lubricate aluminum oxide and other man-made hones with petroleum-based oils. These oils tend to mix with residue, to congeal, and then to glaze into a hard coating that is neither abrasive nor possible to remove entirely. In effect, using a medium like motor oil to lubricate an aluminum-oxide or similar synthetic stone will likely render it useless. Some machinists swear by mineral oil, but my own experience in that field causes me to avoid any liquid honing solution that is not water soluble (dish soap is preferred).

A typical aluminum-oxide hone, with a coarse grit on one side and a finer grit on the other. This is the primary honing tool, necessary for re-setting a dull knife's edge before it can be made properly sharp.

A short note about grits, that is, the coarseness of a stone (or sandpaper). The lower the numerical designation, the rougher and more abrasive the surface. For example, 220 grit (my preference for applying a rough edge to axes) is much coarser than the 400 grit I use for knives. A 1,000 grit is often preferred for polishing the edge of delicately built Japanese kitchen cutlery and straight razors. Think of it as a numerical guide to building a sharp edge: the duller the edge, the lower the grit number; the sharper an edge, the higher the number. As an edge becomes more keen, it requires less metal to be removed, and more polishing, so you move up to a finer grit.

By the same token, if you attempt to sharpen a dulled blade using too high a grit, it will not be coarse enough to remove the metal needed to bring an edge to a keen apex, and you may hone correctly all day long without attaining a sharp edge. Many a novice sharpener has been frustrated to the point of giving up, simply because they have attempted the process with too fine a sharpening surface. A sharp edge can be obtained using only a coarser man-made hone, but these are best employed as tools for applying coarse primary edges that are then polished to finer, sharper edges using harder mediums.

Diamond Hones: A latest generation hone is a plate of steel that has been embedded with a layer of industrial diamonds to form a honing surface that never wears out (diamonds are indeed forever). Although not as coarse as a rough aluminum-oxide stone, diamond hones can polish dulled knives to a very keen edge.

Like other synthetic hones, diamond-plated hones may be used dry or wet, but need to be kept wiped clean with a damp cloth to maximize their effectiveness. The powdery residue that

The Edge-Tek from Buck Knives is a three-sided stick with three grits that can take a knife from very dull to extremely keen without the need for a different tool; this tool occupies a permanent place in the author's kitchen drawer.

accumulates on the hone's surface is comprised of metallic particulates from a blade being abraded over its surface, not from the honing surface.

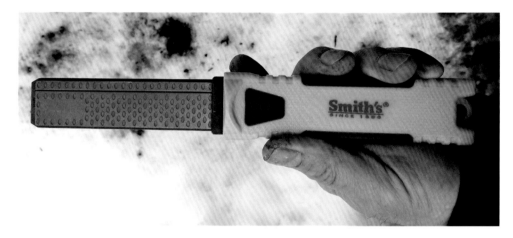

As versatile and portable as they come, this new-for-2017 Smith's Pack Pal has two diamond grits and a serrated rod sharpener to put a razor edge on almost any knife, and it stores in its own handle. Definitely two thumbs up at $25.

I especially like that a good diamond hone never wears out, but its diamond coating must be applied well and with attention to quality. Permit me to relate that I have a Diamond/Carbide Tactical (there's that word again) retractable sharpening rod from Lansky Sharpeners, and the 600-grit diamond coating on the retractable rod began to flake off almost immediately with the first use. On a personal note, my first report of this occurrence to Lansky went ignored; my second complaint was met with a rather bored "Send it back and we'll replace it." I expect a better and more personal level of customer service

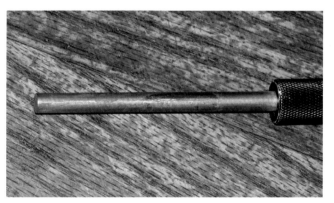

The supposedly lifetime diamond coating on this Lansky Diamond/Carbide Tactical sharpener began to flake off almost immediately, rendering the sharpener mostly useless. That failure has never occurred before or since, but be aware that it did happen once.

from this brand. I have not experienced this flaking problem with any other of the numerous diamond hones I own, but be aware that it can happen.

Arkansas Oilstones: An example of harder polishing mediums are natural stones, commonly known as Arkansas oilstones, after the region where they were first mined and produced. These, too, are available in a range of harnesses, from soft to hard, but all of them are natural stones, and are generally harder with a finer structure than manufactured stones. I generally use plain water to lubricate Arkansas-type stones, but their denseness permits them to be lubricated with almost any liquid. As mentioned, Arkansas stones aren't abrasive enough to sharpen a dull knife, but they will polish a rough edge to surgical sharpness.

Although the most common name for a natural stone is oilstone, it's not necessary, or even recommended, that you use anything but water as lubrication.

Harder naturally occurring "oilstones" like those on the Smith's Tri-Hone are used to polish the rough, but sharp, edges created by using an aluminum oxide hone. (Photo courtesy of Smith's EdgeSports).

Ceramics: Ceramic hones are made the same way as the ceramic blades that they are often used to sharpen. A powdered form of *zirconium dioxide* (ZrO2), or zirconia, is injected into a die, then baked under pressure into desired shapes. Any shape can be molded, but the usual is rod-like.

A classic example of a ceramic sharpener is Spyderco's Triangle Sharpmaker, a polyethylene case containing two coarse and two fine triangular rods that it holds upright at fifteen- and twenty-degree angles. Also useful is the eight-inch-long round ceramic rod that resides in my own kitchen drawer.

Like an Arkansas oilstone, ceramics aren't good choices to re-hone a badly dulled knife, but there's nothing better for smoothing a rough edge into polished razor sharpness. Rods will become noticeably marred by dark residue as you use them, and should be kept clean using soap and a damp cloth.

As with diamond hones, the dark stains on the ceramic are actually powdered metal abraded from a blade.

This Tri-Angle Sharpmaker from Spyderco is arguably the most effective ceramic edge-polishing system created.

Honing Techniques

The hand-honing tools described here are a system. Presuming a very dull edge (it was not so long ago that every knife came from the factory with a dull edge, for reasons of presumed liability), you begin with the coarsest hone to establish rough bevels. A master honesman can achieve a very sharp edge with the coarsest stone, but the normal routine is to use three or four hones, ascending from coarsest to finest, to create a super-keen polished edge that shaves strips from a sheet of notebook paper.

Whetstones are the most difficult of sharpening tools to master because they are dependent on their user. Recent years have seen the advent of machines that feature both blade and honing tools to hold them at precisely the desired angles while metal is abraded from a blade's cutting edge. The better of these machines are excellent, applying as exact and as sharp a cutting edge as you can get from any source in the world. One especially large and expensive (about $500) system is the Wicked Edge (wickededgeusa.com), which has proved to be foolproof in field trials, allowing the greenest beginner to achieve a shaving edge on the first try. Numerous other less sophisticated and less expensive manual sharpening machines have delivered relatively good results.

Large, heavy, and pricey—$325 as shown—the Wicked Edge sharpening system (www.wickededgeusa.com) is the most effective sharpener yet devised, enabling the greenest beginner to achieve a razor edge on any knife with the first attempt.

Despite their difficulty to master, handheld whetstones are my personal choice as sharpeners because of their versatility. It is true that a square, flat honing surface is desirable, but many a razor edge has been created using a stone that looks dished and worn out. The original sharpeners were nothing more elaborate than carefully selected sandstones, usually picked from riverbanks and lakeshores where the effects of water had shaped them to more or less round and flat, palm-sized configurations. Make no bones about it, an incredibly sharp edge can be coaxed from these imperfect handheld sandstones.

Avoid the mistake of using too small a stone. A larger stone takes off more metal with less work, and quicker results mean less frustration. An awful lot of beginners complain that a knife doesn't seem to be getting sharper because they haven't removed enough metal to create a bevel. Working-size hones are at least eight inches long by two inches wide. I prefer double-sided stones with a coarse (200- to 400-grit) surface on one side, and a finer (800- to 1,000-grit) surface the other.

In recent years an awful lot has been made of holding blades at some particular angle while sharpening, largely because the human mind demands reference points and constant values to use as guides. For that reason, irrespective of the fact that it is impossible for a human to accurately determine or maintain a tolerance of even ten degrees using only hand and eye, degrees were selected as the measuring point.

Recognizing that no one can maintain an exact angle, sharpener manufacturers—notably the giant Smith's—are focusing instead on establishing the bevels necessary to creating a keen edge. Angles mean nothing to a sharp edge; it's the apex where those angles do or do not meet that determines the sharpness of an edge.

Key to mastery of handheld whetstones is learning to feel a blade's cutting edge as it mates with the surface of the stone. A blade whose cutting edge is held too steeply or too shallow does not mate with stone's surface, and it feels choppy, skittering unevenly as you drag it against the stone's surface.

Conversely, when metal and stone match, the result is a smooth, even drag that skilled hones-men claim has the same addictive quality as popping bubble-wrap. It just feels good. When you've achieved this ideal tactile match-up of steel and stone, you're sharpening the knife's edge.

The easiest method of learning to grind bevels onto a dull blade is to press a cutting edge, as close to where it terminates at its outer edge against a stone; you can visually confirm that to a close degree. The objective is to grind an angled bevel onto each side until, seen end-on, it resembles a keenly pointed triangle. The tip of that triangle, where the bevels meet, is the cutting edge.

Just grating the edge of a blade back and forth up and down the length of a blade, until a bevel with an even angle and width has been created on both sides, and the two bevels terminate in a sharp point, is the easiest method of sharpening to master. I often employ this simple back-and-forth technique when a blade of hard steel is very dull and needs some earnest abrading to remove enough metal to get a coarse edge. This practice allows hard pressure (BE CAREFUL! More force equals more slips!) to be applied, lessening the time spent achieving the bevels required for a sharp edge. Try it for yourself; you can both see and feel when you've brought the bevels together to meet at a keen point, and you'll be surprised at how sharp an edge you can acquire using only a coarse stone. Short of performing heart surgery, you can get skillful enough using this method on a relatively coarse (220- to 400-grit) honing stone.

Once you've achieved a keen rough edge, you might notice that it feels sharper on one side than on the other. This is known as a rolled edge, defined as a potentially sharp edge that has a burr facing the side that seems sharpest. Some neophytes say that this seems backward, but the side that feels sharpest is the side that needs to be honed—"stood up," in the vernacular of old Great Lakes fishermen. The objective is to even-up the edge bevels on both sides, so that their apex is as sharp and polished as you can get them.

Every honing stone should be washed with soap and water, and wiped clean after each use. Regardless of how much they cost, every honing tool should be treated as the valuable component that it is. Do not apply oil or honing solution, just clean and dry.

Pull-Through Sharpeners

Pull-through sharpeners have been around for many decades, starting as interlocking rows of carbide or hardened steel disks in the sixties, to the carbide V-shaped pocket hand-mills popularized by Lansky in the eighties, to the diamond-hone vector-sharpeners of recent years.

Easily the most effective pull-through sharpener on the market, this Smith's Edge Pro retails for just $20, and in field trials, everyone got a shaving edge with it on the first try.

Every pull-through sharpener shares a milling-style operation to bevel an edge on the blades that it sharpens. What that means is that it uses cutting surfaces placed along either side made from materials—like carbide, ceramic, or diamond—that are typically harder than the blades they sharpen. As a blade is pulled back, choil (heel) to point, microns of it are shaved off, until a blade has, ideally, been beveled to a keen point. Used properly, a sharpener in good shape, with sharp cutting surfaces, can apply as sharp an edge to a dulled blade as a whetstone. The difference is that a pull-through sharpener

Pull-through sharpeners use the milling action of pulling a blade through super-hard carbide cutters, pre-set at a specified angle, to scrape sharp bevels onto either side.

requires none of the "feel" that a handheld stone requires to be effective, and so is much easier to master.

Pull-through carbide and diamond sharpeners share one secret to effectiveness: patience, especially as carbides become worn. The first thirty or forty passes of a blade through a sharpener, with moderate (not hard) downward pressure, might not feel as though it is doing anything, but don't lose faith. Eventually you'll feel portions of a blade "catch," offering resistance that indicates one or both bevels are being scraped down to a sharp bevel. As you continue to draw a blade through the carbides, more and longer sections of its cutting edge will exhibit resistance. When you feel that resistance evenly along the entire length of a blade, the ball of a thumb will confirm that it's sharp.

Electric Sharpeners

Not so long ago, electric sharpeners were usually poorly made, poorly designed, ineffective on several levels. Today's versions reflect the general advances in technology and precision manufacturing. Having evaluated numerous models from Shun, Smith's, Chef's Choice, WorkSharp, and so on, I feel secure in saying that most of them are quite good (with the exception of one short-lived Shun that Williams-Sonoma

Beware electric sharpeners, and never attempt to apply an edge using a bench grinder; this Shun-brand wet Edge rotary sharpener was dropped like a hot potato by Williams-Sonoma after the author's review of it in Tactical Knives *magazine revealed that it was difficult to use and destroyed knife blades.*

dropped like a hot potato after a column by me in *Tactical Knives* magazine revealed that it destroyed knife blades).

One electric sharpener that should never even be considered is a bench grinder. An untold number of priceless Samurai katanas were destroyed by GIs returning from the Pacific after World War II when they tried to resharpen their laminated blades on electric bench grinders. I can personally attest to the same where hunting knives are concerned—to hold a blade steady enough to apply an even bevel as you stroke it across a rotating grinding wheel is a very difficult skill to learn. Many a teary eyed deer hunter has asked me if I could fix a fine blade that had been horribly scarred by a power grinder. If you feel that you must try it, do so using a knife that has little value.

Strops

A strop is used to polish an edge after it has been applied using another type of honing device. Most often seen attached to a barber's chair, where it's used to "stand up" the edge on straight razors before they're used, a strop is nothing more than a usually wide length of leather, about one and a half inches wide by eighteen inches long. One end has a more or less ergonomic handle for holding it taut while the other end is clipped or tied to a stationary anchor. By stroking a blade

along a strop's length *with*—never *against*—the cutting edge, a sharp razor or knife can be quickly polished to hair-splitting keenness.

A strop has been a crucial part of my own sharpening kit for as long as I can remember. But rather than pay $12 to $40 for a factory-made model, I've usually just employed an old leather belt. The results have been the same, and you can find suitable leather belts for just a couple of bucks at resale shops across America. There have been times when I pulled the strop I used from my own belt loops.

Using a strop is simpler than it might seem. Again, forget about trying to hold an angle—all you want to do is gently stroke the apex of the bevels. Lay your blade flat onto the strop, at just enough of an angle that its spine doesn't scrape against the leather. The strop—be it a belt or a purpose-made strop—will bend to conform to your edge. Strop your blade back and forth a few times, enough to cover the entire length of the blade on both sides, then check the edge. Even if your knife wasn't truly keen when you started, you'll almost certainly notice a marked improvement in its sharpness. If your knife was honed skinning sharp, stropping its blade a dozen times in each direction will elicit an exclamation of surprise from most people who test its edge.

Every barber knows how to use a strop to get a polished, face-shaving edge onto a razor, and you can use an old leather belt to achieve the same thing with a favorite knife.

Some strops are made by attaching a length of leather to a flat board, providing a hard surface to polish against. One fellow got himself a bit of press by using plain blocks of hardwood to polish his edges. And you've probably seen skilled honesmen strop a freshly sharpened blade against the thigh of their trousers a few times, to squeeze just a bit more sharpness from it.

CHAPTER NINE
COLLECTIBLES

What makes a knife collectible? That question is both simple and impossible to answer, but I felt obliged to include a short chapter on the subject.

If you're just an aficionado of the edge, like me, anything that has an edge must be at least represented in your collection. This type of eclectic collector is just crazy in the most romantic sense about things that cut. Often they can and do sharpen every tool they have to the keenest edge possible, and most of them actually use the knives in their collection.

A one-of-a-kind handmade knife that was intentionally crafted to be a user.

But using a collectible knife disqualifies you as a purist collector, who typically saves knives as they came from the factory, edge, box, and all. This type of collector might even wear white cotton inspection gloves when handling blades to prevent them from being marred or rusted by acids in skin oils.

See the marks of fingerprint acids on the blade of this old, entirely collectible slipjoint Case XX? Collectibles should always be handled while wearing nitrile or cotton inspection gloves.

Definitely a collectible, even though it might never have much of a resale value, this Chris Hayes Damascus-steel wallet knife is a welcome and valued addition to the author's collection.

This Scottish dirk, made from Damascus steel, is one of a kind; there's not another exactly like it on the planet.

Then there are the esoteric collectors, whose collections are specific to one class of cutting tools. A fan of lumberjacking may include axes in a collection. Old West collectors focus on knives of that era, or which eras interest them. Many collections are specific to antiques, or to blades that might now or someday fetch a handsome financial return at auction.

Stamps and Toolmarks

All collectors can find information about a knife they're holding on its choil. Typically the flat, unsharpened, reinforcing area located directly ahead of the handle. Stamped, sometimes etched with acid, into this area is information about the maker, blade alloy, sometimes the designer, and other abbreviated information that its maker deems most boast-worthy. Almost every knife made today bears such stampings on its choil.

Handmade knives sometimes lack such markings, but every factory-made knife bears markings of its model and manufacturer to identify it.

Antiques

Antique, especially military weapons might carry tool marks on not only the choil, but the finger guard, pommel, and even handle. It is of special significance to collectors when bayonets and swords bear tool marks that match up in some way (region, maker, facility, etc.).

Antique knives and swords are usually most collectible if they are not restored, but are left in the same condition in which a collector found them. That means that rust and pits are best left unmolested, blades should not be polished, wooden handles should not be sanded or refinished. An antique found in pristine condition is a rare find, but in most instances, a historic collectible is worth most in its original condition, regardless of how blemished that might be.

Just because a knife is old does not mean that it possesses any particular monetary value, even if it's a rare find. This is just an example of how fickle and illogical the collecting game can be.

Seventy-three years old at the time of this writing, and exceedingly hard to find, this Western Bird & Trout knife nonetheless has little monetary value as a collectible.

Other Marks of Collectability

Other collectible knives include any knife that has been discontinued. The practice of serial-numbering knives has helped collectors, because a low serial number, indicating that a collectible of any kind was one of the first to be manufactured, has always been a mark of value. Knives that were owned by notable people (I regret to say that a knife owned by Len McDougall doesn't seem to possess extra value) are collectible, as are those made in limited quantities, or which possess some factory-created flaw. Knives that have been modified from their original state (file work, jeweling, etc.) may or may not have increased collectability—in fact, sometimes customizing a knife ruins it value.

This first-run Onslaught model from Benchmade definitely has collectible, perhaps even monetary, value.

Collectability is *not* necessarily the same as financial value. In this, collecting is very much like playing the stock market. If you're looking to get rich from collecting blades, it's probably not going to happen. Consider yourself lucky if you can recoup your investment. A better strategy is to collect knives simply because you're a died-in-the-wool knife nut like myself, and you just like to collect knives. And if you happen to hit upon one of those thousand-years-old Samurai swords that were captured during WWII, and which happens to have a $5 million resale price, consider yourself lucky indeed.

Another unique custom-forged knife, this Damascus steel, clip-point hunter might or might not be a sound financial investment.

Display Cases

A fine knife collection deserves to be shown off and for that you need a display case. For portability and to contain small collections, I like the convenience of the classic knife roll, typically a fabric-and-leather package with elastic bands sewn to its inside. A knife roll can hold a dozen or more knives, depending on their sizes, then rolled into a compact unit and buckled shut. Knife rolls begin at about $15.

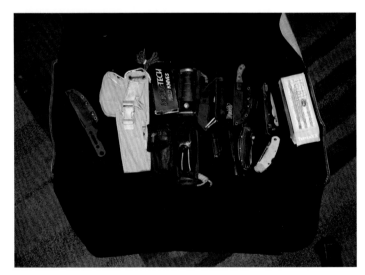

Available inexpensively at knife shops and online stores, a knife roll is a convenient way to carry some of your collection.

More ostentatious—which in this instance is a desirable quality—are stand-alone or wall-mounted display cases. These are made in a wide array of sizes and styles, from pegboard-and-hook configurations to velvet-backed cases, available in your choice of colors. Prices begin at around $40 for a small wall-mount case, up to several hundred dollars for a furniture-grade cabinet.

For the safety of others, I recommend a glassed-in door with a lock, because some folks can't resist handling a knife on display, even when a sign tells them not to.

CHAPTER TEN
KNIFE REVIEWS

The proof, as they say, is in the pudding, and nowhere is that axiom truer than when applied to knife quality. A few readers may recall that, aside from occasional reviews in magazines and books, I wrote as a field editor for *Tactical Knives* magazine for several years, before that popular magazine was discontinued by its publisher. For my part, I refused to romanticize the "tactical" aspects of edged weapons in my columns. I mean, how often do knife experts actually go into battle using a blade against other human beings, or any living creature, anyway? The majority of my own experience derives from dispatching animals that were destined for my dinner table.

Instead, I wrote that magazine's "Survival" and "Keen Edge" (edge sharpening) columns. Field work and butchering meat for the full-blooded timber wolves we raised under license ensured that my blades needed frequent re-sharpening, so both those columns were up my alley. The knife reviews I wrote were reports of how a tool had performed during actual uses that had left it scarred, scratched, and sometimes broken, as opposed to typical magazine product reviews that mostly dealt with fit, finish, materials, and various aesthetic aspects. The attributes of toughness, strength, and practical usability that I considered important are possibly not of interest to collectors, but they demonstrate how reliably a blade performs under real-world conditions.

Following is a compendium of real-life field trials, reviews of knives that have been tested over a period of years—because you cannot get to know a knife over a few days, not any more than you can intelligently evaluate a potential spouse. The best—or worst—friends can only be found out with time and experience. Any knife can look beautiful in a box, or on a rotating pedestal under colored lights, but a jewelry-like appearance is not the measure of a knife—not unless that knife is intended solely to remain on a pedestal, or in a showcase. The presumption here is that most knife owners want *Go*, at least as much as *Show*, from the blades they carry.

Because I do not perform what I refer to as "armchair field tests," a few of these knives, as indicated in my reviews of them, have been discontinued, and some look in their photos as if they might have endured a thermonuclear war. Magazines are on deadline schedules, and all of them are trying to scoop their competitors by being the first to tell readers about some new item that's going to change life on earth as we know it.

Being in a hurry by itself invalidates magazine product reviews, because it's impossible to make a lifelong friend of someone you've only known a week. And you wouldn't let some dude that you just met today babysit your kids. By the same token, I refuse to bet my future on a survival knife based on what some writer claims about it after using it a week, and I won't tell you that you should, either. Even the most honest and knowledgeable reviewer can rarely turn in more than a slapdash, shallow assessment of how good or bad a knife (or any other product) might be.

That is where this book differs from any knife magazine, and from other knife books as well. The knives reviewed here have been around a while, used hard, occasionally abused, and sometimes becoming an old friend to whom I owe my very survival. Individual reviews are combined with a half century of experience using a vast array of different knives for every task from butchering cows to commercial fishing to stringing barbed-wire fence, and that is augmented by what I learned from twenty years in the metal stamping and fabrication industries. Some of these knives have been discontinued by their makers, or supplanted by better models. But many discontinued blades are still available from Internet retailers, sometimes used, and sometimes at lower prices than when they were new. The cutting tools chosen for this chapter are a cross-section of cutting tools, selected to be representative of the treasure trove of fine-edged implements, some underrated, some vastly overrated by their manufacturers, that are available to you today.

Finally, this is the greatest time in history to write this type of no-kidding, real-world knife book. For all the evils that mankind has wrought, our species' pursuit of tools that will make our lives easier has begat the finest cutting tools that ever existed. Even the inexpensive knives of today are better than the best knives we had when I was a kid. Every part of some knives is made from materials that didn't exist even a generation ago, manufactured to precision tolerances that were impossible to achieve, using methods that had yet to be discovered. Based on what I've seen in my lifetime, I envy coming generations for the knives they will have available to them. I hope that the timeless skills and information presented in this book will continue to serve those lucky future generations of knife owners.

Benchmade *Type 62 Bali-Song:* As mentioned earlier, the balisong, or "butterfly knife," is mainly attributed to natives of the Philippine Islands. Its design is ingeniously simple, yet superbly suited to every use from butchering game and cutting vegetables to killing an enemy on a battlefield or in a back alley. It can be deployed or retired in the blink of an eye—many an American sailor who has anchored at Subic Bay can attest to this—and its cantilever design makes it nearly as strong as a fixed blade.

The Type 62 Bali-Song is a revamped version of the classic Type 42, the knife on which Benchmade built its reputation in the late 1970s. It was largely considered a novelty then, alien to most Americans for whom a large folding knife had always been a more complex jackknife. And it was expensive in comparison to other knives, which reflected the hand-fitted craftsmanship

Beautiful enough to be considered jewelry, Benchmade Knives has revitalized this superb weapon/everyday knife with modern alloys and manufacturing processes.

that has become a given with Benchmade knives. Several companies have even cashed in on the popularity of the discontinued Type 42 by producing clones that look like it, but they are just not Benchmades.

Like its predecessor, the Type 62 continues to be entirely made in the USA, but its blade of D2 tool steel, with an impressive 60–62 Hrc, reflects the innovations that have occurred in the knife-making world in recent years. The Weehawk-style (a modified stiletto) blade is 4.25 inches long, 0.125 inch thick, and shaving sharp out of the box; unfortunately, most first-time owners are going to find that out for themselves, unintentionally. Overall length is 9.20 inches open, 5.27 inches closed.

Although not considered to be a glass-breaker, a .250 knob in the center of the closed blade makes an effective hammering weapon before the knife is deployed. As one martial artist stated: "A closed balisong makes a great punch weight, and also a great striking weapon." A closed butterfly knife has also been employed for nerve strikes and to accentuate the pain caused by joint locks. With a weight of 6.33 ounces, the Type 62 also adds a bit of weight to a punch.

The Type 62's trademark perforated stainless handles are a hand-filling 0.48-inch thick, and more ergonomic than they might seem. Most people carry the knife in a pocket, but it comes with a nylon belt sheath.

Martial arts with the balisong is not traditionally a part of Arnis or Escrima (Filipino Stick Fighting), and probably no Japanese Ninja ever

The original ultra-fast one-handed tactical folder, Benchmade's Bali-Song is the equal of any everyday working knife.

laid eyes on one. But it definitely has seen use as a weapon in Filipino culture, and combined with modern-day materials and manufacturing methods, as it has been in Benchmade's Type 62, the balisong is versatile as any knife in existence.

Like all Benchmades, the Type 62 Bali-Song comes with an unconditional guarantee, so long as it has not been modified in any way. The warranty includes Benchmade's LifeSharp re-sharpening service; just ship your knife to the factory, using the forms available at www.benchmade.com, and they'll return the knife, sharp and with whatever repairs you've requested. Retail is $375.

Columbia River's *Hisshou Close Quarters Combat Knife:* Before firearms, a large fixed-blade knife was part of every man's daily apparel. Most famous of these are the Scottish dirk and the Japanese tanto, but the Moro barong, the Chinese dadao, and the Ghurka kukri are examples of the value that every culture placed on a shortsword.

Like the six gun of the old West, having less steel in a holster meant a weapon could be brought to bear before an enemy could deploy his own. A dirk was handy, deadly, and quick. So feared were these small swords that in 1837 the Alabama legislature made any killing with any dirk a hanging offense, regardless of circumstances.

Designed by Master James Williams at the behest of the United States Army, the Hisshou's thirteen-inch YK-30 blade is purpose-made for close-quarters battle. This blade is not a toy for mall commandos.

Columbia River Knife and Tool's patented Hisshou (Hee-show) fighting knife is an example of how formidable a dirk is today. The brainchild of James Williams, developer of the System of Strategy combat technique, the Hisshou is pure weapon (its name means "Certain Victory"). As CRKT asserts, "The Hisshou demands respect, and is certainly not a sport or work knife, but it can truly be a lifesaver for the military professional."

In a darkened room, the Hisshou actually outclasses a gun. In contrast to hitting a target with a bullet whose path of destruction encompasses less than a half-inch, the Hisshou's thirteen-inch blade of YK-30 stainless (Hrc 57–59) describes a radius of lethality that extends more than three feet.

The Hisshou has garnered accolades from martial artists. Its balance point is 1.620 inches ahead of the hilt, making it blade-heavy, but enhancing tip control. An upswept point maximizes the length of its usable cutting edge, and a weight of 16.4 ounces provides the mass necessary to sever muscle and bone. A precisely applied 14-degree saber-ground edge, extending .750-inch up the 1.312-inch-wide blade (at the choil), provides fearsome cutting power, while leaving plenty of brute strength in the .260-inch-thick spine. The blade's point is upswept, a full 2.050 inches off-center from the hilt axis; this detracts from the dirk's stabbing power, but that small demerit is offset by its very sharply pointed tip. Etched into the choil on the blade's left side is the CRKT logo, and just ahead of it on the spine are the Japanese characters for the word "Hisshou," The English version of that word is etched into the opposite side, and ahead of it are a pair of four-inch Fuller grooves cut into the spine, ostensibly to add stiffness to this already brutally strong blade.

The Hisshou's 6.200-inch handle is tightly wrapped in a layer of abrasive black ray skin, over-wrapped in twisted black nylon lacing. The hilt is a fist-filling one-and-one-half inches wide and one inch thick, and provides a secure grip, whether bare-handed or with heavy gloves. The tang terminates in a rounded bludgeoning pommel.

The Hisshou's black Kydex scabbard is formed to hold the blade snugly enough to prevent rattling. A formed mouth with indents at the top of the sheath grasps the hilt firmly and holds it under pressure from either side when the knife is inserted fully, even in the upside-down position, but eleases smoothly with a quick upward jerk on the knife's handle.

A hard Kydex belt loop is reversible, or it may be removed entirely. A nylon strap attached to the belt loop connects with an adjustable quick-release clip, enabling the scabbard to be fastened to any strap. Three long slots on either side permit affixing the sheath to a backpack, harness, or even a personal flotation vest. Or you might opt for CRKT's versatile Van Hoy Biotac fixed-blade carry harness.

When not in service, the Hisshou can be stored in its handsome black-lacquered presentation box. Stored with the box's brass-hinged lid shut, it shows the Japanese characters for the word "Hisshou," the word itself spelled out in English, and the translation of that word, "Certain

Victory," painted in gold. At the opposite end of the box lid is the CRKT logo, also in gold. Leaving the box's cover upright showcases the dirk against a form-fitting bed of red crushed velvet.

The Hisshou has already seen duty in Afghanistan and Iraq. My own cutting tests show that this shortsword can sever a deer's neck with a single stroke, and the blade easily stabbed through a ribcage. Suggested retail for the Hisshou is $325.

This knife is very much like a king cobra: beautiful to look at, but decidedly deadly. It's definitely not a plaything.

CRKT's Ruger-licensed Muzzle Brake Knife: New for February 2017, the Muzzle-Brake was designed for Columbia River Knife and Tool, under license for the Ruger firearms company, by noted blademaster Ken Onion.

The Muzzle Brake shares many of the same traits and lines of the USMC Combat Field Knife, with its 7.5-inch long, 1.50-inch wide, 187-inch thick modified-Bowie blade design, and its extra-long 3.50-inch false edge. An oversized blood groove (or fuller) on either side, .50-inch deep by .400-inch wide by 3.100-inch long, reinforces the blade and enhances its good looks.

Instead of the traditional 1095 carbon steel blade, the Muzzle Brake is made from 8Cr13MoV stainless, hardened to an impressively tight 58–59 Hrc, and protected with a layer of non-reflective black Teflon that has proved very tough. The cutting edge is a generously deep semi-hollow

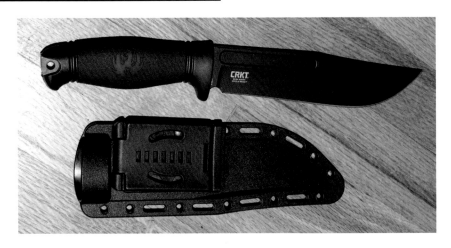

An odd mix of classic field-proven design and state-of-the-art materials and manufacturing, the Ruger-licensed Muzzle Brake is the knife that Han Solo from Stars Wars would have worn.

ground pattern that extends one inch (two-thirds) up the width of the blade. Its 3.8-ounce weight is remarkably nimble.

The handle of the Muzzle Brake is glass-filled nylon construction molded over heavy blade tang. Its sure-grip textured surface is intended to match the synthetic Ruger American rifle stock. A pair of trademark Ruger spread eagles are molded into either side of the hilt. A half-inch notch in the center of the pommel on either side reveals the butt of the tang and a lanyard hole.

The Muzzle Brake's sheath matches its hilt, being molded of black glass-reinforced nylon. Eight 0.700-inch-long slots, and twelve .200-inch-diameter grommeted holes around the sheath's perimeter permit mounting the knife to anything. A very secure quick-release mount attaches to the scabbard in a number of orientations, further multiplying the Muzzle Brake's carry options.

The knife snaps audibly home when pressed downward into a molded blade-width slot. The sheath stays on whatever it is mounted to but, predictably, the knife can be and was pulled free of its sheath during normal activities in the field. Probably as a result of being sheathed and unsheathed so many times, the knife also began to rattle annoyingly while walking.

Both problems were expediently fixed by using a heated .100-inch-diameter steel wire to melt holes through both sides of the sheath mouth. The holes were located even with the top surface of the hilt's molded finger guard. Then I bent the same wire into a narrow "U" whose equal-length sides were sufficiently long to reach through both holes, with a quarter inch sticking out past the hole. A small notch cut into the mouth of the sheath enabled the inserted wire U to be rotated upward, where its other side snapped into the notch. Finally, a light nylon cord tied to the lower U section and secured to one of

The knife is not perfect (as usual these days, its scabbard proved less than ideal in the field), but in the hand, it performed well enough to cause its users to fall in love with it.

the holes in the sheath kept the locking U from getting lost. The knife could not come out of its sheath until "the pin was pulled."

In field trials that ranged from preparing dinner to butchering more than a dozen deer, the Muzzle Brake exhibited exemplary edge-holding ability. It is hard enough to be polished to a face-shaving edge (literally), and its edge geometry holds that edge very well. MSRP is $99. Phone (800) 891–3100; email info@crkt.com; on the web, www.crkt.com.

CRKT All-Cylinders Folding Knife: The first comment heard from several people who handled this knife their first time was "This feels like a Benchmade." That remark is a compliment to the knife, as well as to its designer Bill Harsey—like comparing favorably the road-handling of a budget-class Chevrolet to a high-end Mercedes sport coupe. They were alluding to the smoothness of this folder's action, which does indeed feel like it belongs on a much more expensive knife.

Manufactured in China by CKRT under license from the Sturm-Ruger firearms company, the All-Cylinders is an example of what can come from that big Asian republic with the proper leadership (it's no secret that I appreciate a finely crafted

Everyone who handled this knife was immediately impressed with the smoothness of its operation.

product, regardless of where it's manufactured). With an overall length of nine inches, the All-Cylinder's black stonewashed three-inch drop-point blade, with a two-inch false edge for enhanced penetration, is all-business. Ambidextrous thumb studs allow it to be opened with either hand, but it can also be flipped open with a flick of the wrist. One inch of gimping grooves along the spine opposite its abbreviated choil provide sureness for delicate tip work. A hollow-ground edge extends .625 inch up the one-inch-wide blade to ensure that the 8Cr13MoV blade, hardened to respectable 58-59Hrc, has the geometry to retain a sharp edge as long as possible.

The bolster hinge responsible for the All-Cylinder's smoothness is unique—and in this author's opinion, very cool. It is shaped to look like a revolver's cylinder when viewed end-on, and is easily adjusted with a dyke (wire-cutting pliers) to screw the blade looser, allowing it to swing more freely, or tighter, to make it pivot less freely. Although I like the versatility of that feature, be aware that the bolster can loosen with normal use, causing the blade to simply flop open by itself. I rectified the problem by adjusting the bolster to the desired tightness, then locking it in place with a drop of instant glue.

Two-tone gray handle scales are made from dense and hard G-10 material (G-10 is woven fiberglass, saturated with epoxy resin, then baked under pressure). A wood-grain-like finish makes

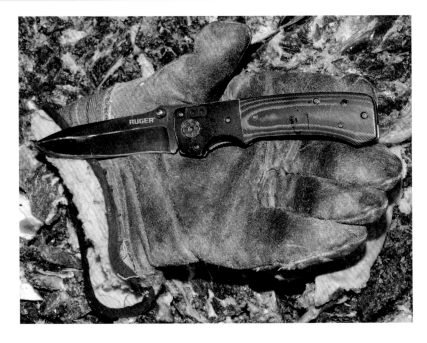

An old idiom says that the proof is in the pudding, and the All-Cylinders knife is a very good pudding indeed.

the scales more eye-catching. The final 1.75 inches at the bolster-end of the handle are made of aluminum to give extra lateral strength, and has an indented finger choil. A stout spring-steel pocket clip next to the hinge bolster can be mounted to either side of the knife to keep it securely in a pocket.

In actual use, the All-Cylinders was a pleasure to use. It's nimble and transitions quickly between grips, its balance point precisely one inch behind its choil pin. The liner lock is sure and tight, with no blade wobble, and the knife is easy to deploy and retire with one hand. My one complaint is that the edge seems to dull more quickly than I would have expected, but re-sharpening is easy enough, and the edge can be made as keen as any.

Retail for the All-Cylinders is $90, but shop around, because I've found them for less than $60. www.crkt.com.

Corona Tools *Twelve-inch Diamond-blade Steel Spade*: What is a shovel doing in a knife book? If you had ever seen me skin a deer—in all honesty, I was just showing off—using my entrenching tool (folding shovel), you'd know the answer to that question. Or, perhaps more "real," if you know how many enemy soldiers have been killed by American GIs with their shovels from WWII through Vietnam, then you know that these lowly tools of war and peace are indispensable tools to combat soldiers. Before that, pioneers who were shaping homes from untracked wilderness learned the value of grinding a keen cutting edge onto their digging implements. When tree roots needed to be removed from soil before it could be tilled into farmland, a shovel capable of cutting and chopping was valuable.

An old episode of The Beverly Hillbillies depicts Jed Clampett sharpening the edge of his spade on a treadle-type grinding wheel, but today's world by and large has forgotten that the shovel is a cutting tool.

It has been observed by people who use them that a military-style entrenching tool is not a shovel; it's what you use when a shovel isn't available. When you're carrying home on your back, and ounces count, a folding entrenching tool may be a necessary evil. But if you're at home, or if you're equipping a backcountry four-wheel drive, there's little sense in handicapping yourself with a teaspoon.

The Twelve-inch Diamond-blade Steel Spade from Corona Tools of Corona, California, is an all-steel answer to the boondocker's prayers. Corona calls the metal used in its wire-welded construction "Aerospace Grade Steel." In fact, that is a hedge to allow the company to change alloys as it sees fit (there are numerous alloys that would do the desired job). My field-test unit appears to be made from knife-grade 420 stainless, based largely on its refusal to rust. The 12 gauge (.105 inch thick) blade is seven inches across, with two folded-forward foot supports, each drilled out to accept a hard-rubber footpad that decreases sole fatigue after a long day of turning soil with the six-pound tool.

The Diamond Spade is sold with a heavy battleship-gray baked-on powder coat that functions more as an esthetical enhancement than for any real protection. The business end of its seven-inch-wide pointed blade has two thirty-degree edge bevels, 3.75 inches long by .750-inch wide, which serve to make short work of the tree roots that make digging through unbroken soil such miserable a task. The bevels are also protected by a battleship-gray coating, and when this coating inevitably wore off from the friction of digging, I eagerly applied my own honed bevels using an aluminum-oxide stone. I was pleasantly surprised that the edges quickly and easily attained a sharpness suf-

ficient to sever a quarter-inch braided nylon rope in a single pass.

A twenty-six-inch tubular steel handle shaft, seam-welded at every junction with the blade and its comfortable (except in the winter cold) all-steel D-handle, gives the shovel immense strength and prying power. There is not a crack or an opening in the shovel's construction where mud might become wedged, making cleanup as simple as brushing off the dirt. The final eleven inches of shaft and D-handle are painted bright red to make the Diamond-blade spade hard to lose track of in thick undergrowth.

Price of the Twelve-inch Diamond-blade Spade is $91. For more information, visit www.coronatoolsusa.com or call (800) 847–7863.

Many a soldier in many a war can—or could, were he alive to do it—attest to the lethality of a shovel as a weapon, and none more so than Corona's Diamond Spade.

The Survivor Survival Knife System from Dajo Adventure Gear: The best knife is one that is with you when you need it. If a knife is clumsy, heavy, or uncomfortable, it's more likely to be left behind. No knife can be a good survival knife if it's not there when you need it.

The Survivor from Dajo Adventure Gear is a polished, full-tang, skeletonized blade of 7Cr17MoV stainless steel, 3.75 inches long (7.50 inches overall), 1.25 inches wide, .125 inch thick, and hardened to Hrc 57. The hollow ground edge is .750 inch wide, holds an edge well, and re-sharpens easily. The tip of the Survivor is 2.5 inches from the choil, the edge sweeps upward thirty-four degrees, almost like a tanto, to form a second flat cutting edge that extends 1.25 inches to the tip. A false edge, 1.75 inches long, brings the blade to a point that's slightly offset on the high side, but Dajo's Survivor has enough penetrating power for opening cans, drilling holes, and other chores that use a knife's tip.

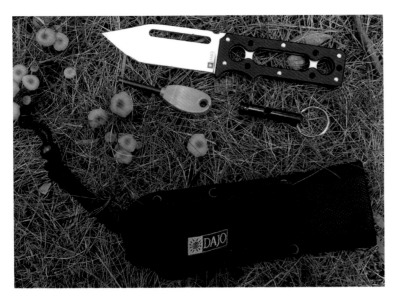

A 2.0- by .25-inch slot in the blade's spine acts as a fuller to help stiffen the blade, but also serves as a wire-bending jig. The handle is skeletonized; its full tang has a 1.75-inch by 0.50-inch slotted hole in its center, bordered fore and aft by two separate 0.50-inch round holes that work well for shaving and straightening

With a fire-starting tool, an emergency whistle, plus an ideal size and price, the Dajo was selected as the first survival knife for the author's grandson.

field-expedient arrow shafts. Five 0.20-inch holes spaced from hilt to pommel along both sides of the handle are ideal for lashing the Survivor to a shaft for spear-fishing. A rounded notch in the spine, opposite the choil, accommodates the included FireSteel sparking tool.

The handle of the Survivor is covered by two black scales of G-10, skeletonized to match the tang beneath, and secured by six round-head rivets; handle scales are not removable. The scales are textured to provide traction against skin, while a generous detent just behind the choil acts as a finger guard. The handle cut-outs increase grip security by impressing into their wielder's skin. This secure grip makes it easier to overlook the knife's 3.75-inch handle, which isn't as long as an average man's hand is wide. Girth—and versatility—can be added by wrapping the handle with cord, but I think most users will find the handle easy to work with.

The Survivor's black ballistic nylon sheath is pure function. A Velcro-flap accommodates belts two inches wide. Lifting the sheath's front flap reveals a spartan survival kit comprised of an aluminum whistle and a FireSteel. At the bottom of the sheath is five feet of nylon cord with a cord-lock.

In the field, the Survivor performed well; it accomplished most cutting chores adroitly, withstood light prying, held an edge well, and re-sharpened easily. The whistle can be heard from half a mile, and the FireSteel started a fire moderately well. Notably, I crawled into my sleeping bag and slept the night through with the Survivor on my belt. This survival knife provides no reason for leaving it at home; and a price tag of $38.95 gives Dajo's Survivor mass appeal.

If you'd like more information about owning a Survivor, visit www.dajoadventuregear.com or call (719) 371–1139.

DiamondBlade *Pro Series Summit*: This knife is a remarkable example of where knives are headed in the near future. This knife was a last-minute addition to this book, because it would have been irresponsible to leave it out. What makes this knife different is a process that DiamondBlade Knives calls Friction Forging (patent number 8,186, 561, inscribed on the blade).

According to DiamondBlade's founder, Charles Allen, "Friction Forging is a direct offshoot of the advanced friction stir process technology developed

Just the look of its blade immediately said that here was something that truly was new, even before patent holder Charles Allen confirmed that his design was unsurpassed for edge retention and strength. This knife promises to change everything.

to help further the space shuttle program and to join exotic, high strength materials, not easily processed using conventional means."

More simply, Friction Forging uses pressure and heat along blade's edge zone to produce nano-sized (microscopic) grain structures that are harder and can be polished sharper than normal steel alloys. Friction Forging is the next evolution in Zone Hardening, and I suspect that we will be seeing a lot more of it. Be warned that this knife's hardness makes it require more patience to re-sharpen.

The 8.75inch-long Summit sports a 3.75-inch-long drop point blade of D2 steel, 1.20 inches thick and 1.00 inch wide. The blade is flat-ground at 4.5 degrees, with cutting edge bevels of 18 degrees. Spine hardness is a tough and flexible 45 Hrc, extending downward to an obvious lighter-colored hamon. From this hamon down to the cutting edge the metal is an astounding 65–68 Hrc. Edge retention is nothing short of incredible, yet I did not get the edge to chip in the two weeks it took to dull it, and the blade demonstrates remarkable flexibility.

For me, the Summit's Suregrip rubber handle scales were icing on the cake. Their soft, grippy texture combined with a four-ounce weight, and the compulsory lanyard hole, give the knife a very nice feel. I once heard an expert on the TV show *Forged in Fire* remark that he thought having finger indentations in a handle diminished its versatility, but that opinion is more wrong than usual where the Summit is concerned. This knife is beautifully nimble in every grip position, and it transfers from one grasp to another as smoothly as any tactical knife. If I were selecting a knife to serve as a personal defense weapon, this knife would certainly be in the running.

The Summit's molded Kydex sheath is a deep friction-fit type, but even without a retaining strap, it holds the hilt high up

Our Diamondblade Summit was pushed hard through normal uses that dulled the best knives made, and it easily surpassed all of them, which was both a surprise and a disappointment; it would seem that this knife represents the next step in blade evolution.

and secure. In field trials, the knife stayed put, without even a rattle. The quick-release slide-clip on the sheath is removable and reversible with two Chicago screws, and is one of the more secure and workable designs in the industry, having been used for other knives in the past.

The warranty is rather vaguely worded, but does guarantee against defects in materials and manufacturing pertaining to only the knife for an undefined span of time. However, my dealings with Charles Allen make me believe that he will stand behind every knife he makes as well as any manufacturer. Since each knife is handmade and serial-numbered, the manufacturer recommends that you allow them time when ordering or when sending a knife in for service. Prices vary with handle and blade materials used, but the price for our sample was $199.

Knives of Alaska Magnum Ulu: Known best as a knife of the Inuit and other Eskimo tribes, the Ulu is unique among knives. Its curved cutting edge is parallel with a handle that fits in the palm, instead of being positioned ahead of the handle, as on a more conventional knife,

and the two points at either end of the blade are useless for stabbing, although they work quite well for drilling and digging. Eskimo hunters employed more

The classic Eskimo skinning knife, taken to new heights with a TPR molded handle and a D2 tool steel blade, Diamondblade's Knives of Alaska Ulu would beautify any deer hunter's belt.

traditional-looking knives, too, but for the large prey, like whales and sea lions, which served as the mainstay of aboriginal diets, a blade dedicated to skinning and slicing was the tool most needed.

Knives of Alaska's (a division of DiamondBlade) 6.4-ounce Magnum Ulu is a reproduction of the Eskimo hunter's most valuable skinning knife that anyone who'd ever skinned a bowhead whale in past generations would have loved to own. To begin, the Magnum Ulu's 3.375-inch blade is fashioned from D2 Tool Steel (one of this author's favorite knife alloys), and is .100-inch thick. The blade is double draw-tempered to align the grain microstructure and then cryogenically treated to give it an impressive hardness of 59-61Hrc. The Knives of Alaska snarling grizzly bear logo is handsomely etched on the front side of the blade, with "Made in USA" on the other.

The Magnum Ulu is hand sharpened on just one side with an eighteen- to twenty-degree edge bevel. At first, this Soviet favorite edge grind might seem difficult to re-sharpen, but I believe that the tendency for D2 to burr on one side on a two-bevel knife actually makes this ulu easier to get sharp. Simply hone the bevel until it reaches a sharp apex, and then strop the un-sharpened side to a razor edge.

I mentioned earlier that I'd once read a quote from a knife expert who claimed that "D2 takes a lousy edge, and it holds it forever." He was half right. D2 is unmatched at remaining as sharp as it has been made, but it is deucedly hard to sharpen—the same toughness that enables it to stay sharp makes it very difficult to abrade away the metal necessary to form a sharp apex. The tricks are to hone at the correct angle and to not give up. I've used this ulu for everything from cutting a chicken into sections (it sheared right through bones) to whittling an impromptu wooden tent stake, and it holds an edge with the best of them.

The handle is comprised of ergonomically contoured Suregrip rubber slabs over a full tang. A brass-grommeted .250-inch-diameter lanyard hole allows the knife to be let go to hang from a wrist while skinning. The handle might seem a bit awkward at first, but in no time you'll find that the ulu is versatile enough to be used with a number of grip positions.

Ergonomic, beautifully constructed, and made from exceptional materials, the Knives of Alaska Ulu is a utility design that performs equally well for hunters, anglers, and home gourmet cooks.

The Magnum Ulu comes with a nicely stitched triple-thick brown leather sheath, with a belt loop and a snap-down retaining strap. The Knives of Alaska bear is embossed on the front, with the reminder "Made in USA" on the back.

The Magnum Ulu is priced at $64.99. Visit knivesofalaska.com for more information.

The Xtreme Model V Survival Knife from Knives of Alaska: Largest in its line, the Model V shares the same ultralight skeleton design and strong D2 tool steel construction of its four brethren, except for a blade length of five inches, and an overall length of 10.50 inches. Hardened to a respectable Hrc 59–61, the edge-holding flat-ground blade measures .120-inch thick by 1.325 inches wide at the choil, with a twenty-degree cutting edge that was shaving-sharp out of the box. The spine of the blade arcs gently downward in a drop-point configuration that provides both good piercing power and a generous belly for skinning game or processing food.

The Model V's strong one-piece construction extends into a skeleton handle that is the same thickness as the spine, with the outer edges of the grip area broached to form a progression of tooth-like cut-outs that provide purchase against skin when slippery. A weight-reducing slot, 3.650 inches long by .700 inch wide at the pommel, tapering to .540 inch at the choil, also enhances grip. A pair of .160-inch-diameter holes just ahead of the slot's choil end are sized to accept lines up to parachute cord-diameter, and are especially handy for securing the handle to a spear shaft. The center of the pommel is pierced with a .400-inch diameter hole to accommodate a lanyard.

Although functional enough as-is, the Model V's handle is most comfortable and secure when wrapped with a cushioning layer of heavy cord. Six feet of parachute cord are included for that purpose, but use your imagination: our test knife's handle carried twenty feet of fishing line (with two hooks) and ten feet of nylon string, wrapped under eight feet of parachute cord.

Because D2, for all of its other great qualities, is a high-carbon steel, it rusts quickly if not cleaned and dried after each use and stored in an arid environment. That problem is all but eliminated everywhere except on the polished cutting edge by a layer of super-tough Emralon resin-bonded fluoropolymer from Acheson Colloids. Fine gold detail on the blade's left side shows the Xtreme and Knives of Alaska logos, while gold lettering on the opposite side identify the steel as D2, with a quality control tracking number, and the words "Made In USA."

The Xtreme Model V is carried in a hard Kydex scabbard that holds the knife with a strapless friction-fit, and fastens to any belt or strap up to two inches wide with a sliding panel and locking quick-release tabs. It's held together by six roll-staked rivets and a grommet at the tip that doubles as a lanyard hole. Four slotted holes at the sides of the scabbard allow you to strap it onto a day-pack or personal flotation vest. In the real world, where avoiding bad situations might depend on having a knife, I'd back up the scabbard's friction fit with a cord that lashes the knife more securely in place.

If you're putting together an ultralight backcountry survival kit, the near-weightless, tool steel, working-size Xtreme Model V is a contender for the job. Priced at $79.99, the Xtreme Mode V has been discontinued, but you may still find one at retailers on the Internet. www.knivesofalaska.com, or call (903) 786–7366.

ESEE Knives CM6 Survival Fighting Knife: New in 2016, this drop-point stiletto-style knife was designed by Terrill Hoffman to be "the joining of tactical and practical, making this knife at home in the woods or on the battlefield." While I feel confident in stating that very, very few can

As skeleton knives go, the discontinued Extreme Model V was king of the proverbial hill, and if this is your kind of knife, track one down on the Internet.

prove the latter half of that claim from the purview of experience, I right now have a year of experience using the knife for less combat-related tasks.

The CM6's overall length of 11.125 inches, with a textured black powder-coated 5.875-inch blade that feels balanced enough for its ten ounces to seem weightless, with a point nimbleness that every designer of working knives strives for. This knife is extremely agile, with effortless tip control that won't tire your hand on big jobs, like butchering an elk—or a half-dozen whitetails, in my case. A hardness of 55-57Hrc means that it will take and hold an extremely keen edge. Handsomely etched on one side is the Chestnut Mountain Proving Grounds logo, the knife's serial number on the other. Like all ESEE knives, it sports a unique serial number.

The drop-point 1095 carbon steel blade is 1.250 inches wide, and .188 inch thick, with one inch of its upper tip sharpened to a short false edge (rather incorrectly known as a "swedge" by some in the knife industry). This design gives its blade the puncturing power of a dagger, without sacrificing strength. This configuration is perfect for knife fishing, a super-stealthy survival tactic that I've used often, and which I've described in numerous survival manuals, for putting food on the table. The hilt, with its gray canvas Micarta slabs held in place by three Allen-head Chicago screws, lacks a lanyard hole—taking a combat lanyard off the table as an option.

The ESEE CM6 model Survival Fighting knife is a superbly built knife, but lacks a vital lanyard hole and a functional sheath, and is far from field-ready as sold.

The CM6's black molded Kydex sheath is friction-fit, with no retaining strap, and is reversible for right- or left-hand carry from its spring-steel belt clip.

If you carry the CM6 afield without significant modification, I promise that you will lose it, probably right away. During field trials, the belt clip came loose of its wearer's belt three times in one hour, just from normal actions like bending, kneeling, and sitting. Typical of friction-fit sheaths, the knife can be pulled from its sheath by rubbing against heavy brush or belly crawling. Also, I recommend mounting the plate which contains the belt clip with a locking solution on the threads of its four machine screws—one of them fell out unnoticed in the first week, through no actual fault of the knife.

Fortunately, the add-on belt loop/retaining strap, described earlier in the Sheaths chapter, remedied the CM6's security problems, and it quickly became a habit-forming tool. It could very much use a lanyard hole, especially since one of its intended purposes is as a fighting knife—there's no way to attach a combat lanyard, as described earlier. Aside from those obvious discrepancies, it's a very well-engineered knife once you've taken precautions to avoid losing it.

The CM6 is entirely crafted in the USA and, like all ESEE knives, it carries a no-questions-asked lifetime warranty, regardless of abuse. ESEE's asking price for the CM6 is $246.78. www.eseeknives .com.

No trials test a knife's agility like preparing a meal, and the handling characteristics of ESEE's CM6 proved outstanding in the kitchen.

ESEE Knives *Izula II*: With an overall length of 6.75 inches, and weighing in at 3.2 ounces (knife only), the Izula II is hardly a Rambo knife, but neither is a cat's claw—or the stingray barb that killed crocodile hunter Steve Irwin. What this knife lacks in size, it makes up for in pure utility. Its 2.88-inch long, one-inch-wide drop-point blade is the type preferred by hunting guides in the Rockies. The spine is a beefy .156-inch thick, with 0.5-inch of gimping grooves cut just ahead of the handle.

The Izula's flat-ground 1095 high-carbon-steel blade will rust, so blade and tang are black powder-coated with a textured finish. On the left side is a rendition of the knife's namesake Isula fire ant and, under it, a serial number that makes the knife indisputably yours.

Although its blade alloy might be classic, the Izula II is a beneficiary of state-of-the-art smelting and hardening processes that have kept 1095 at the forefront of preferred blade steels. Hardness is a flat 57 Hrc, denoting a homogenous stock, and Rowen Manufacturing's proprietary heat-treating process. In trials, the surgically-sharp cutting edge held up like 1095 should, and re-sharpening back to razor keenness was quick and easy.

The Izula II's ergonomic canvas-Micarta handle slabs are held in place by two flathead Allen-type Chicago screws. Or you might opt to leave off the handles entirely, and wrap the skeleton

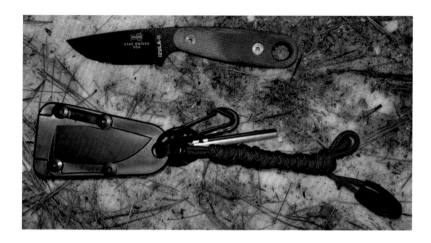

Small, but functional, with a friction-fit molded sheath that proved capable of keeping its knife, ESEE's Izula II earned the right to be carried as a survival blade.

frame with the included five feet of parachute cord. A .550-inch-diameter hole through the pommel accommodates a lanyard.

The Izula II is housed in a molded sheath that is comfortable to wear, virtually unbreakable, and secure during strenuous activities. (Few emotions are so black as reaching for your knife while far from home, and finding it gone.) The knife refused to fall out when shaken, slapped, or jerked in earnest, yet it still came loose with an easy yank on the handle, even in subzero cold.

The sheath offers numerous carry options; a backing plate and a stout 7/8-inch-wide spring steel clip can be mounted to either side of the blade scabbard with four Allen-head Chicago screws, and in either direction for point-down or point-up carry on almost any belt or strap. Remove the clip

Field-proven to be reliable, you could do a whole lot worse than adding an Izula II to your survival kit.

and plate, attach the included five feet of parachute cord and cord-lock per the instructions, and a conventional belt loop can be fashioned. Or you can hang the sheath around your neck for everything from jogging to daypacking.

The Izula II kit includes: ambidextrous molded sheath, clip plate and screws, five feet of parachute cord, sliding cord lock, signal whistle, a molded snap-hook, a one-inch diameter split-ring, and another 1.25-inch split ring holding a magnesium-and-flint fire-starter. Included is a waterproofed instruction card with valuable information, such as how to signal aircraft. A detailed instruction sheet illustrates how these accessories can be used for multiple purposes. The Izula kit retails for $134.20, knife and sheath alone for $117. www.eseeknives.com

Gerber *US Assist Assisted Opening Folder:* New for 2017, this knife appears to be a slightly smaller, sportier offspring of Gerber's popular 06 Combat Folder, which, despite its macho moniker, proved to be such a user-friendly brute of a working knife that I've worn a half inch off its S30V alloy blade.

Beneficiary of some forward-thinking innovations, the new-for-2017 Gerber US Assist folder is a bit less than perfect.

The US Assist also boasts an edge-holding CPM S30V blade, 3.00 inches long by .900 inch wide by .100 inch thick, stone-washed, with the word Gerber etched on the left side and "Made in USA" proudly etched on the other. Total open length is 7.200 inches, with a forgettable weight of just 3.9 ounces. It has the same push-button lock-release on its left side, which Gerber calls a "Plunge" release. Despite a few complaints, this release button is convenient for right- or left-handers (I'm a southpaw, and to watch me unlock and retire the knife, you'd think that it was designed for lefties).

One new innovation that has been a long time coming is the ball-bearings and race, similar to the wheel bearings on an automobile axle, that surround the blade's bolster pivot. Gerber calls this design B.O.S.S. (Balls Of Stainless Steel) Tech. A typical spring-assist folder's action can be hampered by contaminants, sometimes to the point of overcoming the spring and refusing to open the blade. But the near frictionless action of the US Assist means that it's nearly impossible to gum-up—a potentially lifesaving feature for those who tend to neglect their EDC knives.

The US Assist also has a crossbolt safety just ahead of the lock button. Just like the crossbolt safety found on the trigger guards of many firearms, push it to one side, and a red line indicates that the safety is disengaged, enabling the blade to move normally. Push it to the opposite side and the blade is locked in either its fully open or fully closed positions.

A spring-wire skeleton pocket clip enables the US Assist to be carried point-up or point-down, but only from the right side of the knife. Again, this isn't a problem, it simply requires a little adaptation from its user. The wire pocket clip is strong, sure, and snag-free.

Not quite as good in field trials as the 06 Combat Folder that it was intended to succeed, Gerber's US Assist folder with S30V blade qualifies as a working knife.

The US Assist's only demerit is that someone at Gerber thought that it would make the knife easier to open if they sloped the thumb studs, making the blade swivel open from pressure on the top of the stud, instead of from the side. In theory, this would seem to make sense: sloping the stud's top increases its surface area, and a half dozen gimping grooves increase traction even more.

But the real world has slapped down more than one engineer, and in the field not one person did not complain that the studs made the knife hard to open. Ramping the stud made it shorter, and having to press downward on the stud meant that most force needed to push the stud forward to open the blade was being wasted. The shortened, ramped thumb stud is not a good idea.

All in all: Two thumbs up for the US Assist. Gerber's asking price is $119. www.gerbergear.com.

Gerber *LMF II Survival Knife:* Survival is one of the disciplines for which I'm best known, so I'm discerning when I select a knife that serves as my most trustworthy friend in potentially dangerous environs. That's an assignment for which not many knives (including survival knives) can qualify—and none do perfectly. By definition, a survival knife is not a specialty blade, meant to perform a few cutting tasks. It has to do anything that I might require of it—like prying open a jammed car door or breaking its windshield—while remaining unbreakable.

That knife has always been secreted in Zeus's vault, but there have been some good attempts to deliver that Survival Knife of the Gods into our hands. Gerber's LMF (Light Multi-Function) Mark II knife is one of those.

Designed by Jeff Freeman with military use in mind, this 11.00-inch field knife, with its 4.840-inch long blacked-out drop-point blade of 420HC, is a beefy .190 inch thick. The forward plain edge is 2.800 inches long, with a generous belly radius that makes it ideal for hunters who still skin their own deer. In back of the plain edge are 1.800 inches of serrations that rip through tough materials, like garden hose or tire sidewalls. Weight is 11.670 ounces, 24.280 ounces with sheath.

The LMF II's hilt is a composite, comprised of a steel tang overlaid with fiberglass-reinforced nylon, which is itself over-molded with a layer of tough alloy of synthetic TPV (thermoplastic vulcanite—a baked elastomer) rubber. A robust steel polyhedral pommel incorporates a shattering wedge, a flat hammer face, .750 inch across, and a more rounded striking surface of the same width.

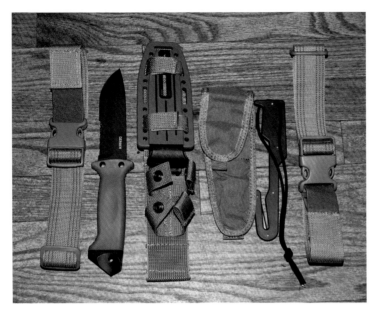

Overbuilt enough to be inconvenient, the new-for-2017 LMF II is a very good survival knife, with a secure, quiet-enough sheath, and a nice cargo pouch, but its two quick-release straps, redundant snap-down retaining straps, and unreachable integral pull-through sharpener are just inconvenient.

At the request of special forces troops, the steel pommel is electrically isolated from the tang, so you can safely cut live wires (just don't touch the blade!). A .200-inch-diameter lanyard hole serves as a simple wire-bending jig. A pair of same-size holes through the handle in back of the choil serve to make the knife easy to lash to a spear shaft.

The LMF II's sheath is well crafted, if a bit over-complicated. Its super-heavy construction, tight friction fit, and strong retaining strap with snap virtually guarantee that your knife will be there when you reach for it. Two elastic-and-nylon straps with non-slip stitching and quick-release buckles enable it to be carried on the ankle, quickly tied down

The rubber covering on our sample LMF II's hilt, near its choil, began to pull away after three days of drawing and re-inserting the knife.

to the thigh, or fastened to almost any piece of equipment. The cargo pouch is ample enough to carry the other two components of *The Basic 3* (fire starter and compass), although the Velcro-type flap is anything but stealthy. A pull-through carbide-blade sharpener built into the sheath helps to keep the knife sharp anywhere you go.

Gerber says this knife has been "thoroughly field tested by American troops in the Middle East." Domestically, the rubber began to pull away from the hilt from the force of inserting and drawing the knife. A drop of Gorilla Glue and a tight wrap of electrical tape to hold it until it cured fixed the problem until the sheath was broken in. After four months of normal use, the LMF II is virtually ideal.

Retail is $124. www.gerbergear.com.

Gerber's Trio of Working Axes: I have a collection of axes, but it would be less accurate to say that I'm a collector than to describe me as a user.

It began fifty years ago, this year. The first efficient-burning "air-tight" woodstoves were a decade away, and two-story farm houses were commonly heated with a single cast-iron pot-belly wood burner. They consumed wood at a frightening rate—about a quarter of a cord each day—and they were cold each morning, not a single ember remaining. That promoted real family togetherness on cold mornings, as everyone gathered around the newly fired stove, trying to absorb warmth.

I was eight years old when it became my daily chore to fill the woodbox after school each day. It was a big job for a little boy, wielding an axe with a three-and-a-half-pound head that he could barely swing with a modicum of control, let alone power.

But I learned. By the time I satisfied the childhood fantasy of forging a log cabin homestead from wilderness, using only hand tools, the way my forebears did, it was with a real appreciation for the skills that I'd developed. (That fifteen-month ordeal is described in the book, *The Log Cabin*, available at most book stores.)

When I left civilization, I took with me two axes, a Dayton-style single-bit and a double-blade Michigan. But, with the exception of having hammer-forged

Axes are one of those tools that remained relatively unchanged for a century, but old lumberjacks from the timber country of northern Michigan have judged this trio of innovative Gerbers to be just a little better than superb.

steel heads (versus the cast-iron of pioneer days), or the individually made, blacksmith-forged steel heads of the timbering heyday, only a yellow fiberglass-core plastic handle distinguished either from any axe made for one hundred years prior.

Gerber (Division of Fiskars) changed that with its 2015 Type II line of redesigned axes. We put the three most popular models through their paces in the timber country of Michigan's Upper Peninsula. This is what we found:

Splitting Axe II: Except for changing the rather drab black-and-gray colors of its original vibration-absorbing, hollow Fibercomp ™ polymer handle, the Splitting Axe II remains unchanged from the award-winning design that was introduced almost a decade ago.

The new Splitting Axe II has an extra-long haft that delivers increased power to its keen flat-ground 420 stainless-steel head (55Hrc). The center of the head flares out to incorporate a splitting wedge into its design, enabling the axe to pull double-duty as a real chip-making felling axe, and an effective splitting maul. Gerber says the axe is "Built to withstand the abuse that regularly breaks wooden-handled splitting mauls and axes, this was made with loggers, arborists, landscapers and homeowners with wood-burning stoves in mind."

That's an extraordinary claim. I personally go through at least two handles a year. My favorite axe actually wears, right now, a hand-whittled haft carved from maple. The biggest cause of handle failure is striking its bottom edge against a log that's being split, which repeatedly splinters that edge, until it breaks.

But Gerber says that it has resolved that problem with a super-tough handle and a mounting that holds handle to head with a strap over the top, instead of a hole in the bit. A polytetrafluoro-ethylene (PTFE) "lubricious" coating helps to keep the head from sticking in a log when it's being split, as splitting mauls, and especially, axes, are wont to do. A lanyard hole in the end of the handle provides another option for hanging or carrying all three of the axes we evaluated.

Also protecting the handle from overstrike damage is a flared-out head design on either side, forming a splitting wedge that's wider than the handle. Before the head can sink far enough to reach its handle, a log would have to be split apart too far to make contact.

But any splitting maul can say that. What impressed us the most is that the Splitting Axe II is sharp, easy to re-sharpen, and that it chops wood like a felling axe. No maul can do that.

In fact, the Splitting Axe II chops wood better than most felling axes, even though its more compact handle is five and a half inches shorter than a standard Collins axe. Not having a hole through its head enables greater weight in a smaller package. An ultralight handle causes it be especially end-heavy, which results in increased centrifugal force.

Bottom line: this sucker splits firewood like a maul, and makes chips with the best felling axe. I have a new favorite for axe work at home.

Overall Length: 28.5 inches
Blade Length: 3.2 inches
Weight: 86.7 ounces
Head: Forged Steel, 57 ounces
Handle Material: Glass-Filled Nylon
Price: $75

XL Axe II: The next step down, in size, the XL Axe II is what is known as a "canoe axe." That eclectic name, in fact, describes a short-handled axe (sometimes with a full-size head) that took up less space and weight when either was limited.

Don't let its small size fool you. Although it's two pounds lighter than its bigger brother, this little axe delivers tremendous chopping power. Even swung with one hand—do not try this—it kept pace with a well-honed, but otherwise standard, three- and one-half-pound Dayton axe (one of my personal axes) in a chopping contest.

The XL Axe II's remarkable efficiency is due to the same hollow Fibercomp handle, which amplifies the speed, centrifugal force and, therefore, the striking power of its smaller stainless head. A PTFE coating makes it as friction free as its bigger brother, while a slimmer, more acute grind makes it so sharp that trees are scared of it.

Although more engineered to chop than to split, the XL Axe II performs really well as a kindling maker. This little guy can ride along in my kayak any time.

Overall Length: 23.6 inches
Blade Length: 3.5 inches
Weight: 53.6 ounces
Head: Forged Steel
Handle Material: Glass-filled nylon
Price: $71

Sport Axe II: Smallest of the trio is the Sport Axe II, which is actually a large hatchet. Six inches shorter than the XL Axe II, with a slightly smaller clone of that model's head, the Sport Axe II boasts a saber-ground stainless blade, frictionless PTFE coating, with the same over-the-top mounting system and a hollow Fibercomp handle. A shock-corded polyethylene edge-guard snaps into its hollow handle.

The Sport Axe II is almost a pound lighter than my oft-proved roofer's hatchet. But Gerber says that it will deliver three times the cutting ability, per swing, and field trials showed that claim to be more than idle boasting. Like each of the trio we evaluated, the secret lies in an ultralight hollow handle that places most weight at the end of the haft, where it generates far more speed for the same expenditure of energy.

Add to that a semi-hollow ground head design, with a 3/8-inch bevel on its cutting edge, and you could literally skin and butcher a whitetail with this outstanding tool.

Overall Length: 14 inches
Blade Length: 2.6 inches
Weight: 22.6 ounces
Head: Forged steel
Sheath: Formed plastic
Handle: Glass-filled nylon
Price: $62

But nothing is perfect, and if all three of these otherwise superb choppers fall short, it's with the biohazard-green molded polyethylene carry cases. Differing from one another only in size, each secures its axe with a rotating thumb-lock lever, and each has an integral carrying handle with finger detents.

If you want to carry your Gerber axe on your person, or attached to your backpack, you'll have to figure out a way to do it. Even the molded edge-guard of the Sport Axe II, meant to make it safe during carry, offers no way of actually carrying the tool on your body.

In fact, we resolved the carrying dilemma pretty readily. Most backpacks are versatile enough to strap on an axe, and for shoulder carry, the field-expedient dog leash carrier that works for snow-shoes, even firearms, made each of the axes readily portable.

In the final analysis, the new Gerber II line is a successful next step in the design of mankind's oldest environment-manipulation tool. Priced to be a bargain, and each with a lifetime guarantee, Dan'l Boone would have approved, I think.

Chris Hayes Custom Knives: It doesn't require much more than a bench grinder, a chunk of scrap steel, and a little time to make a knife. That's a fact, and there have always been a few "custom" knife makers who prove that. I've made more than a dozen knives myself, and I regret to admit that none of them were good enough to serve my needs in the field. Practically any shard of 1010–1008 (the alloy used to make soup cans) bar stock can be shaped, polished, and fitted with a pseudo-antler resin handle, then passed off as a "mountain man's" Bowie—and that describes a few "custom" knives.

What separates the pros from the amateurs is not how pretty the finished product is, but how well it performs. Perhaps most "custom" knives aren't fit to take deer hunting.

But some are. I came across this blademaster entirely by chance, and his expertise, born of years of study and practice, was so evident that my wife, Cheanne, (who once asked for a new chainsaw for her birthday) commissioned him to make her a one-of-a-kind clip-point, fixed-blade hunting knife. Why? Because the best feature of a quality-made custom knife is that you own the only one; no one else can have the same knife at any price.

Another great advantage is that you can have the knife *you* want. You don't have to shop around to find the knife that most suits your desires, you can have the knife of your dreams made to perfectly match your desires. Cheanne's choice was a fixed-blade clip-point hunter, with a mild bolo shape to its blade, made from Damascus, because she likes the looks of it, and with a hilt made from elk antler, shaped by nature. They designed her knife over the phone, and Chris got it right on the first try.

Actually, it was his second try, because Chris Hayes was so dissatisfied with his first attempt that he scrapped it and started anew. The knife that arrived via FedEx two weeks later was twelve inches overall, a 6.500-inch saber-ground blade that exhibited a very noticeable

This Chris Hayes-made Clip Point Hunter is a beautiful one-of-a-kind hunter with 57Hrc hardness that any hunter could wear with pride.

Another satisfied customer for Chris Hayes, custom knife smith.

hamon where Chris had differentially hardened its 5.250-inch cutting edge to blend maximum sharpness with maximum toughness and strength. A slightly concave false edge, 2.750 inches long, gave the blade good penetration ability, and imparted a classic Bowie-type look to the knife.

Being nature grown, the elk-antler hilt is irregularly shaped, but averages 1.100 inches thick, tapering outward toward its pommel. Only its choil end has been sanded to mate precisely with a solid, polished brass fingerguard, .250 inch thick by .750 inch wide, and 1.193-inches long to offer solid protection for your hand. A flat, polished brass pommel plate is held to the .500-inch tang with a brass nut. Chris picked this handle carefully; it transitions well between grip positions, it's comfortable in the hand, and it provides a sure grasp when slippery. Jim Bowie would have carried this knife. Price for this one-of-a-kind, made-to-order piece of working art was $250. Lifetime warranty except in cases of outright abuse. www.chrishayesknives.com.

KaBar Zombie Knives: Regardless of how silly the basic concept behind it might be, where there is a market, there will be suppliers. One notable, if unexpected, entrant into the arena of zombie-fighting gear is knifemaking legend KaBar, with the company's new Zombie Knives line. Said to have sprung from a flip comment that KaBar needed to make knives capable of killing already-dead zombies, the ZK line achieved the lofty goal of standing out from the crowd—incongruous lime-green handle scales with their pebble-grain finish accomplish that much by themselves.

In keeping with the ZK line's apocalyptic theme, each of the larger fixed blades is named for one of the four great plagues

Made fun of by knife snobs on Internet forums, Kabar's Zombie line has proved worthy to wear the Kabar name, despite their somewhat preposterous monikers. This War Sword has butchered more than a dozen deer to date.

of Biblical lore: the Pestilence Chopper, War Sword, Famine Tanto, and Death Dagger. Smaller companion knives include the Kharon tanto-style folder with AUS 8 blade (Hrc 57–59), and the Acheron skeleton-style backup knife that is included with each of the four larger fixed blades. The Acheron's 3.125-inch blade (6.375 inches overall) of 5Cr13 stainless steel (Hrc 54–56) makes it easy to carry as a neck knife in its molded sheath, or as a backup knife inside the secure inner liner that is integral to all of ZK's sheaths.

This Kharon folder served well as an everyday work knife for three years, before being retired, sharper than the day it was unboxed.

The Kharon folder after three years of hard use doing everything from whittling tool handles to wiring fences.

The Acheron skeleton frame backup knife is included with each fixed-blade Zombie knife.

Each of these Four Horsemen knives has a full-tang blade of SK5 high-carbon steel, .200-inch thick, hardened to 52–54 Hrc. A Japanese version of American SAE 1080, this alloy can be hardened to Hrc 60; KaBar's milder temper reflects a strategic balance between sharpness and edge retention, but with an emphasis on withstanding abuse without chipping or breaking.

Because unprotected SK5 will rust without regular care, ZK blades are shielded from corrosion by a matte-finish baked-on black epoxy powder-coat. The powder coat is broken on the left side by KaBar's ZK biohazard logo, and the name KABAR on the choil; on the right choil are the model number, and country of manufacture—Taiwan, in my samples. Be aware that each of these

Actually a single-edged dirk, the Zombie Knives Death Dagger is a superb sidearm.

markings is formed by unprotected metal contrasting against the black coating, and those places need to be wiped clean after each use to fend off oxidation.

ZK fixed-blades are sold with "Biohazard Green" handle scales made from super-tough GFN-PA66 injection-molded polymer that can resist abuse, chemicals, and zombie fluids. Contoured to give fingers purchase in any grip position, handles feature a hand-filling palm swell, with a bumpy lizard-skin texture that makes them easy to hang onto and manipulate while wearing gloves. If green handle scales don't suit you, each of the Four Horsemen comes with a set of identical black scales that can be installed with an Allen wrench.

Touted as knives that can serve with distinction through apocalyptic times means the zombie fighters need a carry system that does more than just hang from your belt. Most impressive for survival knife guys like myself is the single giant cargo pouch at the front of each black sheath. This is not a small pouch that never seems large enough to accommodate a really useful stayin' alive kit, but a voluminous bellows pocket that can swallow your hand up past the wrist, and is big enough for a compass and fire starter, with room for fishing tackle, flashlight, cord, even a small radio receiver or MP3 player. Included in each sheath is eight feet of zombie-green braided bootlace cord. A shorter section of the same lacing on a sliding cord-lock fastener cinches the mouth of the cargo pocket securely shut.

Attach points include a conventional hip belt loop, sixteen vertical MOLLE-type, ALICE-compatible strap-loops on the sheath's backside, and under those, three strap-loops that mount easily to almost any backpack. Knife retention is accomplished using two snap-down straps around the handle, one at the fingerguard, another midway up the handle. The Zytel liner is detented to accept the radius of its knife's handle, and with both retaining straps snapped-down, my knives didn't rattle while hiking. A pair of grommets at the bottom offers further tie-down options, including the thigh-tiedown preferred by professional zombie fighters.

At present, there seem to be no zombies anywhere, so field trials had to be limited to use in Hiawatha National Forest. Best liked as a survival knife was the bolo-style War Sword, whose 9.750-inch blade (15.125 inches overall) was well liked by people who don't normally favor large knives. The Pestilence Chopper's 10.250-inch hooked blade (15.750 inches overall) is a natural for brush removal and light pruning. The Famine Tanto's 7.625-inch blade (13.125 inches overall) is suited to full-time carry in dark alleys. The Death Dagger, which is actually a single-edge dirk, was my favorite among the Zombie line; it sports a wickedly pointed 8.500-inch blade (13.635 inches overall) that exemplifies the combat traditions for which KaBar is famous.

There are better outdoor knives, but not for the price; each of the fixed blades carries an MSRP of $75, the Kharon folder goes for $41, and the Acheron backup knife sells alone for $10. Shop around, though, because I've found them all for considerably less than suggested retail.

Despite being ganged up on by fashionistas on Internet knife forums, actual field trials prove that the Zombie Knives are deserving of the KaBar logo they bear, and are in keeping with the knife maker's reputation for making no-nonsense blades that a person can count on while doing the hard stuff. I'm not willing to hold my breath until hordes of bloodthirsty zombies descend upon humanity, but I won't mind keeping on hand the knives KaBar has made for combating them. www.kabar.com.

Kershaw Launch 6 Auto: While folders equipped with spring-assisted opening, Carson flippers, and just thumb studs in general, have reduced or negated altogether the speed advantage of automatic-opening "switchblade" knives, there is just something very cool about a keen blade that springs open at the press of a button. Actual trials reveal that although this type of folding knife is universally maligned by lawmakers and social sybaritics for a century, it possesses no real speed advantage over other one-hand deployment designs.

A few states have already acceded to the obvious and removed restrictions against switchblade ownership, but governmental change has always been notoriously slow, and many still regard automatics as weapons of mass destruction. Even while lawmakers in the US show indications of becoming more sensible, there is a powerful movement in the United Kingdom to classify every type of knife as a criminal weapon so the battle is far from over.

Kershaw's new-for-2017 Launch 6 is fast, sure, and has such a powerful spring that it can jump right out of your hand on opening.

New for 2017, Kershaw's Launch 6 automatic is a very smart, exceptionally stylish automatic-deployment cutting tool. With a closed length of 4.90 inches and a two-position spring steel pocket clip that permits point-down carry on either side, the Launch 6 is as fashionable for the inside pocket of a suit coat as it is on a MOLLE vest. Its ambidextrous release button is nestled into a recess on the left side, above a beefy bolster, where it is within easy reach of a right-hander's thumb or a southpaw's index finger, yet difficult to depress accidentally.

However you depress the Launch 6's release button, it causes a flat-ground 3.75-inch drop-point blade of .120-inch-thick CPM154 stainless with a black DLC (Diamond-Like Carbon) coating to energetically spring open to an all-business length of 8.70 inches. The blade's cutting edge sweeps upward to a very pointed tip, and is clearly marked with the Kershaw name on one side and "Made in USA" on the other. The butt end is perforated with Kershaw's trademark oval-shaped lanyard hole. This is a knife that you'd appreciate if you were surrounded by unfriendly crackheads in a dark alley.

The Launch 6's 4.95-inch black aluminum handle is machined to be both eye-catching and ergonomic. A variety of planes, angles, and inlets give the knife a stylish appearance, but handling it reveals an intent behind the design. Tip control is precise, and transition between grips is fast and sure.

Most surprising, the balance point of this 3.8-ounce folder is at the knife's physical center. If you were of a mind to do it, this folding knife behaves like a throwing knife, with uncanny spin consistency. It is a prodigious performer in almost every capacity, from skinning a squirrel to whittling a toy sailboat, and its geometry helps to give it impressive edge retention.

Flaws were difficult to find with this beautiful piece of work. However, one time it did open while in my hip pocket, a potentially touchy situation with a surgically sharp cutting edge. That aside, I simply cannot fault this knife for anything beyond the irrational fear its design engenders in some politicians. In fact, it is further endearing that it carries a limited lifetime warranty that includes free sharpening and a $10 replacement fee for broken blades.

The Launch 6 retails for $170. In some places, it is available only to law enforcement (in my opinion, a switchblade knife is not the weapon of a good guy) and some military personnel, so check with local laws before attempting to purchase one. kershaw.kaiusaltd.com

Kershaw Launch 4 Auto: Smallest sibling of the Launch line, this knife inspires remarks about how cute it is, always paired with the adjective "little." But looks are magnificently deceiving in this instance. The rather plain penknife-looking unit has a closed length of just 3.20 inches. Press its recessed release button with your thumb if you're right-handed—your index finger if you're a southpaw—and a 1.90-inch dagger-shaped single-edge blade of CPM154 stainless snaps out of its recess to create a knife that's 5.10 inches long. Pressing the button in its locked position unlocks the blade so that it can be retired.

The sharply pointed blade is .760 inch at its widest, .125 inch thick, and coated with a black DLC (Diamond-Like Carbon). The bolster is identical to the one used on the Launch 6, which makes it exceedingly strong. The left side of the blade is etched with the Kershaw name, the other with KaiUSA, and the blade alloy. Total weight of the Launch 4 is a mere 1.8 ounces. Any lighter, and it wouldn't exist.

The Launch 4's spring steel pocket clip is also the same as that used on its big brother, making it more than up to the job it was designed to do. The stout aluminum handles are coated black, too, but are sans machining and contouring that would remove material from a hilt that benefits from having all the surface area it can get. The pocket clip is on the right side and is oriented for point-down carry on that side only. That feature didn't inconvenience this southpaw in the slightest, and in fact would have been my preferred carry mode had I had the option of a reversible clip. An American flag etched on the left side of its handle serves to further remind you that this knife, like all of the Launch series, is entirely manufactured in the USA.

Like its Launch siblings, the Model 4 carries a limited lifetime warranty against defects that includes a free sharpening service and, and most attractive, a ten-dollar blade replacement fee.

Although you're unlikely to need it unless you're willfully abusive, inexpensive replacement is a very

Small enough to be carried unnoticed in a sock, Kershaw's Launch 4 has the potential to inflict lethal wounds, but it could use a stronger actuator spring.

attractive feature to have in a knife that you're likely to fall in love with, as I did. Be aware that local laws might require that knives sent in for service or repair be returned to an authorized dealer instead of their owners.

This knife is not just a "cute little knife," as so many describe it the first time they see it. Viewed through the eyes of a street fighter, the Launch 4 is a decidedly lethal back-up weapon. In the right hands, it can open a carotid, eviscerate an adversary, sever an Achilles tendon, or kill in a dozen ways. Anyone who sees the Launch 4 as less than a potentially deadly weapon doesn't know what they're looking at.

One serious flaw that I've found with the Launch 4 is a too-weak deployment spring. I recommend spending a lot of TV watching and other free time working the knife. Its mechanism requires as much breaking in as you're willing to devote, and it's absolutely imperative that you keep it clean and free of any oil, dirt, or other contaminants that might hinder its action to even the slightest degree. That includes making certain that the release button spring moves up and down freely. Depending on its owner, it may be imperative that this knife fully open and lock when its button is pressed.

Unfortunately, like most automatics, the Launch 4 relies solely on its spring to deploy its blade; there is no other mechanism for opening a stuck blade short of grabbing it with pliers and pulling it open. I've complained about this problem, recommending the addition of a thumb stud, or even an old-fashioned thumbnail notch, but to no avail. I'd also like to see a lanyard hole that would give me the option of hanging the knife around my neck on a lanyard.

Based on a year-long trial, I recommend using no lubricants whatsoever (not even FrogLube) on any automatic knife. Keep its actuating mechanism clean and scrubbed with hot, soapy water, and maybe solvents now and again. Beyond that, it appears that you cannot give the knife too much exercise, so feel free to give it exercise.

Nor could I avoid falling in love with it, even though I must admit that the new knife demanded an inordinate amount of breaking in before I would trust it enough to rely on it. I regret to say that the Launch 4 is not a candidate for everyday carry. Retail for the Launch 4 is $120. www.kershaw.kaiusaltd.com

Kershaw Link Knife: Kershaw gave this folder the name Link because, according to the company, it represents the missing link in knives "between a quality made-in-the-USA knife and a price that most consumers can afford."

I have to admit right up front that I really like this knife. The plain-edge version has been my everyday work knife for more than six months now. Aesthetically, the Link is handsome, with a flat gray three-planed handle whose backside swells outward to provide a palm-filling grip. A stout spring-steel pocket clip (identical to and interchangeable with that used on Kershaw's Launch series of knives) is reversible for right or left tip-down carry. An American flag etched on the right side tells you plainly where the knife was manufactured.

The Link is fitted with a relatively inexpensive (compared to other alloys) blade of 420 High-Carbon stainless steel, 3.25 inches long, 1.15 inches wide, and 1.10 inches thick, hardened to

Equipped with a blade flipper and a spring assist, Kershaw's Link is a self-defense knife masquerading as a work knife.

With a stout pocket clip, a lanyard hole, and an adjustable blade bolster, this knife can proudly wear the US flag imprinted on its side.

55-57Hrc. Its configuration is a modified drop-point with an unsharpened false edge that stops a half-inch from an extremely keen point to maximize tip strength. Fully open, the Link extends to 7.60 inches, closed length is 4.40 inches. Total weight is 4.8 ounces.

The blade surface has a non-reflective black stonewashed finish that Kershaw calls BlackWash. This finish does little to protect the blade from corrosion, but it looks handsome. Wide, flat saber-grind type bevels provide a steep cutting edge for surprising edge retention, and re-sharpening is fast and easy.

The Kershaw name is etched on one side of the blade, but the other carries the Link's intentionally patriotic model number—1776—and the words "Made in USA," and the perhaps surprising word "patented." That last word refers to the fact that this knife is unique in that it is not only equipped with a spring assist, but a Carson Flipper. As described earlier, a Carson Flipper is a spur on the bottom (cutting edge) side of the blade that forms a finger guard when the blade is open, or a trigger-like lever on the top when the knife is closed. Kershaw also refers to the flipper-style opener as SpeedSafe opening, because fingers never need come near the cutting edge when deploying the blade.

By combining the Flipper with a spring assist, Kershaw has made the Link every bit as fast as an automatic, maybe even faster when one considers ease of deployment. Importantly, the knife is equally easy to operate with either hand. Personally, I prefer a larger, heavier blade as a working knife, but the Link has served me well for everything from opening bags of sled-dog food to cutting up wild game and slicing vegetables in the kitchen.

The Link is available in plain-edge version with aluminum handles, as described, or with a partially serrated blade. Retail price for either of these is $40. For about $6 less, you can have a version with a fiberglass-reinforced nylon handle. All have the black stonewashed blade of 420HC, and all carry a limited lifetime guarantee against defects. www.kershaw.kaiusaltd.com.

Mission Knives' ***Katrina MPK10-Ti Search-and-Rescue Knife:*** January 1968, Khe Sanh Valley, South Vietnam. A C-130 sent to resupply leathernecks was shelled as it landed on the steel tarmac, bursting into flames. A marine hammered his Kabar knife against the plexiglas cockpit, trying to break it, but was forced to retreat from flames after the blade snapped.

Lessons like that have not gone unheeded by knife makers, who have always understood that a knife intended for combat must withstand abuses that would destroy a traditional hunting knife. In recent years, steady advances in metallurgy have come far toward achieving an unbreakable blade that never needs maintenance.

There is no perfect knife, but the MPK10-Ti (Multi-purpose Knife, 10 Inch) from Mission Knives represents one of the most tantalizing attempts yet. Its 5.75-inch-long, .250-inch-thick blade is made from Beta Titanium, developed by the Navy for the landing gear of carrier aircraft. It's also known as 6–4 titanium, which translates to 6 percent aluminum, 4 percent vanadium, and 90 percent CP (Commercially Pure) titanium. The result, said its creator and my friend the late John Moore of Mission Knives, is "the strongest spring ever created."

In service with the Navy SEALs and USMC since 1995, the black-handled MPK10-Ti knife has never broken in the field, despite being run over by tracked vehicles, even hit by bullets. In Naval lab tests, the blade withstood bending of thirty-five degrees with no permanent deflection. With the blade secured one-quarter inch from its tip, a load of 850 pounds was required to break it (the existing SEALs' dive knife failed at 350 pounds), with a tensile strength of 230,000 pounds. Technicians judged the MPK10-Ti "a superior design," and it was assigned Government-Issue number NSN-1386-01-417-1263.

Our test knife was sunk one half inch into a poplar log more than fifty times, then snapped sideways. In every instance, the blade tore free, ripping out sizable chunks of wood. The 3.00-inch false edge delivers great penetrating power, while 2.00 inches of serrations enable it to rip through tough rubber hose.

Explosive Ordnance Disposal (EOD) personnel appreciate that titanium is non-magnetic per MIL-M-19595, and the full-tang insulated handle enables it cut live wires. In subzero temperatures, good field knives have become brittle, while titanium has tested stable over a range of -100 degrees F. to 700 degrees F. Saltwater divers like that titanium is unharmed by seawater and acids.

The MPK10's blade has a hardness of only 47Hrc, but the blade sharpens easily and holds an edge well enough—comparable to 440A stainless. The MPK-10 can skin a whitetail before re-edging is needed, but little more. John Moore told

Despite strong arguments from its maker, the molded friction-fit plastic sheath that was first offered with the Katrina search-and-rescue knife did not keep its knife secure, and was replaced by a conventional survival sheath.

me that he was currently experimenting with an anodizing process that would bring hardness up, but that dream seems to have died with him.

The keenest edge for titanium has thus far been achieved by first standing up the edge with a mid-grit aluminum-oxide stone, lubricated with water, honing with the edge. That rough edge is polished on a medium-hard oilstone, again honing with the edge, then stropped to deer-skinning sharpness. Once polished, the slightly dulled edge is easily re-sharpened using a ceramic rod or chef's steel.

The handle of an MPK10 issue knife is identical in shape and composition, with full-tang seating, and Hytrel-impregnated Kevlar construction. Impervious to the elements, age, most chemicals, and abuse, the molded hilt is beefy enough to fill large hands, but comfortable to grip with shorter fingers. The hawk-bill pommel flares outward to keep the knife secure in its user's fist during hard use, and to provide a wider hammering surface. A lanyard hole allows the knife to hang from a wrist when both hands are needed, and lateral grooves in the handle's sides maximize the torque that can be exerted when ripping through the metal siding and OSB of a house wall, or splitting a log in search of fish bait.

The compact molded Hytrel scabbard of the Katrina model is stoutly built of two form-fitting sides, fastened together with rolled hollow rivets that double as eyelets for tying on cord and gear pouches. A hinged quick-release Tek-Lok fastener, similar in principle to the M9 bayonet scabbard, enables the sheath to be attached without unbuckling your belt, and an adjustable spacer ensures a slop-free fit on narrower pack straps. After my field trials showed that it wasn't secure enough, John bolstered the existing friction-fit design with a retaining strap that insured the knife remained sheathed when a job called for low-crawling through the rubble of a collapsed building. The issue MPK10 comes with a more conventionally military hard scabbard, with snap-down retaining strap.

While not an uncommon element, titanium is presently difficult and expensive to refine, so expect that knife blades made from it will not be cheap. With a price tag of $426, the Katrina knife and MPK10 rank among the most expensive real-world survival/rescue knives, but reliability in the field make that a price that many professionals have already shown they're willing to pay. If your daily job might involve anything from prying open a smashed car door to cutting through an airplane fuselage, the Katrina knife can do the tough stuff, and still have enough edge to slice through seat belts. The same toughness and strength makes either MPK10 a pretty great wilderness survival tool, for times

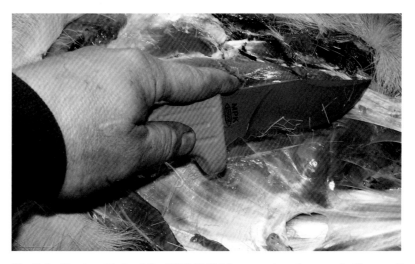

The Beta-titanium blade of the MPK-10 Katrina search-and-rescue knife wasn't hard enough to hold an edge, but it was easy to re-sharpen and it proved impossible to break.

when life might depend on having the most unbreakable tool for shaping an environment to meet your needs.

The Katrina knife, by that name, has been discontinued, but it lives on in the orange-handled MPK-TI, available in overall lengths of ten and twelve inches. If one sounds like a knife that would fit your own emergency-response kit, you can get information about all of Mission Knives' ground-breaking titanium blades by emailing the company's inconvenient (and decidedly unfriendly, I think) message board on their website at: http://www.missionknives.com/

Mora **Bushcraft Survival Knife:** Mora of Sweden has been one of the more innovative knife makers for decades, and Morakniv's new Bushcraft Survival Knife follows a company tradition of making knives that git 'er done in a fashion that would make Larry the Cable Guy proud. Latest in the Bushcraft line, Morakniv's Survival model boasts the same 4.25inch-long clip-point blade as its siblings. A Scandi (a wider, sharper saber grind) edge extends .250 inch up either side of the 9.25-inch-wide blade, whose spine thickness of .100 inch ensures a sharp, thin edge that cuts longer and sharpens fast.

One of the thinnest fixed blades to enter an arena that has been traditionally populated by thick, brutish blades—the Bushcraft Survival boasts a full-tang blade of Sandvik 12C27, hardened to Hrc 57–58. This alloy is renowned among commercial fishing crews for its resistance to corrosion, and for its ability to stay on the job longer between re-sharpenings.

Trials with the Survival included skinning and cutting up almost a dozen whitetails, and the cutting edge stayed shaving sharp through not one but two deer. Even then, it needed only a quick touching-up to restore the original razor edge. The clip point, which follows the knife's center line, demonstrated impressive penetrating power, easily punching through whitetail ribcages.

In keeping with Mora's tendency toward working knives, the Survival keeps the same 5.00-inch handle as its Bushcraft brethren. A core of high-density thermoplastic over the tang is covered by an ergonomically contoured outer layer of very grippy textured black rubber that maintains

The Morakniv Bushcraft Survival knife is another of those that gets brayed about by Internet experts, but it accredited itself well on the ice fields and in the woods.

traction in the hand even when coated with blood and fat. A molded finger choil reinforces the Survival's security in the hand, and molded traction grooves round out the knife's ability to remain firmly gripped in any position.

The Bushcraft Survival's black, molded friction-fit scabbard complements the knife's performance as a field blade with a tab-locked collar and a molded recess for the embedded 2.00-inch x 0.750-inch diamond hone, and an interlocking multi-clip to secure the included Morakniv Swedish Firesteel. With a compass around my neck and this knife, there aren't many wilderness situations that I'd consider life-threatening.

It's my nature to distrust a case that doesn't keep my most prized possession with a retaining strap, but in past years it has been my pleasure to be proven wrong a number of times. Encompassing three inches of the Bushcraft Survival's handle, Mora's scabbard kept the knife through shaking, smacking, even tossing the sheathed blade through the air.

Carry options are provided by a keyed hole that will accommodate a fatigue-style button for the belt-less carry that's popular in Scandinavia. A molded belt loop and belt clip (included) carry cam-locking studs that insert into the scabbard's keyhole at a ninety-degree

Add a compass, and the Morakniv Bushcraft Survival Knife is all you need to keep breathing in any weather.

angle, and tighten as they're rotated into position. For low-carry, the belt loop can be locked to the belt clip, enabling the sheathed knife to be quickly taken off for cleaning without unbuckling your belt. The molded belt clip is too narrow to accept the wider trousers belts preferred by American outdoorsmen.

It has been an enjoyable pastime for self-avowed knife experts who hang out on Internet knife forums to bad-mouth this knife, although few detractors have seen it, and fewer still are experienced in woodcraft, but this is one survival instructor who would buy this knife for his grandchild. Retail for this half-pound of good life insurance is an affordable $54.65. For more information contact: www.moraofsweden-usa.com; telephone: +46 250–59 50 00.

Pro Tool Industries *J. Wayne Fears Ultimate Survival Knife:* The Ultimate Survival Knife. That's a pretty huge title to claim in this world of super alloys, automated machining, precision hardening processes, and so many synthetic materials that the words plastic and steel aren't even applicable anymore. So when I set out to evaluate Pro Tool Industries' J. Wayne Fears Ultimate Survival Knife, it was with the slightly raised eyebrow that I might present to someone who'd just claimed to have invented the Internet.

It wasn't really surprising that the USK's 5.00-inch-long, .120-inch-thick blade (9.75 inches overall) full-tang blade was ground from 1095, the original high-carbon knife steel, hardened to 58–59 Hrc. 1095's properties of edge retention and strength are surpassed by few modern alloys. Pro Tool's Mark Scheifley explained to me that 1095 was mandated by the Fears design team because

"It embodies the traditional values that are a hallmark of the Fears line." Scheifley added with pride that not only is the Ultimate Survival Knife made in Pottstown, Pennsylvania, USA, but so are all of the components used in its assembly, including blade steel.

Critics point to 1095's tendency to rust, but that's less a concern in the field than during storage, because a worn knife is typically used numerous times throughout a day, and at least wiped against a trousers leg after each use.

What it states on the box is a mighty, mighty big claim.

The Fear's survival knife's semi-hollow-ground edge extends .440 inch up its 1.040-inch-wide blade, creating a good balance between a strong spine and a sharp edge. To provide maximum strength, the spine remains full thickness until it meets the concave ground edge, 1.00 inch into its 1.625-inch-long clip-point tip. Black baked-on powder coat protects the blade except where it's hollow-ground, and adds a nice two-tone scheme for a short time.

Also mandated by the Fears team is the USK's "man-size" 4.750-inch-long contoured handle consisting of hunter-orange G-10 scales mated to a full tang by Allen-head screws. G-10 material has already proved to be all but indestructible for handling knives that see rough use. Remove its handles, and the USK's tang can be comfortably wrapped with ten feet of para-cord, which can serve to lash the blade to a staff when a spear is needed.

Our sample's sheath was a simple affair: black Cordura shell, double-stitched piping over all exposed edges; a pair of one-inch Velcro-fastened straps secured the hilt, top and bottom. Carry options are limited to whatever utility you can get from the sheath's conventional 2.50-inch belt loop. When walking, our knife rattled against the molded insert that protects the outer sheath from the USK's edge. It has no pouches for survival tools.

A light-bladed, fairly decent knife in a pretty lousy sheath; this knife is absolutely not the ultimate survival, hunting, fishing, or apple-peeling knife.

Pro Tool Industries' ad claims, "Whether the day calls for digging, shelter making, prying, fire building or cleaning game this knife can do it all." After lengthy field trials, I'll only say that you could do worse than the J. Wayne Fears Ultimate Survival Knife in a survival situation.

Priced at $149.95 (plus s&h), the Fears Ultimate Survival Knife, bears a lifetime no-questions-asked replacement warranty. For more information: www.protoolindustries.net or (800) 708–5191.

The Ritter **RSK Mk-5 from CRKT:** The woodsman lost his rifle while scaling a rocky cliff face; so he speared fish, snared game, and made a bow and arrows. Next, his backpack was swept away while fording a swollen river; so he built shelter, twisted cattail fibers into rope, and ate wild plants. Then one day the woodsman misplaced his knife; after that, he died.

The Ritter Survival Knife, Mark 5 reflects an understanding of the life-saving value a cutting tool has in daily life, whether the jungle is concrete or forest. Created by Doug Ritter, of the Equipped to Survive website (www.equipped.org) in collaboration with designer David White—himself creator of the Shrewd Survival Knife (SSK), the RSK Mk 5 reflects Ritter's credo that "If it isn't with you, it can't save you."

Latest in a line of survival knives born of Ritter's creativity, this survival knife defines bare-bones practicality. With an overall length of just 3.81 inches, the Mk. 5 is hardly a Rambo knife; as CRKT states, "this is not a knife you would use all day for normal work tasks." The little skeletonized knife isn't intended to be the best knife, it's intended to be the one that you have with you. Its 1.75-inch long blade can't whack through the pelvic bones of an elk, but it guarantees that you always have a cutting tool. The contoured skeleton handle and 1.74-inch-wide blade are ground from a single piece of 3Cr13 stainless, hardened to Hrc of 52–55, and stone-washed to a non-reflective satin finish. Gimping on its spine provides grip and control.

Capitalizing on survivalists' penchant for attempting to turn hinged-top metal Sucrets (later Altoids mints) boxes into survival kits, survival authority Doug Ritter partnered with CRKT to produce a miniature survival system.

With its 2.06-inch-long handle held by the first two or three fingers on one side, and thumb pressure from the opposite, this little knife rates being called a survival knife. The skeleton frame of the handle can be wrapped with cord, increasing its girth, while ensuring that its user has a ready supply of cordage.

The lanyard that comes with the RSK Mk5 is a functional part of the knife: By holding the cord in your fist, or looping it over one finger, the lanyard helps to keep the knife more stable in your grip. And I like the fact that the multi-colored cord makes the knife harder to lose.

Because no piece of gear is useful if it isn't available, the Ritter Mk. 5 offers two habit-causing carry modes: around the neck on a lanyard, safely in place but available in a molded glass-reinforced nylon sheath, or as part of a survival kit in the included hinge-top metal box. The box, identical to Altoids-brand mint cans but marked with the CRKT logo, exploits the compulsion of outdoors lovers to organize equipment into kits. Altoids and Sucrets boxes have been used for pocket survival kits for generations. Our test knife fit into the box with room left for a full-size disposable butane lighter, a small compass, a dozen fish hooks, split-shot, and a twenty-foot coil of fishing line. A length of paper towel folded into the box's bottom keeps contents from rattling, and elastic hair ties hold the lid shut through hard knocks. The kit also contains a list of survival tips composed by Doug Ritter.

Although it would never be a first choice, the little Ritter knife could actually be made functionally stable by wrapping its short lanyard around your fingers.

Buttoned down in a breast or cargo pocket, this kit holds the Basic Three— knife, compass, and fire starter—plus a few amenities, and carries unnoticed. Suggested retail for the RSK Mk. 5 is $26.99, which includes hinged metal box, knife, and friction-fit molded sheath. https://www.crkt.com/rsk-mk5

Schrade *Viper, Out-the-Front Opening, 3rd Generation:* Schrade's Viper line of out-the-front knives are cool on the level of a Star Wars light saber. They're completely legal (except in California, New York, and Massachusetts), meeting the requirements of an assisted-opening knife, but the authoritative "snap" as the blade springs out to its locked position might make it appear to be an automatic to untrained eyes. We evaluated the Generation 3 version of the SCHFOTF3B model for more than six months, and this is what we found:

With a closed length of 5.300 inches (8.800 inches open), a width of 1.00 inch, and a thickness of .600 inch, the 3B Viper is a fist-filler. Its aluminum handles are inletted with circuit-board-like lines that actually increase grip traction. A stout steel pocket clip, .400-inch wide by 2.400-inch long, mounts securely to the Viper's butt end for right-side tip-down carry only; as a southpaw, I did not find that at all inconvenient. On the opposite side of the butt is a safety lever with a red dot. When the dot is covered, the blade is locked inside; when the dot is revealed, the blade is unlocked.

Mounted to the end of the butt is a solid steel conical stud, .200 inch tall by .250 inch in diameter. Schrade can't seem to decide whether or not this is a glass-breaker—and the tactical crowd predictably claims that it's a skull-breaker; in fact, it works well in either capacity. A mass of just 4.90 ounces requires that you wield it with a purpose, though.

Schrade's 3rd generation Viper gets points just for being cool.

A large slide-button, .700 inch long, .200 inch wide, and .250 inch tall is located on the top side at the knife's butt. With the safety disengaged (red dot showing), slide the button forward .350 inch, and its spring takes over, propelling the blade forward until it locks. There is no more spring tension than is needed to engage the blade lock: Tests show that opening force is barely sufficient to drive the point one half inch through a paper plate. The point will draw blood if you open it against your palm, but little more.

Our Viper's spear-point (dagger) blade is 3.500 inches long, .700 inch wide, .120 inch thick, and double-edged. The bottom, main cutting edge is 3.500 inches long; the upper, secondary edge is 2.750 inches long. The blade's alloy is 4034 (equivalent to AISI 420J), hardened to 50-52Hrc. This is the steel that many Gil Hibben-style fantasy knives are made from, and although it can be made very sharp, it cannot be expected to retain that edge beyond a single use.

In this instance, that alloy is a good choice, because a double-edge configuration is inherently weak, and a harder alloy with better edge retention would be likely to snap off at its tip. In our tests, the tip bent slightly, but did not break.

This is not a knife that you'd choose as an everyday work knife—lack of edge retention alone disqualifies it on that count. But if you want a backstreet get-out-of-trouble coupon whose formidable looks and authoritative "snick" as its blade suddenly appears and locks into place are sufficient to buy you at least a little time, there are certainly worse choices. For $64, the Viper may be the least

It wouldn't be the first choice for an everyday carry knife (many regions forbid carrying double-edged knives in any case), but it wouldn't be an unwelcome possession in a dark parking garage late at night

expensive insurance you can buy. The warranty is a little fine-printy for me, since Schrade changed hands from Taylor Brands to Battenfeld Technologies, but you'll probably never need it. www .btibrands.com

Schrade's **NaviTool:** There has never been an ultimate survival tool; the very concept is a chimera. If you think of the needs of living as an inverted pyramid, with the most essential need as its cap, and lesser requirements following in order of importance, even the most spartan survival kit needs to perform a half-dozen tasks.

Schrade was a contender for the title of Ultimate Survival Tool with their re-engineered NaviTool. Schrade fans might recognize the NaviTool's configuration from an original version that didn't exactly take the outdoor survival market by storm. Morgan Taylor, then president of Schrade's parent company, Taylor Brands, LLC, described the resurrection as "just reproducing something originally conceived by Schrade before we took over."

There has never been a survival tool that could serve every need, but the Schrade Navi-Tool came pretty close.

"It has been a nightmare to produce and might still need tweaking," Taylor said. This second generation didn't make much of a splash, either, and has since been discontinued—a loss for recreational outdoor adventurers, I think.

The NaviTool that I took into the field measures 6.9 inches long, 2.4 inches tall, and 2.5 inches wide, and weighed 8.1 ounces. The housing is black plastic, with a crenellated rubberized grip strip on the palm side. The unit may be carried in its black ballistic nylon belt case, or it can be clipped to a belt or strap using a spring-loaded clip.

On the blade side are six locking fold-out tools, made from 3Cr13 stainless, hardened to 54–56 Hrc. There's a classic thumbnail-notch, 2.7-inch-long drop-point work blade; a combination Philips screwdriver/bottle opener/wire-bending jig; a sharp scissors with spring-loaded handle; a 2.7-inch saw blade with aggressive multi-bevel teeth; and, finally, a working can opener tipped by a flat screwdriver.

On the outer side is a large knob with Schrade Tough printed in white at its center. Twist the knob a quarter-turn, and it comes free—tethered to the unit by its own lanyard to the heavier wrist lanyard—to reveal an induction-dampened, declination-adjustable, luminous, rotating-dial compass, 2.6 inches in diameter. Opposite that, inset into the body, is a 1.4-inch-diameter stainless-steel mirror that lacks the sighting hole needed to send intelligible flash signals. Also attached to the lanyard is loud signal whistle.

Below the compass knob is a push-button red LED map light that enables the NaviTool to perform the seldom addressed function of night navigation. Bright enough to read compass and map by, the infra-red spectrum doesn't trigger radical pupil dilation and loss of night vision like white light. On the other end is a flip-top compartment, 3.0 inches by 0.6 inch by 1.0 inch, that can accommodate numerous small items.

In field trials, the NaviTool performed up to expected Schrade standards. The saw cuts wood easily, the knife is sharp, the can opener actually works, blade locks are positive, and manufacturing tolerances are apparently tight. It is a good idea to check the snugness of the Allen-head screws used to assemble the NaviTool, though; the corkscrew on our sample had a tendency to loosen at the hinge screw.

The NaviTool is too convenient and too useful, with too many carry options, for it to ever be left behind. It isn't the ideal tool for any of the functions it provides, but it has proved itself capable of performing a multitude of tasks with the efficacy needed to earn a thumbs-up from this old cynic. Suggested retail for the NaviTool was $53.95. www.btibrands.com

The Navi-Tool traveled many miles through the million-acres of Lake Superior State Forest, and its numerous capabilities proved their usefulness many times.

Schrade Phantom Spear: After six decades in the woods, I rarely get impressed by a cutting tool, but the Phantom spear from Schrade (now a subsidiary of Battenfeld Technologies) has become a must-have in my outdoor kit.

Several companies have made spears for decades, but their focus has been on re-creating replicas of spears that have been used historically. The result has been that spears, as valuable as they have been in the development of humankind, have remained essentially unchanged.

Schrade, under the creative genius of Taylor Industries, has reinvented the spear with their Phantom line. The three models in the line are fitted with double-edged blades of 3Cr13 stainless, but the SP1 has a more contemporary smooth dagger-type blade. The SP2 and SP3 carry an oversized arrowhead and a dagger blade, respectively, but both of these have the appearance of knapped stone. We took the SP1 version—which has since been inexplicably discontinued (the SP2 and SP3 have not)—into the field.

The SP1 has a 7.220-inch-long double-edged blade, 1.500-inch wide and .310 inch thick. A fuller, .040 inch deep and .210 inch wide extends 3.860 inches down the center of the blade, 2.750 inches from the tip to give it plenty of strength. A black textured powder coat protects the blade

All but lost in the mists of time, a sharp, short-handled spear was the original and perhaps deadliest of close-quarters weapons against man or beast.

and makes it invisible at night. A full tang seats the blade 4.250 inches into the center of the shaft with three star-drive Chicago screws; if necessary, the blade could be mounted to a short handle and converted to a knife. When not in use—or when I'm using the spear as a hiking staff—its sharp head is covered by a thick form-fitting rubber boot.

The round spear shaft is 36.940 inches long, with a diameter 1.050 inches. Three molded-in bumps just below the head help to locate a wielder's forward hand in the dark, as do two nine-inch wraps of parachute cord on the shaft. The spear shaft has a fiberglass core over-molded with fiber-reinforced nylon in a system that Schrade designers call an Enhanced Flexibilizer. A 15.650-inch-long (10.90 ounces), paracord-wrapped, screw-in extender can be added to the spear for $25, increasing its total length to 52.590 inches.

A buttcap at the end of the shaft, fitted with a .200-inch-diameter lanyard hole, screws off to reveal a 1.760-inch by .240-inch flint rod embedded in the cap. Beneath that, in the shaft, is a 5.700-inch-deep cavity. This cavity houses a cylindrical 2.160-inch-long capsule containing fishing gear and needles, with room to spare for other small items.

As a close-range weapon, whether for hunting, fishing, or close-quarters combat, a short spear has few equals. Fish have always been heedless of being speared, a spear can reach into a hiding rabbit's den, and it has historically outmatched most cutting weapons. The trick is not to throw it, except as a last resort, but to use its reach advantage to slash, stab, block, or even bludgeon with the butt end. A Quirinus ("Wielder of the Spear") footsoldier was a formidable enemy, alone or in ranks.

Adding versatility that our forebears never had, the SCHFSP1 Spear incorporates a fire starter and a survival tools capsule under a screw cap in its butt.

Retail for any of the Phantom spears is approximately $65, although at the time of this writing, with Battenfeld having recently taken over the Schrade name, that price appears to be on the cusp of changing. For the latest information, visit www.btibrands.com.

SOG *Strat Ops Auto Folder:* This automatic is all business. From its sleek, slim style, with an obvious eye toward leaving no protrusions to its buffered action to superb fit-and-finish, if I were going to describe the new-for-2017 SOG Strat Ops automatic-deploying folding knife by using a single term, that would be "simple elegance." This tool is all-go, with lines that are just plain pretty in the same way that a ballcap-wearin', bib-overalls-clad young woman with a sharp knife on her hip, bright eyes, and a pigtail is exceptionally attractive to rank-and-file American males.

The Strat Ops has a 3.5-inch-long, .870-inch-wide, .110-inch-thick clip-point blade of S35VN, with 2.00 inches of false edge. Closed length is 4.400 inches and total weight is 3.70 ounces. Its

SOG's Strat Ops Automatic is beautiful in its plain, no-frills, all-business approach; it flicks open smoothly, with nothing to snag, catch, or impede its speed of deployment.

independently tough steel blade carries a protective black coating of Cerakote—a rugged, wear-resistant thin-film ceramic often used to lubricate and protect hard-working, close-tolerance fire-arms. It has a very respectable hardness factor of 59-61Hrc, but S35V is renowned because it is tougher and holds its edge better than its older brother, S30V. Ten gimping grooves, extending .480 inch along the spine from the choil, provide no-slip security

The *"N"* in S35VN's designation represents the addition of Niobium—a very hard refractory ceramic used on drill bits—to a homogenous powdered alloy. Niobium helps metallurgists to control a metal's grain length and size, which assists in regulating hardness, and tightening hardness disparities that might occur along the length of a blade. It also adds some very hard carbon nodules to the mix. Gone (hopefully) are the days when even reputedly good knives were both hard

The SOG Strat Ops isn't a wilderness survival blade, but if you're in a community of any size when the proverbial ball drops, this might be the knife you'd most want under your palm.

enough to chip and soft enough to bend on the same blade, and the Strat Ops is demonstration of that.

The Strat Ops black linen-micarta handles are so precisely machined that they don't look like linen-micarta, but rather aluminum. They're .850 inch wide by .450 inch thin, and .850 inch at its thinnest point (center), swelling out a little wider at the choil and butt. Aside from four inletted .100-inch wide by .025-inch deep, these "traction bars" enhance grip, while keeping the knife sleek and smooth. SOG claims that these handles become more attractive as they wear—we'll see.

Experiences with automatic knives that have tried to deploy in a pocket indicate that a safety mechanism might be a welcome addition. More experiences have shown them to be correct. The Strat Ops safety locks the blade both open and closed. It is simple to reach, strong, easy to find by feel, without looking, and it stays where it's put.

Dependability, speed of deployment, and top-of-the-line from its cut-on-touch S35VN blade to the deepest-riding pocket clip on the market, SOG's Strat Ops automatic makes a statement that says, "I'm here to do business." This is the knife that an Old West gunfighter would have carried.

Retail is $254, and the Strat Ops shows no sign of being discontinued any time soon. www.sogknives.com.

TOPS ***Armageddon:*** "Big, thick and heavy. This is the North American version of a machete." Based on a magazine article, this is TOPS's description of its relatively new Armageddon survival knife.

Based on its looks alone, this knife is a hit with almost everyone who saw it even in a photo. Designer Trace Rinaldi hit a home run so far as aesthetics. The big knife measures 16.500 inches long overall, with a blade length of 10.630 inches, of which 10.000 inches is cutting edge. Its semi-bolo, clip-point blade is forged of TOPS's trademark 1095 carbon steel, .750 inch thick, with Black Traction Coating protecting it from the elements. The left side of the blade, just ahead of its choil, bears the trademarks of Trace Rinaldi and TOPS in gold.

Although advertised as an "American Machete," TOPS's Armageddon is too hard for hacking woods, and is quite clearly a big fighting knife.

With a weight of twenty-four ounces, the Armageddon has the inertial punch to serve as a typically heavy North Woods machete, but 1095 steel hardened to 56-58Hrc proved to be a bit too brittle for use as a machete—I broke a small chip out of mine. However, a unique edge grind that tapers wider as it approaches its bolo tip makes the curved belly—typically the most difficult portion of a knife to sharpen—easy to get a shaving edge onto. A finger choil —a half-moon shaped indentation—allows an index finger to get a secure purchase nearer to the blade's balance point. The geometry of this blade makes it versatile for everything from butchering a deer to trimming branches from a shelter support, but it would not be my first choice as a machete. The niche of North-Woods machete is already claimed by a number of big knives that do the job better.

The Armageddon's black linen Micarta handle is 1.5 inches wide by .830 inch wide. A second, deeper finger choil in the handle, behind the one in the blade, provides for multiple grip positions, with enhanced tip control. A lighter colored gray spacer separates the Micarta scales from the tang, making it easier to remove the three Allen-head screws and disassemble the knife for cleaning. The pommel is an extension of the tang beyond the handle scales; a pair of .250-inch lanyard holes make the knife easier to tie to a spear shaft. A steel hook formed into the bottom of the pommel ostensibly helps to keep the knife from sliding forward in your grip, but knives with that feature have always proved to be hard on a user's little finger.

The Armageddon's ballistic nylon sheath is a little light for my tastes, but pretty well designed, with two large clip-shut gear pouches that can hold the Basic Three, as well as more than a few other small items. The back of the sheath is MOLLE compatible, which essentially means that it will mount to almost everything. The Armageddon, as released by the factory, scores high as a candidate for a no-bull backwoods survival knife.

In field trials, the Armageddon shone brightly as a flesh-cutting knife.

The Armageddon was released with a retail price over $300. At this time, TOPS has a price tag of $295 on the knife. If you like what you see (a surprising number of people have fallen in love with this blade), visit www.topsknives.com/armageddon.

TOPS *Tom Brown Mini-Tracker #4:*

The Tom Brown Mini-Tracker #4 from TOPS Knives is a miniaturized version of the Tracker knife made famous by Benicio del Toro in the movie *The Hunted*. As the movie depicted, a knife's effectiveness as tool or weapon depends on its wielder, and the Mini Tracker has proved more useful than its larger, more unwieldy predecessors.

Despite being made into a movie star, the TOPS Tracker #1 is not a first choice among experienced survival instructors, but the smaller size of the Tracker #4 makes it a truly functional anytime/anywhere survival knife when a full-size blade isn't possible.

With a blade length of 3.25 inches, the Tracker #4 is legal for open carry in many municipalities, while an overall length of 6.50 inches makes it both concealable and comfortable enough to wear all day. Being a fixed blade, the Tom Brown Mini Tracker enjoys the strength of full-tang design, backed up by a blade of classic 1095 high-carbon spring-steel, .125 inch thick, and hardened to an edge-holding 56–58 HRC.

Directly ahead of the choil is a small notch that will accommodate most flint-rod fire starters. Ahead of that is a recessed draw edge, 1.50 inches long, for whittling and scraping tasks. From there the blade widens to 1.30 inches and forms a sweeping belly, 1.90 inches long, that is ideal for skinning and filleting chores. Five gimping grooves opposite the choil provide purchase for finger or thumb. Ahead of those is a gentle depression, 1.50 inches long by .140 inch deep, that accommodates an index finger for delicate chores. Broached into the spine near the blade's tip are six very aggressive teeth.

The Mini's blade is protected from the elements by TOPS's non-reflective Black Traction Coating. For collectors, etched into the left side of the blade is a facsimile of Tom Brown Jr.'s signature and logo. Below those is the Mini Tracker's part number and name.

The knife's gray linen Micarta handle scales are held in place by three Allen-head Chicago screws; the TOPS logo is pressed into left-side scale. A red spacer between tang and each scale makes a pleasant contrast between the two. The lanyard hole is lined with brass, 0.80 inch in diameter. Handle dimensions are 3.14 inches long by .440 inch thick, but the smallish size is compensated for by a smartly ergonomic handle that provides a secure grip in all positions, even when your little finger is curled over the pommel end.

The Tracker #4 is encased by a folded one-piece Zytel friction-fit scabbard whose edges are secured by three roll-staked brass grommets. A blued spring-steel belt-clip, 1.25 inches wide, with three round and two slotted mounting holes, enables the case to be attached in a variety of orientations to almost any belt or strap using the two included Allen-head Chicago screws.

I'm suspicious of friction-fit scabbards without retaining straps, but the Mini Tracker #4's sheath refused to come loose from my belt. Or you can remove the clip and hang the sheathed knife from around your neck by its lan-

The Mini-Tracker #4 from TOPS proved itself to be just the thing for a lady on an ad-hoc blueberry-picking excursion.

yard hole. The knife, which pushes into the sheath with a reassuring snap, never came loose, even when worn inside a sleeping bag for several nights.

Retail for the Mini Tom Brown Jr. Tracker #4 is $170. For more information about the Mini Tom Brown Jr. #4, visit www.topsknives.com or call (208) 542–0113.

Randall's **RAT Pack Survival System:** The human compulsion to organize equipment is instinctive: In a wilderness, where what you brought is what you'll use to shape an environment into something less hostile, a survival kit must be practical, packed with items that are essential in most circumstances. At least as important, those tools must be ensconced in a unit that is handy, and too convenient to ever leave behind.

The RAT Pack survival kit from Randall Adventure Training and Escuela de Supervivencia, Escape and Evasion, discontinued almost immediately after being introduced, is designed to meet the most basic survival needs in any situation. The outfit begins with a heavily zipper-shut case of rugged ripstop Cordura. In the front is a quick-release buckled flap over a large pocket; the outer pocket carries four heavy elastic bandolier loops, and four separate elastic pockets below them. The closed kit is MOLLE compatible.

Unzip the kit and it opens like a book, revealing one large eight-inch-long by seven-inch-deep pouch between the kit's inner and outside walls. Inside are mesh-covered pockets, two on the right, one full-length pocket on the left. You may select either an RC-6 flat-ground or RC-5 sabre-ground survival knife, both with a heavy baked-on black powder coat over high-carbon 6.5-inch blade of 1095 spring steel (HRC 57). Slab Micarta scales and contoured handle ensure a firm grip when the knife is slippery. An overall length of 11.75 inches gives the RC-6 leverage for prying open rotting logs to find insects, while a blade width of 1.56 inches and spine thickness of .188 inch provide brute strength for hard use. Instead of a conventional retaining strap to keep the knife's blade caged in its simple Zytel sheath, the knife is retained by twelve inches of elastic shock-cord wrapped around its handle and secured to a buckle at the kit's outer hinge point.

Oddly, the RAT Pack didn't catch on with outdoorsmen, despite its convenience and life-saving versatility, and it was discontinued, although a few can still be found with Internet sellers.

Randall satisfies the need for fire with a beefy flint-and-steel sparking tool. The tool's .375-inch-diameter by 1.75-inch-long flint rod produces arc-welder-like sparks when scraped hard with a knife blade. The sparks are bright enough to signal across open spaces at night, and the 2.750-inch by 1.00-inch handle is marked with small but clear survival tips.

Inside the fire starter's screw-capped handle rests a .750-inch diameter compass. Small enough for a kidnapped DEA agent to swallow, the little dial compass enables a survivor to navigate almost any wilderness. Its black dial is contrasted by the four directions in fluorescent green, with white graduations of ten degrees marked around the bezel, and midpoint (NE, SE . . .) markings. There was still enough free space inside the handle to accept a Wetfire chemical tinder cube, too, which gave the fire tool all-weather capability.

Included with the RAT Pack is a Smith's Diamond Retractable Sharpener: carried inside its own anodized aluminum handle is a diamond-impregnated sharpening steel, tapered on one half to accommodate serrated edges, and round with one flat honing surface at the other. A longitudinal groove in one side even sharpens fish hooks. The sharpener stores in a tube molded into one edge of the knife's Zytel scabbard, itself fastened to the sheath with a screw grommet that during field trials came loose, letting the sheath fall from the blade while the knife corkscrewed on its unwinding tether.

Standard are two Navy-approved zipper-lock bags, one with a volume of sixty cubic inches, the other 25.3 cubic inches. These bags can contain their own kits, serve as emergency canteens, or can be sealed and tucked inside a shirt as flotation devices.

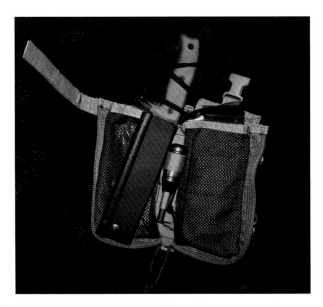

Although the belt-carried RAT Pack came provisioned with basic survival tools, it left plenty of room for additional small items—even snacks.

My sample carried three one-inch-wide "Ranger bands" cut from bicycle inner tube, and a 6.5-inch length of tube from which to cut more—it speaks well that ESEE places function over fashion when lives are at stake. There was room left to tuck away safety tape, a whistle, fishing kit, a flashlight, matches, Fire Wicks, and twenty feet of paracord.

The RAT Pack gets two thumbs up from this survival instructor. It shows a move in promising directions and out-of-the-box thinking. MSRP was $187. info@eseeknives.com or call (256) 613–0372.

Blade-Tech's **RIJBAK Folding Field Knife:** The RIJBAK tactical/hunting folder from Blade-Tech has what it takes to become a best friend. Designed by Canadian backwoodsman Greg Lightfoot, the RIJBAK reflects Lightfoot's unique experience with using a knife as both a lethal weapon and as a tool during the wild boar hunts. Many farmers can confirm Lightfoot's contention that maximum power is required to inflict a fatal wound to these dangerous, thick-skinned animals. Few

Slim and otherwise heavily built, the RIJBAK folder with its S30V blade promised to be an excellent working knife, until its pocket clip broke in two.

hides are tougher on a knife's edge, and no chore is a better test of how much grip its handle provides.

While not a full-size "pig sticker," the RIJBAK is a contender for anyone who needs a knife that can work for a living. The RIJBAK's 3.750-inch spear-point blade is plain, because as Lightfoot pointed out during our interview, serrations tend to snag against hide when skinning. The surgically keen S30V blade is .150 inch thick, with a flat-ground edge hardened to 58-60Hrc. A 2.500-inch false edge, with blade point axially aligned with the handle, gives the RIJBAK penetrating power, while the false edge becomes thicker toward the point to maximize tip strength for stabbing, prying, and drilling. It's a point of pride at Blade-Tech that none of the company's knives has ever suffered a broken tip.

Our test RIJBAK's titanium liner-lock was very tight, right out of the box. Blade-Tech's Mikey Vellekamp told me that this is intentional, the objective being to maximize the functional life of the lock.

"This is a working person's knife," Vellekamp told me. "Our objective is to make a high-quality knife, regardless of profit, and we think the RIJBAK offers a whole lot of bang for its price."

Hinge action of my RIJBAK was tight, even a little gritty, but the opened blade locks with vault-like strength—this lock isn't likely to cave under pressure. Frequent washes in hot, soapy water had my test RIJBAK feeling silky after a few days of normal use.

The RIJBAK should have been a great knife.

The knife's spring-steel pocket clip was a disappointment. It was New Year's Eve, and I was shoveling three feet of wet, very heavy snow from our barn roof. Unseasonably warm weather that hovered at the freezing mark made this snow dangerously heavy to the roof trusses, while rendering the steel sheeting beneath treacherously slick. When my feet went out from under me, I wriggled as I slid toward the fifteen-foot drop until I was on my butt. I slid off the eaves into darkness and landed hard on my left hip. I was uninjured, but the steel pocket clip of my RIJBAK had snapped in half just below its mounting screws. A voicemail left with Customer Service went unanswered; a written email was ignored. I did not feel obligated to take further action.

File-textured G-10 handle overlays provide strong gripping power against fabric. The knife itself is assembled using twelve-point screws, because, as Vellekamp observed, the knife should not be disassembled by its owner.

The RIJBAK gets high marks in ergonomics. During field trials that included butchering two whitetails, the knife never felt slippery, even when covered with blood and fat. A lanyard hole in the butt allows the knife to hang from a wrist, while a large teardrop-shaped thumb hole gives the RIJBAK deployment speed.

MSRP of the RIJBAK is $280. If you'd like more information about the Lightfoot-designed RIJBAK, contact: www.bladetech.com, phone (253) 581–4347.

Rapid River **Redi-Axe:** I'm from Michigan, so it stands to reason that I'd prefer to showcase a knife maker from my home state, already popular—rather, notorious—for automobiles, street crime, and the only melted-down plutonium reactor in the US.

To be bluntly honest (my trademark), it took a bit of searching to find a native knife maker that I'd be willing to brag about. In the end, there was only one. (Two, actually, but Dave Shirley of Northwoods Knives passed away, may his soul rest in the peace he deserves.) If I were to select a knife from a Michigan blade master, it would be from Kris Duerson of Rapid River Knife Works, in Rapid River, Michigan.

The Redi-Axe is a pack axe from a designer who knows how to make knives for the wild North Woods; it more than proved itself in an environment where brutal work is the norm, and in temperatures that have broken many a world-class knife.

Rapid River is noteworthy for preferring A2 Tool Steel as the alloy of choice. A generation ago, a knife made from this alloy was difficult to manufacture, and it was a pricey proposition. Better tooling, and innovations like cutting steel with a super-pressurized stream of water (Rapid River's method of cutting out its blanks), have made it feasible to craft knives and tools from steel. Blades aren't usually notably harder on the Rockwell scale (largely to facilitate ease of re-sharpening), but A2 and its ilk are tougher and offer increased edge retention at the same hardness values as conventional skills.

Having already had a dozen years' experience with Rapid River's classic Drop-Point Hunter, the product selected for review here was the company's new-for-2017 Redi-Axe pack axe. Designed primarily for processing meat, this little axe is just 9.250 inches long and nine ounces, and made from a single piece of steel. Rapid River advertises it at "a full quarter inch thick," but my sample measured from .280-.295 inch—thicker than advertised.

The handle is a beefy .700 inch wide, leading up to a head that measures 1.850 inches wide, with a slightly convex cutting edge that has a linear length of 2.450 inches. Edge bevels are at twenty-five degrees, each extending .310 inch up the blade. Just below the head, mounted into insets in the handle by two Allen head screws, are a pair of replaceable carbide cutters; the cutters are not for the axe, but serve as a pull-through sharpener for keeping your knife keen.

The axe held its functional factory edge well through three deer, including chopping through heavy bones. When it had dulled, a half hour of work on the tool-marked edge with aluminum-oxide stone, a diamond hone, and, lastly, a leather strop, had it sharp enough to skin a deer.

The hand-finished walnut handle on my Redi-Axe, held there by two brass rivets, made it .810 inch thick by .730 inch wide. The handle is too small for my hands, especially while wearing gloves. The head, while light, can divide the largest bone, not as easily or as quickly as a full-size axe, but certainly faster than a skinning knife.

Although its polished wooden handle is display quality, it could use a larger circumference for those frigid temperatures that require heavy gloves or mittens.

The most endearing quality of the Redi-Axe, so far as I'm concerned, is its brute strength. It is as near to unbreakable as a tool has ever been. If you're a fan of batoning wood, go for it. Or, if the little axe lacks the mass to chop through a moose pelvis, it does no harm to pound it through like a wedge.

The warranty is typical, in that it covers only factory defects, not user-inflicted damage. However, Rapid River provides free sharpening and polishing for as long as you own the knife (you pay shipping and handling). Retail for the Redi-Axe is $175. www.rapidriverknifeworks.us; phone (906) 474–9444.

Schrade's ***SCHF9 Extreme Survival Knife:*** Designed by knife maker Brian Griffin, the SCHF9 begins with the foundation of a 6.4-inch-thick blade crafted from the 1095 steel that made the Kabar USMC knife a legend. But the SCHF9 begins with the advantage of being made from more homogenous stock, and hardened by processes that didn't exist when the USMC knife was government-issue. (Note that some early literature mistakenly identified the SCHF9's blade steel as 1070, but Schrade has assured me that it is in fact 1095.)

Made from classic 1095 high-carbon steel, built brutally strong, and designed by Brian Griffin, a skilled woodsman in his own right, Schrade's Extreme Model 9 is one of the world's finest survival knives, despite an almost ridiculously low price.

A blade thickness of .240 inch along its spine gives the 15.9-ounce SCHF9 the backbone to pry open car doors. And because it's hardened to Hrc 57–58, you don't sacrifice the edge retention that continues to make this steel a favorite among chefs and meat-cutters who cannot work without a sharp knife. Rust is kept from the blade by a layer of gray DuPont Teflon. (Do yourself and your knife a favor by not removing this protective finish).

I didn't mind skinning a whitetail deer with the SCHF9; by the end of the job it had lost its keen edge, but a few strokes on a Smith's Diamond bench stone and a quick stropping, and it was back to razor-sharp. A series of five gimping grooves milled into the tang, just behind the choil, are intended to be a thumb- or finger-rest for skinning, but those on my sample were too rounded to provide a secure rest.

The SCHF9's handle is two Kraton scales mounted to a full tang by four Allen-head screws on each side, giving the hilt a beefy feel in the hand. The surfaces of the scales are molded into a pattern of overlapping concentric rings that provide a sticky surface when the handle is greasy. A flared butt makes it harder to lose grip when chopping (many a tired machete wielder has involuntarily launched his blade when fatigued muscles gave out). A cutout in the Kraton scales at the pommel reveals a lanyard hole through the tang only.

In keeping with the pragmatic theme of this knife, the SCHF9's black ballistic nylon sheath is multi-functional. At first glance it appears that the sheath is right-hand only, but the round-head rivet at the bottom of the sheath pries apart, freeing the liner so that it can be reversed for left-hand carry.

The SCHF9's sheath incorporates a detachable cargo pouch for outfitting the knife as a complete basic survival kit. There was enough room in our sample's cargo pouch to hold a Blast Match fire starter and a working-size compass, with space left over for a fishing kit and a small folding knife.

The Schrade's sheath has a quick-release belt loop for conventional wear on the hip, and its back is MOLLE compatible. When worn on the waist, the snapped-in knife "breaks" comfortably at the hip joint, not bridging it and inhibiting flexibility like some sheaths. The hilt's retaining strap is uniquely adjustable.

The SCHF9 performed well in field trials. Its balance point and finger-friendly grip

In the million-plus acres of Lake Superior State Forest, the SCHF9 was a favorite of Cheanne Chellis, the "Wolf Lady of Paradise," who raised and showed full-blooded gray wolves (under license) for eighteen years. This lady knows more about what a wilderness knife needs to be than most.

gives it a nimbleness that belies its weight. The knife transitions easily from one grip to another, and its contoured handle makes it easy to tell in which direction the cutting edge is facing by feel alone.

The blade's point is on the knife's center axis, enabling it to drill holes, while making the SCHF9 a formidable stabbing weapon.

As factory-made survival knives go, I rate Schrade's SCHF9 as a very good choice, and a suggested retail price of $67 only sweetens the deal. For more information about the SCHF9 and other Schrade knives, visit www.btibrands.com

Schrade's **SCHF-42 Frontier:** Schrade's new SCHF-42 Frontier, from blade designer Brian Griffin, is a candidate for backwoods adventures. The Frontier shares the lines of the more beastly SCHF-9, also designed by Griffin, but in a smaller, and arguably more handsome, package.

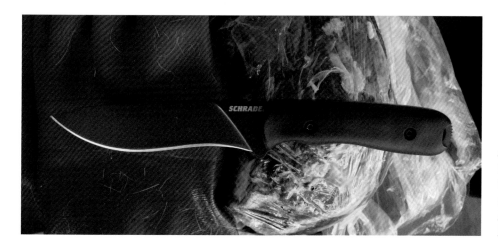

A bit more genteel appearing than its big brother, the SCHF42 is nonetheless capable of everything that a body might need a knife to do in the backwoods.

Like its larger sibling, the Frontier has a high-carbon blade of SAE 1095 steel, hardened to 57-59Hrc. Overall length is 9.95 inches. Its blade is 5.12 inches long by 1.25 inches at its widest, and .300-inch-thick at its choil. Its full-tang, semi-bolo design offers maximum chopping power, and enough belly to serve as a skinning knife, while 2.50 inches of gimping (six grooves) provides forefinger traction for delicate point-work.

The pommel end of the tang extends past a recess in the handle slabs to form a combination lanyard hole and hammer, enabling the butt end to be used as an ice chipper, wire-bending jig, or to secure the Frontier to your wrist with a loop of paracord. Gimping on the pommel consists of nine grooves, .650 inch long. Re-sharpening on a diamond bench stone was fast; within a few strokes, the cutting edge was restored to its original keenness.

Schrade's Brian Boyd said that the handle slabs are molded from a proprietary Swiss thermoplastic known as GV-4H Grivory, a semi-crystalline polyamide whose signature quality has been as a replacement for traditionally die-cast components, like car door handles.

A knife without a sheath is like a gun without a safety catch, so the production Frontier includes a stitched-and-riveted, black leather scabbard of top-grain cowhide, with a leather snap-down retaining strap, attached low on hilt, where it should be for easy, quick-draw access. Schrade's logo is tooled into the front.

At the time of this evaluation, the leather sheath was not yet available, due to instability in the leather market (according to Bryan Boyd), so my sample was carried in a pair of after-market molded Kydex scabbards from Chris Maris at Red Hill Sheaths. These included a handsome RealTree oak-leaf pattern in a low-riding tactical configuration that straps-down to the thigh.

The second Red Hill sheath proved to be habit forming. It was the same Kydex scabbard, except colored coyote tan, and fitted with a hinged quick-release belt clip that made the Frontier into a real grab-and-go work knife around our backwoods home.

Both sheaths are MOLLE-compatible, and attach to any belt, strap, backpack, or vest. Both have six grommeted holes around their perimeters, each with an approximate diameter of .220 inch (.559 cm). The holes are sized for parachute cord, and permit lashing to equipment, or mounting a sleeve holster to carry an on-board sparking-type flint fire starter. Red Hill sheaths can be custom-made to accommodate any knife. Prices start at $12.99. For more information visit www.redhillsheaths.com, or call (208) 946–6108.

In actual use, the Frontier performed well. Its smooth lines and surface texture of its Grivory slabs were like super-fine sandpaper, providing good grip when wet, or when coated with fat. Contours of the ergonomic handle include an integrally molded lateral finger guard, .900 inch (2.286 cm) wide, and curving back to .700 inch, to keep a user's hand from sliding forward. From there, the handle swells to a full inch.

Temperatures during our field trials were typically below zero, Fahrenheit. Heavy gloves were daily attire when opening bags of kibble for our teams of sled dogs, chipping ice from frozen water buckets, and performing the variety of everyday tasks necessary when the nearest town is forty-five miles away. Our Frontier was handy when wearing bulky gloves, secure in the hand, and transitioned smoothly from one grip to another.

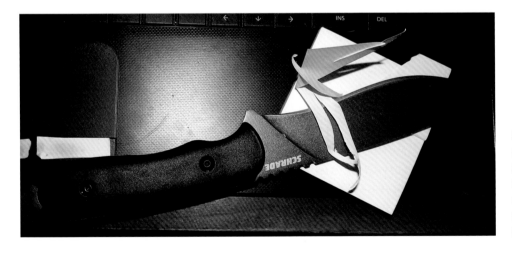

Shaving-sharp straight out of the box, that was a sign of things to come, and the Model 42 performed exceptionally well during the toughest field trials in the business.

Bottom line: Whether it's for hunting, survival, or virtually any other use that needs a sturdy, reliable, fixed blade that holds an edge, Schrade's newest Griffin design will fill the bill nicely. The SCHF-42 Frontier was released in May 2015. Retail for the knife, with leather sheath, is $76. To order the new Frontier, or to peruse the other fine knives being offered by Schrade, visit btibrands.com.

Smith's Survival Lockback Folding Knife: This company is best known for making most of the best sharpening tools on earth. But in recent years, demand for conventional whetstones has been dropping off with the number of knife owners who can use them, and competition from companies making a rainbow of gadgets that promise to turn anyone into a sharpening expert instantly has this company looking to diversify. Smith's is still at the top of their game with an assortment of multi-function sharpeners that range from handy to downright cool.

A legend in the sharpening tool industry, Smith's new stainless-steel folding knife comes with a tapered diamond sharpening rod and a flint striker, making this $20 knife more valuable than most, right out of the package.

Smith's Survival Lockback Folding Knife represents a foray into the unknown for the manufacturer. Proof of the adage that the best survival knife is the one you have in your hand during a crisis, this 4.250-inch closed knife does what it's designed to do. With a 3.25-inch-long drop-point, hollow-ground blade of 440A stainless, .900-inches wide and hardened to a relatively soft 53-55Hrc, this blade needs sharpening almost every time you use it. Ahead of its choil is .700 inch of serrations to rip through tough material like rubber hose, while .500 inch of gimping on the opposite side give an index finger traction for precise point control. Ambidextrous thumb studs enable users to deploy the blade with either hand. Its action is slightly gritty, but the adjustable bolster is tight, with no lateral blade wobble, and the stainless liner-lock is positive and well fitted.

The Survival Lockback's hand-filling one-inch-wide gray polystyrene handle is mated to yellow rubber grips at the handle's blade slot. A stout 2.260-inch-long pocket clip permits left-side, tip-up carry only.

What separates this folder from every other inexpensive lockblade are the tools fitted into two recesses molded into its handle's butt. On one side is a combination 2.060-inch-long by .160-inch flint rod fire starter whose plastic yellow handle is molded to be a loud and shrill signal whistle.

You cannot reasonably expect a $100 knife for $20, but Smith's stainless folder is just one example of the fierce competition that exists within the knife-making industry— and why it's the greatest time in history to be in the market for a new knife.

Opposite it, in an identical recess (the tools are interchangeable from one side to the other), is tapered coarse-grit diamond honing rod. Weight of the assembled knife is five ounces.

Retail of this knife is $20. Made in China. Visit www.smithsproducts.com or call 1-800-221-4156 or (501) 321–2244.

SOG's *Aegis:* In Greek mythology, Aegis (Ee-jis) was a shield, specifically the breastplate worn by Zeus. It was said that when Zeus shook his aegis in anger, "the thunder rolls, and men are struck down in fear." Small wonder that the United States' seaborne ballistic missile defense system was named for this impenetrable shield of the gods.

Handsome, clean, and simple, SOG's Aegis lives up to its name as a shield against dangers that might come when you least expect them.

Small wonder, too, that SOG has awarded that name to its own Aegis, a lightweight tactical folder that comes very close to being an ideal everyday carry knife, capable of serving as an everyday working knife. But this assisted opening folder, with an overall length of 8.250 inches, a clip-point blade 3.500 inches long, forged from AUS-8 stainless (with a super-tight hardness of 57-57Hrc), is obviously meant to be last-ditch life insurance when there's no cop around to protect you. Its flat-ground blade, .130 inch thick, is engineered to minimize penetration resistance. You could fillet a largemouth bass with this knife, but that is clearly not its most intended use.

Ergonomically, the Aegis captures that magical feel-good quality striven for by every knife maker, the elusive tactility that engineers who are not users seldom achieve. It would be less accurate to call the Aegis ambidextrous than to say that it doesn't matter if you're right- or left-handed; every feature seems to be right where it needs to be, regardless of which hand is holding the knife. Its sliding Piston Lock blade release is ambidextrous, as is its deep-riding, point-down pocket clip.

Some folders that bear the tactical label are actually just lockblades that could serve in a defensive capacity if they had to—I once skinned a white-tailed deer with a folding electrician's knife, but it most definitely was *not* a skinning knife. But the Aegis is a thoroughbred folding fighter that also works well for filleting fish or opening boxes. Its thoughtfully engineered titanium nitride-coated flat-ground drop-point blade of is sharply pointed, designed for maximum edge retention, and sharp enough right out of the box to demand respect as a slashing weapon.

Complementing the Aegis's power as a defensive weapon is the patented SOG Assisted Technologies (SAT) opposing-spring action that deploys the blade into its fully locked position as soon as a user begins to push the thumb stud. The Aegis literally springs into action with a distinctive snap that serves to warn anyone present that a sharp blade has appeared—like a viper's rattle, except that bad guys only get one warning in this case. As SOG boasts, this action truly is addictive, and you'll find yourself snapping the blade into battery at every opportunity.

The Aegis's ergonomically contoured Zytel handle, with sticky Kraton inserts, is built for the human hand. The knife feels almost like an extra finger; strategically placed braille-like protrusions at the butt and bolster give added traction when the handle is wet, and the knife changes grip positions almost automatically.

SOG's Aegis is a sleeper in the classic vernacular sense, not looking anything like the effective defensive weapon that it can be when it's not opening mail or cleaning fish.

Available in half-serrated tanto, straight-edge drop-point versions, and six other versions, both black and digital camo, SOG's Aegis is a pure-blooded fighter, built for defense in the jungle or on a dark urban street. Retail for the at-this-time discontinued plain black basic model we tested is $93.25. For more information, visit www.sogknives.com.

SOG Knives *ToolLogic-brand SL3 Fire Folding Survivor:* The new SL3 Fire from the ToolLogic division of SOG Specialty Knives is an ultralight answer to being prepared with the two most critical survival capabilities: cutting and fire-making. Adding a spark striker to a knife isn't an original idea, but the SL3 and its brethren are unique in being everyday carry folding knives designed to be full-service survival tools.

Marketed by ToolLogic as a "complete offroad survival kit," the SL3 Fire weighs in at 2.7 ounces, and fastens securely with a stainless-steel pocket clip. The knife clips only in a tip-up (closed) position, and isn't reversible. A lanyard hole enables it to be carried as a neck knife.

Deploying the SL3 Fire is easy and smooth. The three-inch 5Cr-0.5Mo stainless blade is half plain edge, half serrated to make it as functional for filleting a bass as for cutting a radiator hose. SOG's Chris Cashbaugh told me that "At this point we are not publicizing the Rockwell hardness on these knives." But unofficial tests showed 55-58Hrc. The blade fixes open position with a stainless-steel liner lock; overall length is seven inches.

Advertised as a "complete off-road survival kit," and carrying an on-board flint striker that's large enough to take seriously, SOG's ToolLogic SL3 needs only a compass to make that assertion a fact.

Inserted into a six-sided polygonal tube in its black molded glass-reinforced nylon handle is a magnesium alloy sparking rod that emits sparks of 2500 degrees Fahrenheit when scraped against the blade.

Rated for hundreds of strikes, the quarter-inch sparking rod is held snugly in place by two black rubber O-rings, and not likely to fall out during rough-and-tumble activities. The half-inch-diameter handle sticks out three-quarters of an inch when the rod is fully inserted, and is ridged to provide a sure grip with cold-numbed fingers.

The rod sparks even when wet, and throws a hotter spark the more that it's used. Although not specifically stated in the SL3 Fire's instructions, the elliptical thumb-opening hole in the blade serves as an excellent striker without opening the knife.

There was enough room inside to add about a quarter of a powdered Wetfire tinder cube, which makes the SL3 a never-fail fire-starting kit when natural tinder has been saturated by rain. There's room to add a fishhook and a sewing needle. Replacement strikers are available from ToolLogic's warranty department for less than ten dollars.

Molded into the SL3's handle is a loud, shrill emergency whistle that my tests show can be heard from more than a quarter-mile away. The whistle can be a life-saver; only recently an elderly lady became lost in the forest near my home, and couldn't yell loud enough to alert help. That incident was resolved safely, but she doesn't go into woods now without a signal whistle.

Priced at an affordable $36.25, the SL3 Fire needs only to be added to a compass to make it a functional do-everything survival tool for adventuring a wilderness. The SL3 is sold with a lifetime warranty. For more

With the spaces of the SL3's flint compartment filled with powdered chemical tinder cube, the knife becomes able to strike a fire anywhere, in any weather.

information about the SL3 Fire and other innovative survival tools in the SL line, contact www. toollogic.com, (888) 405–6433, www.toollogicsales.sogknives.com.

Tactical Operational Product Specialties (TOPS) **_Knives Brothers of Bushcraft Field Knife:_** Jagged slabs of Lake Superior ice surrounded our party, four feet thick, weighing many tons. They'd been driven onto the ice shelf to lie strewn, huge frozen monoliths that dwarfed the humans who picked their way between them.

It was cold on the ice. Wind chills drove temperatures below minus-fifty degrees, Fahrenheit. This was a dangerous environment; it could kill you just for standing around. You didn't encounter a lot of tourists out here.

The situation I found myself alone in was scary. I'd traversed a downward-sloping grade at the base of an ice wall, parallel to the ice shelf. The wall ended abruptly at the edge of the ice shelf, where ten feet below were lethally cold waters clogged with large ice chunks that would batter me to death against a sheer ice cliff while I died rapidly from hypothermia. Across the opening where it terminated was another ice wall, perpendicular to the first, and blocking the way. The only way out was up a grade of ice that sloped down to the precipice. Nature had set a trap that I couldn't have seen until I'd walked into it.

Even now, I was slipping backward toward guaranteed death. I knew from experience that going into icy waters wasn't like in the movies. In real life, victims are instantly incapacitated, unable to save themselves, and even if someone extracts them from the water quickly, they'll die without immediate medical attention.

I carried retrieval gear for such emergencies, but it was in a pack on my back. It hadn't occurred to me that the guy who other people paid to keep them safe might be the one in trouble. But then, I'd never encountered a combination of lethal circumstances like the one I faced now. The irony wasn't lost on me as I fell to my hands and knees in a desperate effort to increase traction.

While it is not the enchanted blade it was represented to be by the guys who jointly designed it (the author was delayed in his journalistic review of the BOB knife after destroying his first sample in five minutes), it is hard not to feel warm and fuzzy about a knife that quite literally kept one from becoming a frozen cadaver.

My descent slowed, but every breath sent me slipping inexorably toward the edge. My left hand swept to my waist and yanked the TOPS Brothers of Bushcraft (B.O.B.) Field Knife from its friction-fit Zytel sheath. I drove its 4.5-inch, 1095 blade halfway into the ice. The blade held my weight as I inched up the grade with my makeshift ice axe. It was a mere fifteen feet uphill to the safety of flat ice, and it took less than three minutes to traverse that distance with my makeshift ice axe, but it proved to be one of the longest trials in my life.

The 10-inch B.O.B. Field Knife that saved my life that day was not the magical blade its hyperbolic press had claimed that it was. My review of this knife in *Tactical Knives* magazine was actually late because I destroyed the first sample I received in five minutes (it turned out that I'd been shipped a blade that had been finished without going through heat treatment).

When I finally got a proper sample, the knife world had already elevated the thing to the status of an idol. The Brother of Bushcraft applied terms like "modified Scandanavian grind"—a saber grind—in conjunction with claims of edge retention that simply did not hold true, along with more or less useless features like fire drill divots.

Although the BOB knife was not the Excalibur-class knife that it was rumored to be, the Brothers of Bushcraft knife proved in the long run to be a high-quality TOPS-made field knife that was an excellent keystone in a great survival knife system.

I have since modified my own to have a belt loop that keeps its belt clip from twisting loose, like it has done many times, and I've given it a retaining strap so that it will stay in its scabbard. Thanks to TOPS, it is a good knife at a good price—$200—but numerous pre-existing knives easily best it as a field knife. www.topsknives.com

TOPS Power *Eagle-12:* I don't know that this 17.5-inch knife, with its 12-inch blade, is a "real man's tool," as *Tactical Knives* magazine claimed in melodramatic fashion, but it is most definitely a serious backwoodsman's tool. Designer Leo Espinoza can take a bow, because after six years of tough, brutal use in the largest and wildest forests south of Canada, this big knife has more than proved its worth to me. Of the two I've had, one of them suffered having a one-inch half-moon chip being broken from its 1095 high-carbon blade while chopping through a venison leg bone on a sub-freezing night.

Mike Fuller, president of TOPS, told me that I had the unlikely honor of being the first to break this monstrous knife. TOPS replaced the Power Eagle immediately, and left me with the broken one to "re-profile" into what has since become one of my preferred field knives. A full quarter-inch thick, this saber-ground blade is prybar-strong, butcher-shop sharp, and, mated to a Lost Mountain Iron Works (www.lostmountainironworks.us) survival sheath, it constitutes everything a person needs to get back home, or to survive indefinitely if it came to that. As a weapon, it is lethal; as a tool, it is invaluable.

As it comes from the TOPS factory, the Power Eagle 12 is the basis of a terrific survival knife system, for those who are comfortable using a large knife for everything.

An unadorned tan canvas Micarta slab on either side of the full tang makes the Power Eagle easy to draw and hang on to, even with thick gloves (necessary attire most of the year in these parts). A doubled elastic cord looped through holes in the hilt ostensibly serves to help keep the knife in your grip (similar to the Combat Lanyard described earlier), but in actual trials it proved to be useless, and was removed. The tang-incorporated finger guard is superb.

The sheath supplied with the Power Eagle is minimal for field work, with a generous quick-release flapped gear pouch, a hook-and-loop retaining strap, and light plastic sheath liner. The hook-and-loop retaining strap keeps the knife sheathed. Like most sheaths supplied these days, I find this one inadequate for my needs.

Twenty-six ounces of mass give the Power Eagle lots of energy to impart, and 56-58Hrc makes it hard enough to take a keen edge, but tough enough to take a pounding (it took me a year of such abuse as I described to break it). A textured epoxy powder coat, emblazoned with the TOPS logo and the Power Eagle trademark, protects the blade from corrosion. I've skinned game and filleted fish with it, which demonstrates its handling characteristics, and it has split and fashioned more than its share of wood.

This knife is too long and heavy for most people to carry except as a machete, but if you have the knack for a bigger blade (there are a lot of guys riding Harleys that are way too big for them, so don't let your ego override your intellect), the Power Eagle can do it all. The issue sheath needs

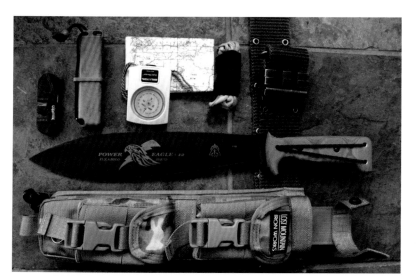

improvement, but properly geared-up, this knife can be your most trusted friend in a survival situation—*any* survival situation. Retail is $290. www.topsknives.com/power-eagle-12.

Outfitted with a Lost Mountain Iron Works aftermarket survival sheath, which was subsequently stuffed like a Christmas stocking with survival gear, the Power Eagle 12 became a near-perfect large survival blade.

TOPS Knives' *XcEST Alpha Survival System:* "The more you know, the less you carry" is a cliche among survival experts today. The romantic notion of a bare-knuckled hard case dominating nature is a gross oversimplification that no aborigine on any continent has ever embraced. A more pragmatic survival philosophy might be expressed as, "The more you know, the better prepared you are to make yourself prepared." The more options one possesses for accomplishing a task, the better the chances for success under the broadest range of circumstances.

As a factory-produced survival knife, TOPS's XcEST Alpha is the undisputed archetype. If you want one more suited to your needs, you have to build it yourself.

One member of an Internet knife group mourned that he had just received his XcEST Alpha, but that he couldn't fit all of the items it came with onto the knife. It does fit, but getting it attached is perhaps a test of a survivalist's ingenuity.

The Cross-Country Emergency Support Tool, or "XcEST Alpha," is TOPS Knives's answer to ensuring that anyone can have an assortment of useful tools on hand for emergency situations. The XcEST Alpha isn't a knife that has been adapted to survival purposes, but a purpose-designed compact survival system that is engineered to perform, from the shambles of a post-earthquake inner city to frozen northern wilderness.

The heart of this belt-ready survival kit is a fixed-blade knife with an overall length of 7.500 inches, and a one-piece skeleton-tang design of 440C stainless, hardened to an edge-holding Hrc 58–59. Its beefy .188-inch-thick blade is 3.250 inches long and 1.500 inches wide. Already resistant to corrosion, the blade and tang are further protected with a baked-on gray epoxy-hybrid powder coat onto which the TOPS logo and model designation are handsomely printed in gold. The point is blunt but strong, for drilling spindle holes in the fireboard of a bow-and-drill or for punching through sheet metal. A notch in the choil accommodates flint fire-starting rods.

The XcEST's canvas-Micarta handle is ergonomic to a variety of hand sizes. A divot on the left-side handle scale serves as a detent for the drill of a bow-and-drill fire starter, and as TOPS's Mike Fuller pointed out, it permits users to tell in which direction the edge faces without looking at the knife.

Removing two screws that anchor the Micarta scales exposes the knife's full-length skeleton tang, with recessed lanyard hole. With the scales in place, there is room enough between them to contain fish hooks and other small items. Without scales, the XcEST can be tied to a sapling and used as a spearhead.

The XcEST's heavy, handsome, ballistic-nylon sheath is available in olive drab or tactical black, and it too is designed for practical efficiency. A detachable full-width flap cover with a quick-release buckle protects the knife and the sheath's cargo pouch. The XcEST is held by a hook-and-loop retaining strap that wraps around its hilt in a conventional manner, so the hook-and-loop fastened flap can be removed without fear of losing the knife. Our field trials found no reason to detach the flap, which not only protects the knife, but secures the cargo pouch.

The XcEST comes loaded with seventeen survival tools that demonstrate TOPS's commitment to making this survival system stand out from the crowd. Included are: a folding hacksaw, two inner-tube Ranger bands, a liquid-filled compass, a length of monofilament fishing line, two mid-size fishhooks, an offset flat-and-crosspoint screwdriver, a P-38 can opener, a length of steel snare wire, an LED squeeze-light, a large sail needle, a flint-and-magnesium fire starter, a razor blade, an aluminum carabiner, two mid-size safety pins, a card-size fresnel magnifier, three feet of 550 parachute cord, a whistle, and a Lansky Quick-Fix pull-through sharpener. None are items I would not include in a survival kit.

It was a challenge to make all of these survival tools fit onto the XcEST sheath as a convenient unit without making the package cumbersome, but it did happen. The assembled system is as functional a survival kit as I could make; and with a price of $149.95, it's even better. For more information about the XcEST Alpha, contact www.topsknives.com.

Ultimate Survival Technologies *3.5 Green Glo Folder:* For almost three decades this company has been associated with producing some of the most effective survival gear in history. Now they've entered the survival knife-making world.

The 3.5 Green Glo Folder that is hanging around my neck as I type this features a 3.0-inch by 1.0-inch by .11inch-thick blade of 440C stainless, titanium coated, overlaid with black oxide protective coating. The blade opens with a thumb stud, but only from the right side; southpaws like myself have to learn to flip it open. A strong liner-lock keeps the blade from closing on fingers. Total weight is a mere 4.4 ounces.

The bead-blast textured two-tone, high-density TPR (thermoplastic rubber) scales are day-glow green on either end, black in their centers, with four oval-shaped holes in their centers to make cleaning easier. This is a handle that you can keep in your grasp. A well-made (so many of them aren't) carabiner at the butt end makes fastening the knife to a belt loop or lanyard literally a snap. Open length, counting carabiner, is 9.4 inches.

I've mentioned that the late and great Blackie Collins once told me that if he had to choose just one knife to serve him for the rest of his life, it would be made from "one of the 440s." I've also mentioned that I disagreed, but it is a fact that during my younger years I used 440C knives to skin, butcher, and sometimes dispatch innumerable whitetails.

Ultimate Survival Technologies, once again under new leadership, has officially entered the folding knife market with its 3.5-inch Green Glo model; after more than a year of steady use, this knife exhibits no more than a few scratches and normal wear.

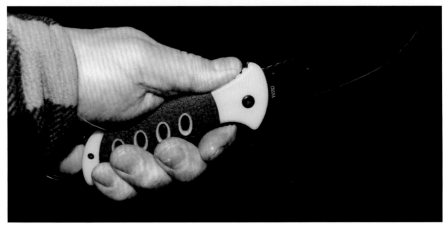

A minority of knife buyers, like car buyers, have expressed a bias toward the Green Glo Folder based on nothing more incriminating than its country of origin (China), but if you want the best value for your dollar, this knife merits consideration.

I eventually snapped the blades on two of my 440C knives, but those knives still hold a pretty special place in my heart. I personally would prefer 440C in a hunting knife, because of its sharpness; it's softer but tougher 440B in a field knife, although my preferred do-it-all knife wouldn't be made of 440 at all. Nonetheless, the bottom line is that Len McDougall is simply not qualified to have an argument over knives with Blackie Collins, rest his soul.

And after a year of working UST's Green Glo Folder above and beyond the call of duty, I have to give it two thumbs up in terms of all-round performance. With nary a drop of oil, only infrequent washing with soap and water, the action has remained smooth, its liner-lock tight and positive. The black oxide-coated blade (not a traditional baked-on epoxy powder coat) has a hardness of 50-54Hrc, perhaps the ideal for a working knife of 440C. Even so, the Green Glo Folder, after a dozen strokes against a leather strop, cleanly shaved off a three-day growth of facial whiskers.

The Green Glo Folder is sold on a blister-packaged card, which I think contributes to its image as a cheaply made knife. Reviews I've read reflect that image. In fact, this is a fine knife for the beginner or the expert. Do not expect a $200 Benchmade when you take this $15 folder from its packaging, but the unit I have is definitely a working person's tool. This knife is available from numerous sellers, or www.ustbrands.com

Ultimate Survival Technologies *Paraknife FS, Orange:* Earlier in this book, we covered

knives that would be suitable for children, or knives that are inexpensive enough to have scattered about, in a car's glovebox, a bug-out pack, or a sock drawer. A very good knife that isn't at hand when you need it is useless.

The UST Paraknife—available in several configurations—meets the criteria of a functional emergency knife. If you can overlook the functionally inconsequential fact that the knife is forged in China, there are some pretty good reasons to have at least a few of these cutting tools stashed in a place where they might be needed.

The Paraknife starts with a 5.00-inch-long blade of 420HC, hardened to 55-57Hrc. The clip-point, hollow-ground blade is 1.050 inches wide, .150 inch thick, with a 1.750-inch false edge and 1.000 inch of serrations just ahead of the choil. A finger choil indented just rearward of the cutting edge gives the knife excel-

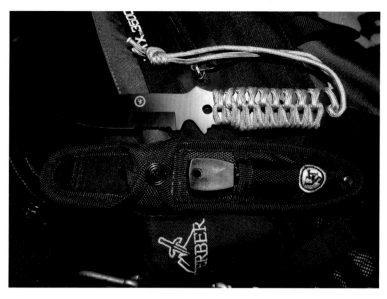

There are better skeleton-frame fixed-blade knives, and there are certainly better survival knives, but with an average price tag well under twenty dollars, the ParaKnife from Ultimate Survival Technologies is inexpensive enough to have two or more spread through your bug-out gear.

lent tip control, and a pyramidal projection opposite that provides a thumb rest. A black polytetrafluoroethylene (PTFE) coating over the entire blade protects from corrosion and reflections. The left side is stenciled with the Ultimate Survival Technologies logo, the other with the word China on its choil.

The hilt is part of the blade, and therefore all-steel. Four slanted oval-shaped holes, .400 inch by .200 inch, with two .300-inch-diameter holes at the choil and pommel, serve to make the Paraknife easy to lash to a spear shaft. As it comes from the factory, the hilt is wrapped with hunter orange pseudo-parachute cord (the most common stuff these days, rated to have a fifty-pound working load, rather than the 550-plus pounds of genuine paracord).

The Paraknife's sheath is made from black Cordura. Edges are taped and nicely stitched, with an interlocking rivet at the bottom to keep the knife's point from penetrating. There is no sheath liner, per se, just a sewn-in length of imitation leather to keep the knife's tip from cutting the fabric. (I made a liner insert from a plastic juice bottle—refer to the Sheaths chapter for instructions). A snap-down integral retaining strap holds the knife securely. An open top pouch on the front holds a .300-inch-diameter magnesium rod with .150-inch-diameter flint rod inset into it.

The Paraknife would not be my first choice as a survival knife, but it would be a tool that I'd be more than a little happy to see if my boat were blown ashore and wrecked on one of the remote wilderness beaches around Lake Superior or on the Pacific coast of Washington State. In any emergency situation, whether it be dispatching a deer that had been hit by a car to figuring my next move in the aftermath of a weather calamity, I'd like to see this in my glovebox or junk drawer.

Prices for the Paraknife vary wildly. UST's site merely directs you to a list of retailers, who set their prices by whatever the market will bear. I've seen the knife advertised at prices as high as $30 down to $7, so shop around. For more information, visit: www.ustbrands.com.

Ultimate Survival Technologies *Saber Cut Camp Axe:* I was dead wrong about this tool. Having grown up in timber country, cutting firewood each autumn, working as a choreboy when I was too young to be legally employed, working as a professional lumberjack until it became clear that it is not a profession from which one retires, I'm something of a snob when it comes to axes. There are no fewer than fourteen in my personal collection, all of them showing signs of a hard life, all of them sharp enough to skin a deer, which I've done on more than one occasion.

Most of what pass for "survivalist" axes these days are cute little fellas that we knew as boys' axes when I was a kid. Their balance is wrong, their very designs prohibit power, and they're just too small. I didn't expect much when I set out to see what UST's hatchet-size Saber-Cut Camp Axe could do.

Made in China, the Camp Axe has an unorthodox design; it begins as a single piece of 420HC steel, 11.750 inches long, with a head that extends 4.125 inches from the back of the haft. The outwardly curved cutting edge covers a linear distance of 4.250 inches. The head of the tool is ground into a chisel head with a .500-inch bevel. Thickness is a seemingly too-light .200 inch. The steel surfaces are protected from corrosion and reflection by a generous PTFE (polytetrafluoroethylene) coating. The UST logo is stenciled on the axe's left side, the word China on the right.

Sometimes a new product is surprising, and the durability and cutting power of Ultimate Survival Technologies Camp Axe accomplished that on two counts.

The Saber Cut Camp Axe is advertised as having thermoplastic rubber (TPR) handle scales, but the hard orange handle with a softer gray rubber insert includes two different, complementary alloys of elastomer. Scales are indented with finger grooves for a secure grip, and held to the matching tang by three star-drive Chicago screws.

The axe is provided with a polymer-lined black Cordura sheath, shaped to fit its head. Two flaps with snaps hold the head securely, and a black ballistic nylon belt loop sewn to the back permits the axe to be worn on your hip. The front of the case is stitched in white with the UST logo, and the words SABERCUT.

The surprise came in the field—or more precisely, in the barn while processing venison carcasses for the wolf pack we kept under license for eighteen years, and for our teams of Siberian sled dogs. Our canids have meat in their diets every day, and the good health they have enjoyed through several generations is proof that this diet works. This little hatchet displayed amazing chopping power for a weight of just twenty-five ounces, attributable largely to its configuration and excellent grip. It took large chips out of the logs it cut, and it had no trouble at all separating ribcages from the spines of white-tailed deer. I was betting that the handle would snap in twain, but after months of excessively abusive chopping every day—in temperatures down to -25 Fahrenheit—it hasn't failed yet.

Shown here with the larger FastAxe from TOPS Knives, the SaberCut axe from UST delivers a lot of power for its size and price.

At this time the SaberCut Camp Axe is still manufactured. If you have need of a hatchet-size axe for your kit, I recommend giving it a look. With an MSRP of $40, you can hardly go wrong. www.ustbrands.com.

Kitchen Cutlery

In these modern times, when the cooking of good, home-made meals has become a lost art to many people, there exists a heartbreaking loss of respect for fine kitchen cutlery. But for the waning number of folks who still can and do render a deer, hog, or Chinook salmon from living creature to the most succulent source of protein that you've ever closed your teeth on, a fine food preparation knife holds the same majesty and grace as any weapon of a Samurai ever did. Just as a professional carpenter, stonemason, or drywaller will tell you that doing a job of which you can be proud demands the tools necessary for doing that job right, so will an aspiring palate-master be only too happy to lecture you on the elegance and necessity of a beautifully crafted set of kitchen cutlery. It is no exaggeration when I tell you that there have been kitchen knives that brought tears to my eyes, so beautiful a job did they make of the meat and vegetable dishes they prepared.

A teenager whose only car has been Dad's rusted-out and rattling old Crown Victoria cannot understand or appreciate the deep passion and love a true automobile maven feels as he runs gloved hands over the fender lines of a Lotus Panterra. No one has more appreciation of a fine knife than a chef in a first-class restaurant, where preparing magnificent dishes that cause guilt in those who would defile them with a fork is reason for living. A sharp jungle machete can be and has been used to slice potatoes, trim the fat from steaks, and to fillet fish, but it is not the best tool for the job.

In general, kitchen knives are more lightly built than outdoor and work knives—although I have always had a suitable heavy outdoor knife in a drawer for separating frozen chicken thighs, et al. A thinner blade is more friction-free, enabling a blade to slice thinly and cleanly, and a lighter design, built for nimbleness and lighter weight, rather than strength, is less tiring and easier to manipulate. They are not built for hard uses like prying and twisting —even though we've all seen our share of kitchen cutlery with bent and broken tips.

The New Millennium is the best time in history to be a cook, in terms of the cutlery available. Just three generations ago, some of the best kitchen blades available were the 1095 carbon steel Old Hickory knives from Ontario Cutlery. Their blades rusted overnight and could be chipped, but they were capable of being made razor sharp, and they held an edge as well as any knives of that era. Old Hickory knives are still popular today, but they are easily bested today by an array of affordable, superior alloys. Following is a representative cross-section of some of the cooking knives available today:

Böker Manufaktur, Ceramic 10.8-inch *Santoku:* When ceramic knives began to appear a score of years ago, some heralded them as the next step in the evolution of of blades—or at least kitchen cutlery. Ceramic is much harder, completely stain proof, and holds an edge for much longer, but the first examples were brittle, even to the point of breaking if they were dropped onto a floor. The attraction, particularly in a world where probably most professional cooks hire-out to have their knives sharpened, was that ceramic blades hold an edge many times longer.

The Kyocera company flatly refused to take part in this book, but Germany-based Boker was eager to place one of their knives into the toughest field trials in the business. Boker submitted their 5.9-inch bladed Santoku, with a total length of 10.8 inches and a feather weight of just three ounces, and it was put to work immediately in a busy kitchen.

The ceramic Santoku handled well. Most notable was its feather-weight; this knife feels virtually weightless—almost dangerously, as if it were a toy. The two-tone rubber and plastic hilt is tough, and very ergonomically-shaped. I like that

Boker's ceramic Santoku kitchen knife.

the handle has a lanyard hole—a useful feature not often seen on kitchen knives. In short, this knife was a pleasure to cut with.

One legitimate concern about ceramic blades is that they can break. That is a fact, but they do not break easily. Just dropping one on a floor is highly unlikely to harm it. *Do not* attempt to use it as a screwdriver or prybar—in fact, do not attempt to use any kitchen knife in such a manner—but if you handle it as cooking cutlery should be handled, it will last forever.

Like other ceramic blades, the Boker was sharp, but lacked the hair-popping keenness of a fine steel blade. It retained that original sharpness through a month of regular meal preparation. The edge still demanded respect from its user when I decided to experiment with getting the edge to my preferred hair-popping sharpness. The first few passes against an aluminum-oxide stone didn't seem to make much difference in sharpness, although the stone left streaks of gray against the white ceramic—those washed off easily enough with soap and water.

Next came attempts with a Smith's carbide pull-through sharpener. It's tough to say which was harder, the carbides or the ceramic, but a chip broke out of its blade almost immediately. The chip was relatively easy to erase using a Smith's diamond-faced benchstone, but no amount of honing, polishing, or stropping produced what I consider to be better than a minimal working edge. The molecular structure of ceramic just seems incapable of being polished to a keen that is truly sharp. The bottom line is that a ceramic blade can be made sharp enough to peel potatoes and slice onions, and it will hold that edge many times longer than the finest steel blades. And because the Boker ceramic Santoku is both non-magnetic (like many cooks, I use big magnets to hold my kitchen knives) and breakable, it comes with a nice polyethylene sheath, so you can toss it into a drawer.

If you're skilled at sharpening your own knives, then ceramic probably isn't for you. But if you're one of the majority of people in the world who aren't, then ceramic is as close to a never-needs-sharpening knife as you're likely to get. Price of Boker's ceramic Santoku is $54. To review this and other Boker knives, visit www.bokerusa *or* www.boker.de or call (800) 835–6433.

Ontario Knife Company Agilite Kitchen Cutlery: Based on more than forty years of experience using OKC's Old Hickory label kitchen knives, it was with more than a little anticipation that I opened the box containing a five-piece set of their new Agilite stainless-steel cutlery.

Ontario Knife describes this latest generation of cooking knives this way: "The Agilite line was designed to be the most lightweight, durable, ergonomic, and advanced cutlery produced by Ontario Knife Company. Engineered down to the edge geometries by blade master Dan Maragni,

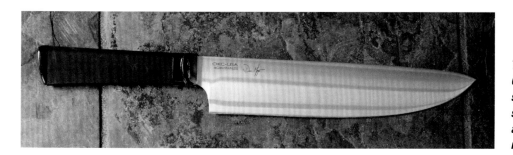

The Agilite kitchen set from Ontario Knives (Chef's Knife shown) sets a whole new standard for that company's already established reputation in that arena.

the Agilite knives are technically superior to almost any cutlery in the market." That is a bold claim, and it is not an assertion that OKC would make blithely.

Among the features common to Agilite line is full-tang blades of Sandvik 14C28NTM carbide steel. Steel-maker Sandvik describes this alloy: "Sandvik 14C28N is the latest development in Sandvik's range of knife steels. Optimized chemistry provides a top grade knife steel with a unique combination of excellent edge performance, high hardness, and good corrosion resistance." Sandvik 14C28N is indeed a remarkable alloy, capable of being hardened to 62Hrc (Agilite blades are 59-61Hrc), without affecting a blade's grain microstructure, and—importantly—without affecting edge stability. Put simply, edges neither chip or burr, and knives forged from it are easy to sharpen.

With the makers of the knives and the alloy used in them both singing the praises of this steel, I set out to see how the blades performed in the kitchen. After six months, the blades, flat-ground and .060 –nch thick, are scratched and scuffed, but only the three most frequently used have needed just one proper sharpening each. That is nothing short of amazing to a guy who had become accustomed to re-sharpening his kitchen knives after every second or third use.

Please note that, because of their TPE (thermoplastic elastomer) composite handles, with clear, hard, amber-colored moldings at the quillon (the blade end of the handle) and the pommel (butt of the handle), and black textured rubber between them, these knives are not recommended for the dishwasher. That's actually okay in my kitchen, where cooking cutlery never sees a dishwater, but is immediately washed, thoroughly dried, and put back into the block.

Those are the features generic to the Agilite line, but the strategy and planning that went into the various pieces in this cook's set warrant individual attention.

Utility Knife: The finer serrations on this knife rip through hard vegetables or any item having a tough outer layer. The sharp points of the serrations pierce before the concave cutting edges slice. The unique serrations of these knives have a smaller proportion of "points to curved edges" to allow a smoother cut with less tearing and deformation of the item being cut. This is likely to be the most used knife in the set for most folks. Retail: $46.

Santoku: Put simply, a Santoku is a Japanese version of the classic European Chef's knife, but generally without the length. The edge is slightly curved to aid in the rocking action needed to quickly turn vegetables into very small pieces. A Santoku has no trouble dicing an onion small enough to be blended evenly into barbecue sauce, while retaining the nimbleness needed to carve a Thanksgiving turkey. OKC's Agilite version is a shorter variation of the classic Santoku design, but shortening the blade does nothing to lessen its performance. Retail: $63.

Chef's Knife: A Chef's Knife was my favorite kitchen knife for decades, able to perform any task from peeling potatoes to slicing a ham. Like the Santoku, Ontario's Chef's Knife is a variation on the classic, mixing the most useful features of a European Chef's Knife with the longer, wider

Japanese Hocho (this is a big knife). The Agilite version has 40 percent of its cutting edge, ahead of the heel, flat to allow it to mate better with a cutting board. Retail: $80.

Bread Knife: This specialty knife is seldom needed in many household kitchens, and some cutlery blocks even lack a slot to keep it. The Agilite version is long, thin, and aggressively serrated to cut cleanly through hard bagels, but fine and sharp enough to slice bread. Retail: $65.

Paring Knife: Design of the Agilite Paring Knife is conventional, being short-bladed, lightweight and easily controlled from any grip position. The general design of this knife fits big or small hands, and allows precise control whether your cutting with the edge or the tip. Retail: $42.

Steak Knives: The Agilite Steak Knife is much like the Utility Knife (and could substitute for it), except that knives are sold in sets of four. This knife has a wide curve at the point and a fine serration to easily cut cleanly through meat without excessive tearing. Retail: $155.

Spyderco: This knife maker's name carries the same impact as Hummer or Browning, and I have never been given cause to expect that the knife I find in a Spyderco box will be anything less than one of the sharpest knives I've ever used. Every Spyderco that I've owned for the past twenty years has been sharp enough to shave my face with, right out of the box.

Spyderco's professional-grade kitchen cutlery did not disappoint. For this book, we selected four of the company's newest and most highly touted models: the K11 Cook's Knife, the Mini-Paring Knife, the Utility Knife 6" Model K04, and the Santoku.

K11 Cook's Knife: Produced specifically for Spyderco by some of Japan's most skilled and esteemed cutlers, this 10.35-inch knife is an ambassador for Spyderco's kitchen knives. Engineered to be a do-it-all utility knife, this versatile 0.870-thick blade is large enough to carve a turkey, with the ergonomics of a much smaller paring knife. Its drop-point, PlainEdge blade is forged from premium VG-10 stainless steel, also known as V-Kin (Japanese for "Gold") Ten. Created by Takefu Special Steel Company, Limited, VG-10 is widely known as one of the "Cobalt Steels," and is highly regarded for its keenness, edge retention, and ease of sharpening. VG-10 has become a premium choice for every type of knife in the world.

Forged of VG-10 alloy with a beautiful ebony hilt, this Spyderco Cook's Knife is simply outstanding on the cutting board.

The K11 Cook's Knife's 5.85-inch blade has a full-flat grind for strength, terminating at a gently cantled (slightly rounded, as opposed to a flat bevel) cutting edge. Thickness is advertised as .087 inch at the heel (the start of the cutting edge, ahead of the handle, for knives that do not have a choil), but tapers down to .050 inch at the tip. This unusual design creates exceptional edge geometry, resulting in low-friction cutting, edge strength, edge retention that is actually a bit surprising, and generally outstanding performance.

The K11's beautiful polished black Corian handle scales mate perfectly to a full tang with non-removable stainless-steel Cutler's Bolts. The handle is contoured to be comfortable, but I found it to be a little too slippery for my tastes, and the way it widens toward the pommel makes it a little clumsy to transition between grips.

In the kitchen, Spyderco's K11 performed superbly for every cooking chore from peeling potatoes to boning raw meat. Tip control, so necessary for cleanly taking red meat from around a bone, with minimal waste, was as good as any knife I've used. The first three inches from heel are flat, to mate perfectly with a cutting board, then sweeps gently upward .300 inch from there to the tip. Edge retention was so good that you might just forget to sharpen this knife. MSRP is $150. www.spyderco.com, phone (800) 525–7770.

Then there is the new (at the time of this writing) MBS-26 stainless steel series of kitchen cutlery. MBS-26 is a proprietary alloy of Masahiro and is a less expensive version of premium VG-10, lacking the Cobalt and Vanadium present in the latter, and with less Molybdenum, and is therefore used to make less expensive knives. MBS-26 blades are hardened in three stages: (1) quenching, (2) sub-zero freezing, and (3) heating and cooling until the steel reaches a hardness of 58–60 Hrc, which Masahiro asserts is the optimal hardness for a kitchen knife forged from this alloy.

Forged of MBS-26 alloy, this Spyderco Santoku performed impeccably in the kitchen.

MBS-26, hardened to the same temper as VG-10, is actually more flexible, which makes it a better kitchen knife, and any difference in edge retention is negligible enough to go unnoticed. Both are easy to sharpen, and both take an edge that has shaved my face clean. Like hunters arguing over whether a 6mm Remington or a .243 Winchester has better ballistics, the experts who argue which alloy is better for kitchen knives are indulging in hair-splitting beyond a typical human being's ability to notice here on earth.

Santoku Model K08: My favorite of Spyderco's MBS-26 K-Line is the K08 Santoku. The overall length of this knife is 12.06 inches. The full flat ground blade length is 6.81 inches (6.36-inch actual cutting edge), with a width of 2.075 inches and a thickness of .070 inch. Weight is 5.2 ounces.

The Santoku's black handle is textured polypropylene plastic, with molded-in vertical ridges, horizontal lines, a finger guard, and a rounded, hooked pommel, all of which serve to make this knife downright graceful in the kitchen.

The K08's sweeping cutting edge is the ideal radius for the long rocking motion that chefs use to expeditiously make large pieces into small ones. The K08 Santoku is made under license for Spyderco in Japan. Retail is $80. www.spyderco.com.

Utility Knife 6" Model K04: Available with both serrated and plain edge, this knife is engineered to be a go-to piece in every kitchen. Overall length is 10.81 inches, with a full flat-ground blade length of 6.50 inches, and an actual cutting edge of 6.00 inches. The blade is 1.160 inches wide and .053 inch thick. Weight is just 2.1 ounces.

The K04's black molded polyethylene handle is virtually identical to the handle on the Santoku described above, making the Utility Knife a pleasure to handle.

We tried out the serrated version of this knife. Its thirty-nine serration grooves, thirteen large and thirteen smaller sets of two, are very sharp, yet shallow enough to allow the blade to peel an apple without removing an excessive amount of fruit flesh. The final .375 inch before the blade is plain-edge and extremely sharp—ideal for one of the more mundane kitchen chores of removing paper labels from steel cans before they go into the recycling bin. This knife is aptly named, able to slice celery or remove the rind from a fresh pineapple with equal ease. MSRP of the Utility Knife is $50. Made in Japan.

Mini-Paring Knife Model K09: This is a very cool little knife—emphasis on "little." With a blade (and edge) length of 2.25 inches, this 6.08-inch-overall knife put off some of the people who tried it out at first. Its .057-inch-thick full-flat ground blade (.005 inch thicker than the Utility Knife above) and mere 0.80-ounce mass just made it seem too tiny to do any kitchen cutting job effectively.

The K09's black molded polypropylene handle is identical to the handles used on the other two K-series Spyderco knives already described, only smaller. Its hilt still fills the hand, though, and surgeons wish that their scapels offered the precision control of the Mini-Paring knife's mildly-curved Hawksbill (Karambit) blade. Peeling a potato with this knife is effortless.

But it's the blade that constitutes this knife's single flaw. Its short concave edge is not accommodating of typical flat honing stones, and you can destroy, at minimum, the knife's good looks by trying to sharpen it like a conventional blade. My best luck has been with a three-sided Edge-Tek diamond rod ($43) from Buck Knives.

Retail of the K09 Mini-Paring Knife is $35. Made in Japan. www.spyderco.com.

W. R. Case XX 7-Piece Household Cutlery Set: Re-introduced in 2011 after a seventeen-year hiatus from making kitchen knives (and now discontinued in favor of a similar nine-piece set), this is a classic ugly duckling of cutlery sets. The Walnut handles of its five knives (plus a honing steel and the walnut block itself) are held to full tangs with brass rivets in three places so that they're affixed with more strength than a wooden handle can provide. The handles are not nicely finished, but look as if they were shaped by someone who was intentionally trying to impart a rustic look; their ends are crudely sanded, and the wood is finished just enough to avoid splinters.

The knives themselves consist of one each: 8-inch Chef's Knife, 9-inch Slicing Knife, 8-inch Bread Knife with Miracl-Edge Serrations, 6-inch Boning Knife, 3-inch Paring Knife, and a 10-inch Sharpening Steel. Their blades are described as being forged from "Tru-Sharp surgical steel" (several companies use such ambiguous descriptions to avoid being legally obligated to use just one alloy). Our set was almost certainly forged from 420HC stainless. Rockwell values were also kept on the down-low, but the feel of blades against stone indicated 55-57Hrc. As homely as their handles are, the blades are things of beauty. Hollow-ground edges have been precisely applied to enable the blades to quickly take a shaving-sharp edge, and retain it for as long as possible.

The "walnut stained" storage block is made from darkened pine wood and looks good on any counter-top, regardless of the motif of your kitchen decor. Rubber feet are intended to prevent marring surfaces, but they stick fast to any smooth surface after a few days, leaving round smudges that require forceful scrubbing to remove. We resolved that particular problem by simply gluing felt to the bottoms of the feet.

Performance of the knives was quite good for a 400-series alloy. The factory edges were usable, out

The ugly duckling of kitchen cutlery block sets, the seven-piece block (discontinued in favor of Case's nine-piece set) is filled with excellent kitchen knives.

of the box, and a few strokes against the honing steel before each use let us use the knives for two weeks before a proper sharpening with a stone was required. These knives are not the finest kitchen cutlery that you can own, but their retail price of $220 is merited, and you can justifiably take pride in having this block on your kitchen counter.

Again, this set is discontinued (although you can still find it online at various retailers), but you can view the nine-piece block, as well as Case's expanding lines of kitchen cutlery, at www.wrcase.com, telephone: (800) 523–6350.